Love Builds Brains

Thank you for registering for our 2021–22 Virtual
Speaker Series.

**DSBN Parent
Involvement
Committee**

We hope you enjoy your complimentary copy of
Dr. Clinton's b

D0967373

Love Builds Brains

Jean M. Clinton, M.D.

TALL PINE PRESS
Edmonton, Alberta

Tall Pine Press
2655 Sir Arthur Currie Way, Edmonton, AB T5E 6S8, Canada
Web: www.tallpinepress.com   E-mail: tallpinepress@gmail.com

Library and Archives Canada Cataloguing in Publication

Clinton, Jean M, 1954, author
     Love Builds Brains / Jean M. Clinton.

Includes index.
ISBN 978-0-9810149-3-7 (paperback)

     1. Social learning. I. Clinton, Jean M., 1954-, author II. Title.

HQ783.B39 2016   303.3'2   C2015-907011-2

Cover Design: Jeff Sotropa

T▲LL PINE PRESS

Contents

Foreword

As I sit at my desk and look out through my window, it might seem to be an ordinary spring day. The birds begin their courting chorus in the early mornings, the new buds on the pin oaks are pushing their wintered leaves to the ground and the daffodils are sprinkling the garden with bright yellow and verdant green. But this is by no means an ordinary spring day—not in Canada and not across the world. We live in various forms of lockdown, connected to each other by using social distancing and through various forms of digital means. We're in a world battle together against the Covid 19 pandemic.

The pandemic has impacted our lives in so many ways already. The future ahead will depend on the resilience and creativity of humanity in ways yet to be understood and explored. For today, we share anxieties for the safety of our loved ones, especially the elderly and those working on the front lines of our healthcare institutions. We do our part by working from home or sheltering in place with a rigor and patience we have never yet tapped. We try to home school our children. We worry about lives and livelihood, in the short term, and about families and the resilience needed to face an unknown future, in the longer term.

I trained as a physician at the University of Toronto and completed residencies in Toronto and Hamilton, training in the specialties of paediatrics and public health. Eventually, I opened a practice in consultant paediatrics in a smallish southern Ontario town for the first half my career. During that time, I had the particular honour of working closely with families and especially moms to diagnose and treat their most precious possessions—their children. During my watch, infectious disease hospitalizations fell due to the success of a series of new immunizations against meningitis, hepatitis, bronchiolitis and gastroenteritis.

But much of my practice focused on behavioural and learning issues as well. I came to understand in a very real way, that whatever the disease or condition at hand might be, attention to the family impact and functioning was critical for a successful recovery. And the supports and resources of the family both emotionally and materially were significant factors in the lives of healthy and unwell children. As my waiting lists for a consultation grew to years in length, I felt I was catching kids at the bottom of a water fall when the real opportunities for interventions were much farther upstream. So I looked for openings to work on and change policies that could make life better for kids and families.

During this time in the early 1990s, I had the opportunity to work with Dr. Fraser Mustard and the Honourable Margaret McCain on an Early Years Taskforce. These were heady days. There was a rapid evolution of neuro-scientific thinking and the growing emphasis on the early development and functioning of the brain and its impact on long-term health and wellbeing. The nature/nurture arguments were in full bloom and science was showing that early environments for animals and for children 'got under their skin' and altered their genes. The knowledge that moms had known forever—that it's relationships that are warm, responsive and predictable that help our children thrive—was standing up to credible scientific scrutiny. Policy makers and governments were examining the implications of this research and realizing that societal investments in the early years made for a healthier and economically more successful population.

It was during some of this work with Dr Mustard at the Founders Network in Toronto, that I came to meet Dr Jean Clinton—a fast talking Scottish child psychiatrist with a curiosity and wit that sparkled and sparked. That meeting began our lifelong friendship with our shared intent to shine a light on the importance of the early years and to ensure that, with deep understanding of the implications of the supportive science, children in Canada and in the world would have their fair shot at healthy relationships within families, within communities and within countries.

Jean describes herself as a "knowledge translator" and indeed, with great admiration, I've watched her do just that. I've seen her present in many formal and informal forums. She's presented her work in one-on-one meetings and also to gatherings of thousands. She's been in-person on Zoom, Youtube, in film and on TV. She's a gifted teacher with a depth of knowledge and a contagious charisma that engages folks with her passion. Her curiosity and energy can be depended on to uplift the room.

One cold, icy February evening, Jean invited my husband and me to accompany her husband and her to a presentation she was giving at an annual meeting for a local service club that works for children and youth. I jumped at the chance to see Jean in action again. We gathered at an upscale local hotel and were shown to the pre-dinner cocktail area where folks gathered with a glass of wine and wandered past to chat with Jean. Some of them had met her before or had heard her before. All of them told her they were very much looking forward to the evening. Jean's focused attention and her sincere interest on their stories and experiences was evident. Connection is central to Jean's work and is both her message and her model.

As we moved to the dinner area, warmth and adoration followed her and she demonstrated once again Kipling's "ability to walk with Kings, nor lose the common touch," as she paused, greeted and listened to people. The dinner was flavourful and delicious. The people at our table were enthusiastic and interesting. The dinner conversation was robust and stayed focused on the lives and challenges for kids in this small town. It was clearly the shared passion for these good folks at the table, many of whom had made a difference in big and small ways in the lives of children over many years.

After some awards and accolades, Jean was introduced warmly and the way she valued and supported early years' workers was particularly noted. She moved to the podium to address the group and began by building the early brain story and tailoring her message to the important work of those in the room. She spoke to the parents, the staff, the philanthropists and the politicians—all of whom had a stake in the well being of children. She sprinkled her talk with humour and shared anecdotes from her childhood. She told stories of coming to Canada from Scotland at age 11, feeling lost at sea and learning to knit at a local Boys and Girls club in Hamilton, which became a place where she "felt connected and felt *felt;*" it was a place where she felt both valued and valuable. The talk moved to her discussion of the adolescent brain which she emphasized was under construction. She reminded all of us that while teenagers' cognitive abilities are growing, they need to feel safe, significant and have purpose. She emphasized once again that building brains is based on relationships and that it clearly takes a village to raise children.

That evening, Jean, as always, modelled compassion, curiosity and commitment and built her talk on our common humanity so that she sent folks off into that dark, cold night with a renewed enthusiasm and appreciation for their roles in the lives of children. It was one of those magical nights, when the message and the medium come together in a unique and very meaningful way.

Jean's book, *Love Builds Brains*, lays out the early years' journey of attachment, self-regulation, connection, resilience and well-being, with scientific explanations that she measures out in understandable doses. We hear her voice throughout the chapters as she tells clinical and personal stories to amplify her points and perspective. She speaks from a population perspective, berating the poor world rankings of Canada on various OECD reports and then speaks to the individual level of our involvement with children suggesting prevention and management strategies. In the book, there's a strong and appropriate emphasis on early years' development, but there's also attention to the adolescent brain. This book is full of scientifically-based wisdom in a conversational style—it's as though you're drinking a coffee and having a chat with Jean as you sit at her kitchen table.

The Covid19 pandemic is the worst crisis in recent human history. It will be felt for decades, if not generations, to come. So understanding and embracing these new approaches to what Jean refers to as "sculpting the brain" and following her wise advice will aid in our ability to anticipate a better future. Over these next years, our children need healthy support and guidance to develop hopefulness, creativity and resilience as we rebuild our society under new economic and health conditions. This book distils important new science and interventions for healthy child development at a critical moment. It's just in time for our children, our families, our country and our world.

Through it all, Jean's lovely mantra, *Love Builds Brains*, can guide us. Enjoy!

Dr. Robin C. Williams, C.M., M.D., F.R.C.P.
Chair, Early Years Taskforce,
Canadian Paediatric Society.

Extraordinary Spring, 2020

LOVE BUILDS BRAINS

Introduction

My father used to tell me how lucky I was to have my passion (working with children and focusing on their healthy development) and my career (child psychiatry) so completely in sync with each other. Over the years, my concern has been not only with my own 5 great kids and 5 grandchildren, but with all children in the world. That's my focus. What a privilege it is now to put my passion and knowledge on the printed page so that I can share my life work with you, my readers.

I count my blessings. I'm so emotionally and geographically close to my 5 grandchildren and I can see, right in front of me, that LOVE BUILDS BRAINS. I see my three year old grandson reach gently over to his little 6 month old sister with love in his voice, his eyes and his body posture saying "I love you Ella Bella." I see her whole body squirm with delight and I fairly glow with pleasure. Where has he learned to be such an empathetic, nurturing child? From his adoring, loving, predictably warm and responsive parents of course.

Then I watch my 2-year-old grandson explain to his Mama that he had a bad dream. He told her he didn't like the brown cow spraying milk in his face from its mouth. Then I see my daughter gently helping him recognize his feeling. "So", she said softly, "you said that made you feel scared, didn't you? And then she asked him, "What can you tell the brown cow next time?" Once she heard him make a suggestion, she replied, "Yes, that you don't like it when the cow does that. What did you do to feel better?" As she listened to her little boy, she continued, "Yes, and Mummy came, didn't she?"

Now that's a parenting high point for me. But don't get me wrong, there are lots of moments of pure chaos and dysregulated behaviour in my children's homes. But I'm so happy to know that, at the heart of their young parenting, there is a desire for their children to feel understood, *feel felt* by their parents. My daughter has learned that when your partner is away and your 2-year-old twins are crying for you as well as your 3-month-old baby, it sucks! But it's life. You do the best you can to help them grow into the realization that bad feelings go away

There are a couple of things that you should know about me before you begin this book that I elaborate in the body of the text. Firstly, I'm an Upstreamist and I'm a brain geek!! I'm an upstreamist because after more than 25 years as a child psychiatrist I recognized that I was in a rushing stream of kids and families trying valiantly to grab and catch as many kids and families as I could. I learned from a mentor, the late Dr Paul Steinhauer, a wonderful child psychiatrist from Sick Children hospital in Toronto, that as child psychiatrists, we need to be upstream, to find out the why of these situations. I realized I wanted to try to stop kids from falling into the river of psychiatric illness and disturbance in the first place.

I have, for the past decade or more been on that mission. I continue my consultation work as a child psychiatrist, but I also work very hard to advocate for children and youth and to translate the sciences that have uncovered more about the workings of the brain and mind. My role is as a Knowledge Translator. That's the brain geek part. I'm a student of the field of neuroscience, not a neuroscientist. I read continuously about the science of the brain and what we're learning and then I try to find ways to bring those insights to groups of people by making that research and knowledge accessible. Why do I want to do this work? Because I know that understanding the brain has been a complete game changer for me—in all the work I do and in the life I live.

Secondly, this book is born from the many requests that I've received over the years after giving talks to a variety of groups of people. I wanted to have a book that captures my translations of the brain research that has changed the way I think and act so completely. Parents and educators want to know where they can turn to get decent, scientifically sound information that can help them do their work to the best of their abilities. This is that resource. It is based on a series of talks that I have given over the years. It's not a continuous narrative but it is based on the topics that my listeners have asked me to provide. The good news is that each chapter can be read as a stand-alone. There are key concepts in each chapter that hold the book together. The most significant of those key concepts is that love builds brains. Let me say it again, love builds brains.In writing this book, I hope to support families and educators as they bring their humanity, their forgiveness and their renewed ability to repair relationships to the realm of raising and educating children. If one parent or educator decides to reach out and hug a child or to stop for a minute to think, "I should connect before I correct this child," my task is accomplished. I would love for readers to stop and reflect on how they see their role in children's lives and to recognize that it's their relationships with children that have a lasting influence on a child's development. It's not the material stuff they have or the fancy vacations or their learning tools; it's the quality of their interactions. If adults can feel increasing confidence in their ability to build and to repair relationships and after doing that, to say to themselves, "Hey I'm not perfect but I sure am doing my best," then I'll have accomplished my goal. My mantra in parenting, as you will read in this book, is for adults to think about "Progress, not perfection."

One of my dear teachers, the late Dr Clyde Hertzman, paraphrased Voltaire once and said to us, "Don't let the perfect be the enemy of the good." I was so struck about how relevant his words were to raising children. Parents tell me over and over that they feel pressure to be this perfect parent, to have just the right balance of activity, love, nutritional meals, oh and don't forget helping kids develop a spiritual side. They're under such pressure that they don't feel they have permission to *just be with their kids*. I hope this book tells you, as readers, that the science behind the whole brain and body story is about *just being with your kids*. The best knowledge about brain development says that creating the relational conditions for children to thrive is the most important thing we can do for them.

I hope you enjoy the flow of the chapters in this book. You'll notice, and I hope you'll forgive me for repeating some key themes throughout the book. Chapter 1 begins by outlining why the science of the early years is so important and sets the stage for the key theme that the brain is physically, literally, built by the experiences that babies and children have. The very architecture of the brain relies on exposure to safe, nutritious, loving, warm and responsive interaction. The concept of the impact of stress on this developing brain is explored and ways to mitigate toxic stress can be managed by creating predictable, warm relationships. I touch briefly on the deep brain architecture story that influences this brain-building activity and on the science of Epigenetics that describes how genes listen to the environment and are activated or silenced by environmental cues.

Chapter 1 leads naturally to a deeper exploration in Chapter 2 of the science and practise of attachment. This is the fundamental building block of who we become, and it's based on the relationship between baby and caregiver and the predictable, sensitive warmth of these interactions that have the potential to lead to a baby who feels secure in the world. Under unfavourable conditions, these interactions may lead to a baby who doesn't feel secure.

Chapter 3 is a discussion on the social brain. As a species, we're wired to connect with each other. But kids come into the world with a lot of their own temperaments and characteristics—as anyone who's raised children knows. This chapter presents the question of how we parent consistently when the needs our children express can be so different. The task of parenting in this situation is always to remember to listen so that you understand the child and to help reframe the behaviour of those challenging kids. I truly believe that all kids will do well if they can and that often misbehaviour comes from a stressor that's overwhelming the child.

In Chapter 4, I explore the concepts of resilience and recovery. For many years, psychologists and researchers focused on what makes children mentally unwell (psychopathology) and they noticed incidentally that some children who are exposed to similar difficult conditions had very different responses to them. Some children seemed to 'bounce back' from adversity rather than be overwhelmed by these often significant experiences. This observation led to the development of the field of resilience.Chapter 5 asks you to think about the power of connecting with children and to reflect on your view of the child. In the chapter, I ask whether you see children as empty vessels to be filled with our knowledge and wisdom, or, do you see them as powerful, curious, competent co-creators of their lives? This question leads to my provocative statement that too often we have been seduced by what I call the *Tyranny of Cognitive Seduction*, which is the belief that our cognitive development is more important than social and emotional development. Unfortunately, this is a particularly evident belief and practice in our current school systems.

The second half of the book addresses specific developmental issues in chapters 6 to 10. These issues include the following: infant mental health, adolescent development, self-regulation and anxiety. Chapter 10 finishes with a look at the present and the future by providing a discussion of the digital culture that we're all exposed to and that will shape aspects of the future. I want to point out that Chapter 6 explores the issue of early childhood mental health and the systemic need for many of our social and educational systems to work together to address the needs of our youngest children and their families. The sense of urgency I feel about the need to redress these systemic issues is one that runs through the entire book.

As I have mentioned before, I'm a brain geek. In order to understand what adolescence is all about, we really need to understand the brain of adolescence as being under construction. But we also must recognize that this magnificent time in life offers great creativity and capacity for passion and change. We need to recognize that adolescents need more of our time, not less of it. Are you hooked yet? Well, don't feel you have to start at the beginning of the book and read all chapters in order. If teenagers are your primary concern and you're struggling with that age group, go to chapter 7 right now.

At this point, I also want to emphasize the role that self-regulation plays in a child's success. Chapter 8 looks at the concept of and framework for self-regulation, which is a key developmental understanding and ongoing competence for all of us to develop. Sadly, self-regulation is lacking in many adults and in many children. The chapter on self-regulation draws heavily on the work of my dear friend and colleague Dr Stuart Shanker and his work in self-regulation as a framework for understanding children's behaviour. In addition, Chapter 9 addresses the question of anxiety and its apparent increase in young children. This topic comes up in every talk I give, so the theme of anxiety, and what we know about it, is an underlying concern throughout the book.

I want to say a bit about chapter 10, which is on the digital age we live in and what it means to be growing up digital. Should we be worried about how much time young people are spending on social media? A spoiler: Yes, if it's excessive. Should very tiny children be on screens for as long as they like? How is screen time influencing the brain? What are the good things about the digital world? How do we find the right balance for each family? I know these questions need to be asked and they need some answers. So, if digital culture is your primary concern, go to chapter 10 first.

I'm aware that life has become very different since I raised my own children. Even in the decade between my oldest child, who was born in the 1980s, and my youngest who was born in the 1990s, life changed dramatically. But have core principles of parenting and education changed significantly? I wonder. We still need our children to develop a positive sense of purpose, of hope, of belonging and of having meaning in their lives, but their paths may be significantly different due to the digital worlds we face now. I sense a seismic shift in education. Perhaps there will be a shift from filling our children with adult-oriented and pre-conceived concepts, as if they're empty vessels and we need to fill these buckets with information. Maybe we can focus on an idea that education is about human development and we will begin to ignite the flame of children's learning and have a more sustained focus on learning itself, both as students and educators keeping in mind that we are all learners.

There are many people to thank who have contributed in innumerable ways to my learning and thinking. In my formation as a child psychiatrist I will be forever indebted to the late Dr Dan Offord and Dr Paul Steinhauer. My understanding of consilience and the integration of ideas across disciplines was profoundly affected by the brilliant, irreplaceable Dr Clyde Hertzman as well as by Dr Stuart Shanker. Mary Gordon, founder of Roots of Empathy has been an enduring friend and inspiration to me as we both have embraced her thesis that Love Grows Brains. Most recently the educational giant Michael Fullan has honoured me by listening respectfully to my ideas on education and relationships and together we work towards a model of education that has as a moral imperative creating the conditions for learners to be good at learning AND good at life. I do not have words for the steadfast friendship and mentorship of my dear friend Dr Robin Williams who I met more than twenty years ago as we worked together with the late Fraser Mustard on the Early years agenda and have continued to learn laugh and love over these many years. This book would not be a reality without the love, guidance and persistence of my dear friend and editor Dr. Joyce Bellous.

My deepest thanks go to my children and to my husband, my life partner and best friend—they've stood by my side through all the ups and downs of life and growing together. I am truly blessed

I do hope this book gives you an opportunity to pause, to think, to reflect on your role as parent or educator. As many people have noted, between stimulus and response there's a space. And in that space is our power to choose our response. That means that in our response lies our growth and our freedom. My wish for you and for myself, is growth.

Jean Clinton

Hamilton Ontario
May 2, 2020

1

Let's Start at the Very Beginning

INTRODUCTION

Gandhi is credited with saying that the true measure of any society can be found in how it treats its most vulnerable members. His wisdom seems a simple enough concept until we consider the conditions in a society, a community, a family, that lead to treating our most vulnerable members well. At that point, we start to deepen our understanding of what well-being requires and we see how profound a statement it is. At its heart, it's an evaluation of civil society itself.

If we think about children, especially very young children, as an example of a vulnerable population, we recognize that many people in Western society believe that the care of children is a parental responsibility. But as we look at what adults require to be effective parents, we realize their responsibility is nested within community support. So we ask a second question. How can communities be supportive? As we ask that second question, we notice that the parental role is nested within social norms and within economic and political realities that shape community support.

One model for considering the interacting levels of support for human growth was identified by Urie Bronfenbrenner (1974). He called it an "ecological model of human development"[1] in which development is influenced by several environmental systems. These

1

systems include the most intimate system, the family (which is a micro-system) and the political forces that influence families. One implication of his model is that, in order to look after our most vulnerable people, we need to have children, families and citizens who care about the welfare of others. We also need schools that provide relational support in their practices and school cultures. To accomplish that educational aim, we depend on apt policies and practices that support human growth.

In this chapter, I propose that in order for our communities to prosper, we must look to what's required to support the development of our youngest children and their families. Why do I say this? What happens in the early years literally builds brains and establishes the pathways that allow the young to develop more and more skills. The interactions that parents have with their children, the connections that teachers make at school—all these links create the architecture of the brain. That architecture houses language and communication skills that impact how children think of themselves and what they think relationships should be like. These interactions build pathways to help the young recognize and manage stress—their own and that of other people.

Why is stress an issue for children? How a child deals with stress has a whole lot to do with how they're able to learn, figure things out, solve problems and be responsible citizens. The issue of early years development isn't just a pleasant idea for getting kids off to the right start. It's about living in a country that can continue to be productive and healthy for a very long time. My purpose in writing is to illustrate some of the social benefits to the country as a whole that result when a society cares for its most vulnerable populations, in this case, young children and their families.

If society intends to support young children, and if citizens want to know how they're doing and how our society is faring with respect to their well-being, children's development must be monitored at the level of the whole population. In Canada, we have a tool for monitoring development in all 5 year olds that's now used in many countries. As a researcher, I used this instrument and, along with other researchers, have observed that almost 1/3 of all Canadian 5 year olds arrive at school without essential skills they need to do well in that educational environment. The instrument, the *Early Development Instrument* (EDI) reflects what children have learned and experienced before they arrive at school. The distressing reality is that vulnerable children who arrive at kindergarten have already fallen behind their peers. They don't always catch up. They continue to have a multitude of problems with learning and behavior. As a consequence of not having these necessary skills, vulnerable children aren't able to get the most out of educational opportunities that schools are set up to provide for them.

But this situation could be addressed. The research of the late Dr. Clyde Hertzman at the University of British Columbia indicates that decreasing the overall vulnerability in the Canadian population by just 1% would increase Canada's Gross Domestic Product (GDP) by 1% over the lifetime of that group.[2] By extension, his work implies that if we brought early childhood vulnerability down from 30% to 10%, we would increase a country's economic growth by 20% over the work lifetime of that group. I propose that Canadians would receive a massive return on their investment in the future if we addressed the source of vulnerabilities picked out by the EDI (*Early Childhood Instrument*). Yet what are effective strategies to create change at a societal level, which is clearly needed if 1/3 of our children aren't doing well?

Canada isn't the only country that has vulnerable young children, but not every country sees the issue in the same way. For example, there was sweeping reform in Sweden during the 1980s when gender equity was the rallying cry. While I was in Sweden I noticed that the brain and its development wasn't at the core of this reform. When Swedish people raised the issues of early years development, they talked about gender equity. That's why they have universal preschool. All of the wonderful things I'm going to tell you about brain development weren't the prime mover of their reform. Rather, they believe women have as much right to be in the workforce, as do men. They also know both moms and dads want their children to be well looked after.

In the United States and Canada the rallying cry is currently focused on building better brains, on school readiness and the impact of early environments on brain development. There's also

3

more attention directed to social and economic conditions that allow early childhood environments to flourish. Nobel winning economists, such as James Heckman, after intense scrutiny of these issues, support high quality early childhood programming for socially disadvantaged children as a key factor in economic prosperity.[3]

The economic argument for developing a comprehensive approach to early years development is massive. If you want to make a difference in your economy, invest early. If you want to get 17 dollars for every dollar you spend, invest early. In Canadian neighborhoods where vulnerability is very high, we know what to do to help children and families so that kids can soar throughout life. President Obama, in a December 2014 Washington Summit on Early Child Development, stated that investing in early child development is one of the greatest investments his country could make.[4] But children, their families and their communities require advocacy if environments where young children grow up are to become as healthy as they need to be.

AN UNEQUAL SOCIETY

I dedicate the work I do as an advocate for children and knowledge translator to my dear friend, the late Dr. Dan Offord who worked at the McMaster University at the Offord Centre for Child Studies in Hamilton Ontario. Based on his experience,[5] he observed that growing up in Canada is like running a race on an uneven playing field. What did he mean? On average, children who suffer the disadvantages of poverty, whose parents didn't finish high school or who experience maltreatment or neglect, do less well. These conditions have a profound effect on a person's life chances. Where you're born, who your parents are, even your postal code all make a difference in how long you're going to live and what kind of job you're going to have. One could think that Canadians' health should be good no matter where people reside, because we live in a country that has universal access to healthcare. But this isn't so. One might also think that, because public education is freely available for every child, educational outcomes should reveal that school experience is equitable. This isn't the case.

When data is examined, there are gradients and slopes as one plots income and just about any other outcome, such as education, illness or employment. The poorer you are, the worse your chances: the fewer your opportunities for good employment, the less schooling you'll get and the more illnesses you'll suffer.[6] These findings aren't due to poor people being born with lousy genes, or making bad lifestyle choices. Social conditions are the determinants of health and have the most impact. That's why Offord dedicated his life to making sure people were thinking about how to ensure that every child, no matter where they live, has the opportunity to arrive at the starting line with what they need to soar through schooling and life.

Let's look at one city. Where I come from, Hamilton Ontario, there are kids who live in poverty. As one example, they don't get to become hockey players because they can't afford the equipment. Even if they get equipment to start with, they can't afford new equipment when their bodies change as they grow up. At school, they can't afford the pizza days other children enjoy unless there's someone on the Parent Council who insists that these days be scheduled on days that are close to the day their parents' support income checks arrive.

What does it feel like to be the child that can't afford pizza day, when that day is so easy for so many other children? What would it be like—day in and day out—to feel that you don't have as much as other students and be embarrassed about your clothing? We're now able to answer these questions, at least in part. The toxic stress of these environments affects how the brain develops, how well students get along with others and how well they're able to delay gratification, all of which are significant features of fitting in at school and feeling you belong. These conditions affect many characteristics that predict success and failure during a lifetime.

EARLY BRAIN DEVELOPMENT

Why is it that conditions surrounding childhood have such a long lasting effect? Scientists from many disciplines are coming together to point out how environments in which babies and children exist profoundly affect health, schooling and employment opportunities. The evidence comes from many sources. Longitudinal research (data that were gathered by following the same group of people over a long time and measuring their physical, educational and social development at different points in time) sheds light on what influences health and development during a lifetime. In one significant longitudinal study, Hertzman looked at results from a British cohort made up of people who were born during one particular week in 1958. In 2014, they were all 56 years of age. Data collected on this cohort covers many factors, for example, smoking during pregnancy, the mother's level of education, occupations in the family of origin, health status and school achievement indicators.

Hertzman focused on specific issues in this data. As an example, he looked at each child's height at age 7 and their math scores and made a guess at what their health situation would be at 45 years of age. During his research, he asked various questions, such as: Could he predict later health problems such as heart disease or asthma? Could height at age 7 (relative to their adult height) and math scores be telltale markers of what their early years were like? Could the relationship between the quality of nutrition they received, whether someone read to them in the early years, how parents spoke to them, all be related to later aspects of their lives? Through his research, and in the data, he found an association between these questions and what he discovered about their health later in their lives. Within the data, if children were doing poorly at age 7, they were more likely to have adult diseases like heart disease, lung disease and addictions.[7] How was it possible for him to propose this connection? The simple answer is that our health isn't based on the quality of our present activities alone. It's influenced by how our brains and bodies developed early in life. Another study, the Adverse Childhood Experiences study (ACEs), made a similar connection between the number of ACEs (adverse experiences) one has and adult health.[8] In this research, the more ACEs that were discovered (e.g., maltreatment, household dysfunction, neglect) the more likely was an occurrence of heart disease, depression, suicide and addiction later in life. In an era of ever-increasing worries about health care costs, we're well advised to focus on building better health for the future by addressing what happens early in life, instead of only treating and managing peoples' poor health once they become adults.

THE TEACHINGS OF THE ELDERS

I'm learning more about the human capacity to care for children from the wisdom of our First Nations peoples. Several years ago I heard Mohawk Elder Tom Porter speak. His wisdom was inspiring. He spoke about being raised by his grandmother. He talked about how much he *felt* felt by her, Porter has written down many of the lessons she taught him in a book he titled, *And Grandma Said...Iroquois Teachings.*[9] What was so remarkable to me was that many of the teachings he described are now supported in scientific literature. His grandmother told him that, when a child is conceived, it's the family who's pregnant. She told him people must look after the whole family that's raising children. Evidence is accumulating on the important role fathers have in the early years of development as well as in the mental health of the children's mother. Porter described his grandmother's advice that a husband should never yell at his wife when she's pregnant. The science of stress shows that high persistent stress in pregnancy is a problem for the developing baby. When they're born, children whose mothers experienced extreme, on-going stress during pregnancy are at an increased risk of being premature, smaller than the norm, with smaller heads, of developing more learning difficulties and are more at risk of developing Attention Deficit Hyperactivity Disorder (ADHD).[10]

EPIGENETICS: HOW THE ENVIRONMENT TALKS TO OUR GENES

There's another First Nations cultural belief that Canadians would do well to adopt. The belief is that community leaders should consider the next seven generations as they're making decisions. The next seven generations? Why is that? It's the kind of belief Clyde

Hertzman was talking about, which was based on his research with children. Essentially, what happens in the early years has a very long reach. The NOVA program (*www.pbs.org/wgbh/nova/genes/*) called *Ghosts in our Genes*[11] tells us that what our grandmother and great grandmother ate has, as one example, a big influence on whether we'll have diabetes later in life.

How are these messages passed along? Chemical message tags get placed on top of Deoxyribonucleic Acid (*DNA*). These 'tags' tell the DNA to be active and make proteins, or they tell the DNA to be silent. What's revolutionary in science is that we can outline how these messenger tags get passed down through the generations. DNA is a molecule that encodes the genetic instructions used in the development and functioning of all known living organisms. A belief that intergenerational transmission of trauma gets passed down through the generations (First Nations peoples have held this belief for a very long time) has scientific evidence to support it.[12] Their wisdom is something we should have paid attention to a long time ago. The best time to influence a child is 100 years before they're born. From the point of view of the best way to care for children, what happens during one generation affects the following one, as well as the generations after that. We have to ask ourselves what it would mean if we took the needs of children seriously. What would it mean for Canadian social policies and practices?

VULNERABILITIES IN THE EARLY YEARS

The wisdom that Tom Porter grew up hearing was based on a cultural belief that children are the sacred ones in a community. During the talk I was listening to, he said that children are the heart of the nation. Child rearing is a sacred communal responsibility. Imagine what it would be like if all Canadians actually believed that children are the heart of the community. If children were at the centre of what Canadians care about, what would we focus on in our newspapers? I think it would be very different from what we now see in the headlines.

8

In 2007 and 2013, UNICEF Innocenti.[13] Reports were made public. These reports addressed the quality of children's lives in developed countries.[14] The research analyzed data on children's well-being in the richest countries of the world and compared outcomes of that research among those countries. The data included measures for material well-being, education, health and safety, behaviors and risk, housing and environment.

In 2007, 21 countries were studied and Canada came 12th out of 21 countries. The more recent report came out in May 2013 and looked at 29 countries. In the 2013 report, the lives of Canadian children ranked 17 out of the 29 countries. Did Canadians hear about their mid-range ranking in the newspapers? No, we didn't. Why was that? When only 45% of 11 year olds, 13 year olds and 15 year olds report their parents spend time "just talking to them" compared to the report of children in Hungary at 90%, or, where we rank 17/29 in child and youth health and safety indicators, I can't help wondering what our young people think and feel about the country they live in. How can they ever think about being good citizens if they aren't experiencing parental support in their lives? Under the conditions reported in the data, how will children and youth come to care about other people, if they don't feel cared about themselves?

When we talk about being ranked overall at 17/29, what are we talking about? We're talking about children living in poverty and taking unreasonable risks that negatively impact their life chances. When the report came out, what hit the paper is that Canadian youth smoke more marijuana than youth in the other 28 countries. That's what hit the newspapers! How is it possible that Canadian children are stuck in the middle of that group of rich nations and their ranking overall never made the newspapers? Further, the report tells us that we're 27th out of 29 in child obesity and 22nd out of 29 in children's mental health. The purpose of doing that research was to provide a platform for the United Nations to persuade these rich countries that, if children do well, their communities will do well and the nation will do well.

As long as we have high vulnerability in our communities, our children won't flourish. When some of our kids do poorly, it affects everyone. I was listening to a presentation by Ed Rolnick, an American economist with the Minnesota Federal Reserve Bank. He observed that people don't even have to like kids to support their needs, but they need to know that children's well-being has an effect on whether there'll be enough dollars around for them to have health care once our country ages and the silver tsunami of Baby Boomers finally hits. Baby Boomers comprise a graying population that will need someone to look after them. Rolnick's point was that the quality of the workforce of tomorrow is based on the well-being of young children today.

There's no question that a lot of money is spent on children and the care of children. Yet it's overwhelmingly spent on physical health care. In terms of health care, about 1,000 cases of childhood cancer are diagnosed each year across the country, according to 2014 data from the Childhood Cancer Canada Foundation.[15] These health care dollars are much needed and well spent. Most people are aware of the need to act fast with good medicines for children who are affected by cancer.

However, other children suffer conditions that lead to a much higher long-term cost to our health budget, our special education budget and our criminal justice budget. Their plight is largely ignored. As examples, in 2008 there were 85,000 substantiated incidents of child abuse across the country. These investigations were complete. Allegations were found to be provable and substantiated. This number doesn't reflect numerous incidents of abuse in which the children withdraw allegations after family members pressure them or if we count cases of neglect where harm is harder to prove. How much are we spending on the well-being of these children and on efforts to prevent childhood maltreatment from happening? Not enough!

THE MAGNIFICENT PLASTIC BRAIN: NATURE OR NURTURE?

I've been saying that what happens in the early years lasts a lifetime. How is it that events in infancy and childhood get under the skin and affect development for life? To answer the question as simply as possible—it has everything to do with the brain. Researchers who study the early years care about the brain because they've come to realize that we are our brain. It's the master organ and is responsible for who we are, how we think and feel. The brain develops during a lifetime and changes through individual experience.

As one example, I'm a Canadian citizen and have lived in this country for over 50 years. Yet, I have a Scottish accent. Why is that? It's due to my early life experiences and their impact on my brain. I spent my first 11 years in Scotland. While I was there, my brain cells, called neurons, got fired up in the hearing and speaking centers of the brain. They were wired up together pretty solidly. All of the neurons that got wired up together cause me to speak with a Scottish accent. If I'd been born in Canada, the firing of neurons would have taken place in a pattern that sounded Canadian. If I grew up in France, I would sound French. At birth, my brain was ready to learn any language, even multiple languages. It was my experience— this exposure to a Scottish accent that sculpted my brain cells and gave me my accent. Neurons that get wired up together so that a person can speak with a Canadian accent didn't get used as I was learning language. They weren't used and hence they got pruned away.

As a consequence, I can only speak with a Scottish accent. My two younger brothers speak with a Canadian accent. My older brothers and sister speak with a Scottish accent. My children are bilingual. They speak with Canadian accents, but do a great imitation of my Scottish accent.

What about your experience? What about your brain? If you were to hear my Scottish accent, some of your brain's neurons would fire up and perhaps would ask you to think about some Scottish comedians. Perhaps you would think of the brilliant role that Robin Williams played as a Scottish nanny in Mrs. Doubtfire. So you'd hear that sound and you think, "Oh there's a Scottish accent." What about Star Trek? Who remembers Scotty? "Och, captain she'll never hold." You hear my Scottish accent and think of your experience with hearing a Scottish accent. As I speak with a Scottish accent, I kindle those neurons, those brain cells and mostly it's funny—if you're remembering Scotty or Robin Williams. So I have lit up the areas of your brain that got wired up earlier to hear my accent and now you think, "Oh isn't that nice." On the other hand, if you have a mother-in-law who's Scottish and is difficult to be around—who you think doesn't like you—a completely different area of your brain will fire up as I'm speaking.

Brains are built by personal experience. What you love, what you hate, what you laugh at—all of it is built up over time through experience. Here's an example of what I mean based on a story I heard from the Chief Justice of Ontario. She talked about a book she'd read that was written by a young man who said he was 10 years old when liberated from a concentration camp during World War II. After the war, he went to Switzerland. One day, his Swiss teacher asked him to come to the front of the class, look at a picture of William Tell and explain to the class what he saw in that picture.

Who was William Tell? He lived in the area we call Switzerland as it was trying to become independent. An Austrian magistrate didn't want independence to succeed. This magistrate tried to exert his influence over people and so he put his hat on a pole in the town square. All the people were supposed to bow as they passed by the hat. William Tell refused to bow. Because he wouldn't submit to bowing, the magistrate told William that he and his son would be executed. He was given one way out. He must shoot an arrow and knock an apple off his son's head. The picture given to the boy who had been in the concentration camp depicted William Tell with a crossbow and arrow in his hands that was pointed toward his son. The image showed him stretching the crossbow bowstring and preparing to shoot the arrow, as the boy stood in front of a tree with an apple perched on his head.

As the boy from the concentration camp stood at the front of the class with William Tell's picture in his hands, he said nothing. He froze. He couldn't talk. The teacher said, "Tell me what you see." He couldn't say anything. Finally he was able to say that it didn't make sense to him. "What do you mean?" asked the teacher. He replied, "They never used ammunition on children. They only gassed them." His brain was constructed by experience. As he looked at the picture, his neurons wired up a primitive, fearful, on-guard, frozen area of his brain. When Swiss kids looked at the picture, they saw one of their heroes and filled in the whole story. They knew William Tell loved his son and would never hurt him. Based on knowing this nationally important story, as they looked at the picture, areas of their brains released dopamine, a pleasure neurotransmitter.

Let's look at the brain from another perspective. I have a degree in music. That was my first degree. Every time I tell this story I hear the William Tell music in my head, which some of us remember from childhood. It was the Lone Ranger theme on television. I listened to that music while I was doing my philosophy and music degree. My brain is constructed by my experience of the story and the music. My brain lights up with dopamine when I think about or hear it.

If you're thinking of children whose life experiences have been destructive to them, there's some good news. Those who do research in the areas of psychology and psychiatry used to think it was genes that were responsible for different behaviors associated with the example of William Tell. Then we thought it was environment that built up these responses to an event. We'd argue about nature versus nurture. Is it our genes or is it the environment that shapes us? We may have had fun in these discussions but it was a waste of time. We now know that it's genes interacting with the environment that builds the person we become. It's nature and how it's affected by nurture that influences human growth. The early years are the greatest opportunity to affect how a brain is molded and constructed by experience.

BRAIN PLASTICITY

To go deeper into nature versus nurture, we need to talk about brain plasticity, which refers to how the brain changes due to experience. That's why we have to pay a lot of attention during the early years. Parent/baby or caregiver/baby interactions literally turn on brain cells and cause those cells to make connections with other brain cells. The more stimuli and experiences that enter, the stronger these signals and pathways become. If children hear lots of words and explanations during the day and are picked up when they're distressed, those related areas in the brain get linked up together. There's good research to show that we can rewire brains by creating new experiences if a child hasn't benefitted from good connections due to early childhood experiences. But just like building a house, restructuring isn't easy or simple. It's harder to reconstruct or renovate a house and a brain than it is to build it well in the first place. Repair takes a lot more energy and effort after the early years have passed.

Can a child who experienced early years neglect ever make up that lost time? The data are very mixed. Some evidence from Romanian orphanage studies shows that children who were removed early and placed in high quality foster care improved significantly compared to their peers who remained in these institutions.[16] Getting it right in the early years matters a great deal. Those who have children under the age of 6 years old, as they read this information, may wonder how soon they can put the book down to go and hug their kids. Those who have kids over 6 years may think they've already blown it. But here's the other big part of this story. Brains don't stop growing. Early years are the greatest period of plasticity but opportunities for change don't stop there.

Another magnificent time for renovation is during adolescence as brains are again under construction. Often parents think that the disruption during teenage years is due to hormones, but it isn't. It's the brain. Research on adolescent brain development has expanded as technology has developed ways to look at the brain in action—this research is relatively new, over the past decade or so. Researchers have learned there's a significant change going on in the brain of a young person, which I will discuss further in a later chapter. Again, experience is what builds the brain. Activities and experiences that young people have sculpt the brain. Suppose it's guitar or drama lessons, those areas of the brain develop. If it's social isolation and/ or violent video games, those experiences profoundly affect brain growth. Whatever gets used gets wired up together. What doesn't get used is snipped away or pruned.

THE BRAIN'S CAPACITY FOR CHANGE OVER A LIFESPAN

As a child psychiatrist, there's a huge part of brain research that's important for me as I work with families. The brain is capable of change throughout life—absolutely throughout life. I have a mantra in parenting: *Progress not perfection*. Another mantra I use in clinical work is, *Never give up on a child*. I have story after story of the power that one person can have to change a child's or young person's life.

As an example, when I work in rural communities, I've seen that the person who can provide the right conditions to change a young person's life might be the school janitor. For another young person, it was a school principal. One principal in a rural school noticed that a particular young man could spend half time in school but would need to de-compress by staying home. She also noticed that the young man loved talking to senior citizens. So she organized his schedule to let him spend half of his day at school and the other half of the day playing bingo, helping to clean up and do other odd jobs at the seniors residence next door to the school.

She used her insight into a strength-based approach and her observation of skill-based preferences to help a young person benefit from schooling. She didn't simply think about the pathology of a boy who wouldn't come to school. She asked herself what she knew about him and focused on what she could learn through careful observation. She helped him change.

This principal shows us that we have good reasons to shift from believing our current assumptions about the children we know or observe. That shift moves us to ask what we actually know about them based on understanding that brains can change throughout life. The good news is that if you're working with people who you believe can't change, you now know they can. But people have to want to change. So, how can we help people want to change? To understand how people might change, we have to start at the very beginning to see how the brain works.

The brain is responsible for what we think. But when does thinking begin? It starts with the infant's development *in utero*.

There's good research to show that if parents read to their baby *in utero,* after the baby is born, he or she will recognize the books parents first read to them.[17] They also recognize mom's voice and dad's voice. That's the positive side. But for babies whose moms are exposed to intense, persistent stress during pregnancy, there are signs they will have more problems later on, partly because stress affects a person's body chemistry. For example, levels of cortisol increase in mothers that experience intense, persistent stress during pregnancy. Cortisol is a body hormone secreted by the adrenal gland. As cortisol increases due to high stress *in utero* it affects the developing brain.

Human babies are born extremely dependent on their caregivers. Their brains weigh only about 1/3 to 1/4 of what they'll weigh by the time a child is 6 years old. That level of brain prematurity isn't seen in any other species. At birth, an infant brain is nine months premature. Researchers believe that human brain prematurity is related to ancestral experiences. As an example, as earlier Homo Sapiens developed new skills, such as using tools and walking upright, the brain was enlarged. An enlarging brain, built by this new experience, couldn't be delivered through the narrow and shallow pelvis of its mother. So the infant is delivered prematurely in terms of its brain. Despite this prematurity, a human baby is well designed to make sure there are systems set in place to have caregivers who are crazy about them and want to look after them.

What does that mean for the first year of life? During that year, babies should be treated as if they were in what we might call an external womb. As a consequence, the Canadian federal policy of 18-month parental leave should support the reality every infant finds itself in. At birth all the billions of brain cells are in place and they have been since about the 20 weeks gestation period, but they haven't made significant connections or networks with other neurons. Many crucial developmental windows, or sensitive periods, are most open and responsive in the first 5 years of life. Research into brain development identifies the experiences children have in their earliest years as the source for making these essential connections among neurons in the brain.[18]

Some practices aimed at paying attention to brain development in the early years are becoming common. As an example, at doctors' visits in the first two years of life, a baby's head is measured. Why do doctors do this? Measuring the brain helps establish that new brain wiring is happening, as it should be. Babies who are extremely neglected show a failure to thrive, which is observable based on the size of their heads and their bodies. Neglect prevents heads and bodies from growing at the right pace.[19]
Sensory experience during these early years builds connections among all brain cells. Development results from all the connections that happen in the brain. Given the profound vulnerability of babies in their first year, we must ensure that we have social policies to support young families so they can stay home or find loving caregivers, get the resources they need, and have the general social support they require. We must support young mothers who develop depression or anxiety *post-partum* because this condition can interfere significantly with their ability to carry out the social interaction babies require in order for early experiences to establish secure brain development.

At birth, everything is in place. But what happens during pregnancy to start the brain development ball rolling? The brain starts to develop as a neural tube within a few days of conception and continues to develop throughout pregnancy and after birth. Brain cells migrate to their appropriate geographic location in the brain during the first 20 weeks of pregnancy, if no toxins interfere with this movement. Alcohol is a known toxin that not only affects facial features in the developing foetus and other physical features as well. It can also affect brain development throughout pregnancy.

Alcohol affects where brain cells go, how they grow and how they communicate with one another. Early in the first trimester of pregnancy the baby's face is developing. If high levels of alcohol are in the mother's blood during this time it can affect developing face cells so that they grow in a way that produces the identifiable features of Foetal Alcohol Effect (FAE). However, at any time during pregnancy alcohol can negatively affect the brain. The majority of people who have foetal alcohol disorders don't have identifiable facial features. They may have a normal IQ but the brain is affected nonetheless. They may have issues that impede their progress, such as attention problems, self-regulation issues, learning difficulties and other developmental challenges. At no point during pregnancy is it safe for mothers to drink alcohol.

During brain development, the first cells to develop essential connections among the neurons are sensory. What do I mean? From the start, a baby's brain cells are in place in various areas of the brain and are set up to expect stimulating experiences to occur. The brain is ready and programmed to receive stimulation. As stimulating experiences occur and enter the brain, they come in first through the senses, as an example, through sound. Signals such as a mother's voice are picked up and sent through fingerlike branches in the brain called dendrites. Stimulation enters the brain and turns on chemicals that initiate a signal. As a signal gets stronger, it reaches a critical threshold and causes a release of other signals to fire off a neurotransmitter, or cell messenger. These cell messengers cause the next brain cell, or neuron, to get into the action and start the firing process too. As stimuli come in over and over again, the signal gets stronger. As this happens, neurons fire these signals and connect with other neurons.

Cells communicate as they send out neurotransmitters into the space between neurons. The space between neurons is called synapses. It's the new synapses and dendrites (connections) that actually cause the increased brain size doctors measure in the first 2 years of life. As parents or caregivers read to babies over and over again, the process of creating synapses takes place. Connections between and among brain cells are re-enforced. If stimuli come in over and over again, they build a huge highway in the brain. This highway is built of all these connections occurring in cells that get used over and over again as stimulation enters the brain. If there is a little bypass that didn't get used very much it shrivels up and goes away: brain cells that fire up together are the ones that wire up together.

What's behind the drive to create these brain highways? Andrew Meltzoff provided some of the earliest work that looked at a baby's drive to connect and imitate what was coming in through his or her experience. In a now famous paper, written in 1977,[20] he included a picture of an adult and a very young baby. In the picture, the baby is clearly imitating the mouth gestures of the adult. I said earlier that a baby has an ability to ask for the environment that helps it survive. What do these requests look like? What's the purpose of imitation captured in Meltzoff's picture?

His picture tells us about a human baby and the brain. His image demonstrates the powerful drive to connect that helps a baby learn it can have an effect on another person so that something happens. This capacity to connect creates a bond that has an adult fall crazily in love with the baby. In this way, babies learn they can make a difference. The baby experiences: "Wow, I do something and something happens back." It was a significant revelation for the whole field of infant studies that babies have this capacity.

With this revelation, people wanted to improve baby brain development. When scientists first started reporting that enriched environments stimulate brain growth in rats, people got very excited. If rats in enriched environments had better memories and bigger brains, wouldn't it be great to create enriched environments for human babies. People jumped on the bandwagon. Products flooded the market, such as Baby Einstein, flash cards and many others. But what if what works with rats doesn't fit human experience?

What babies need to grow great brains isn't fancy programs. They need daily back and forth, serve and return social interaction, that happen during face-to-face interaction with loving, responsive, caring adults. Babies are intensely curious about their environments. They're like little scientists that pick up cues from all around them. As an example, some of the brain research describes babies in India that are able to observe adults precisely. As a result, they shake their heads in a particular way. These infants also note the particular way adults raise their eyebrows. As other examples, little babies can tell if someone they see on a screen is speaking their own or a different language, even if the sound is turned off.[21] As these little scientists notice clues from their surroundings, they learn about the environment and start learning communication strategies so later on they can learn language.

A tiny infant has a remarkable capacity to engage adults so that learning is possible. When I'm presenting to audiences I play a video to reinforce this point. The video captures the experience of a 7-day old child named Jordan who's interacting with his grandfather. As his grandfather puckers his lips, the baby does the same. The infant even reaches out to touch his grandfather. We see Jordan smile in delight in return to his grandfather's smile. When my youngest son was born in 1994 we wouldn't have recognized the social interaction pattern that's so clearly conveyed through the video between Jordan and his grandfather. We wouldn't have been able to read this image because we didn't expect this level of social interaction from a 7-day old infant. We thought it would come much later. In 1994, smiling, puckering, reaching toward an adult face was attributed to tummy gas! We had no idea babies were that competent and capable from birth. What does the video tell us? It tells us that we need environments in which people fall madly in love with their kids through the serve and return of social interaction.

We also need to do more research on the importance of dads in baby's life. We have all kinds of research on the impact of moms and babies and their inter-personal interaction, but we don't have nearly as much on the influence of fathers. I recall hearing Dr. Terry Brazelton say that typically, when moms pick up their babies or interact with them, they use a baby voice. They say things such as: "Oh, you're so cute." When a dad comes in, he's more likely to say something like: "Hey, how're ya' doing kid." When babies are in their car seats, a mom will come in and snuggle up close. Dads come into the car and do this bump, bump thing on the baby's tummy to make the infant laugh.[22] He was describing his experience after having seen thousands of parent child interactions. I also certainly see moms or partners interact in non-gender specific ways.

It's important to infant development that babies experience different ways of interaction. As an example, how often have you seen a parent toss a baby in the air and catch the child? Who is it most likely to be? It's fantastic for babies. The experience of being tossed in the air and caught fires different neurons than those that fire when an infant is cuddled. But when my kids were little, I didn't know it was good for them, neither did my husband. If a dad threw his baby in the air, other people would get nervous and say: "Oh no, don't do that. That's not good for the baby." We didn't have research to tell us it was good. It's important for a baby to have experiences of excitement and high energy and recognize the different ways people like to interact—whether mom, dad or partner. The brain is a social organ. But there's something we need to keep in mind. It's a social organ that's affected by how much stimulation comes in and by how much stress a child experiences.

CONCLUSION

Why do the first five years last forever? The quality of a child's environment builds the infant, toddler and adolescent brain. It's the quality of adult/child relationships during the serve and return, which is the back and forth of social interaction in everyday experience that sculpts its architecture so that, under favorable conditions, the child has a strong, solid foundation for learning, particularly, learning to care about other people.

But the dark reality of brain plasticity is that poor environments create weak foundations. Toxic stress damages that foundation as much as does poor nutrition. So the work of creating civil society is to promote healthy conditions and to prevent adverse conditions during the early years. We must wholeheartedly address barriers that keep adults from being the parents they long to be. The willingness and ability to create healthy relational environments is a responsibility of a civil society.

In this chapter, I've emphasized the role of everyday face-to-face, serve and return social interaction as the centerpiece of healthy brain development. I want to acknowledge the work of a school program called *Roots of Empathy,* which originated in Ontario, but is now worldwide. Mary Gordon developed the program and records its development and outlook in a book by the same name. I heard her tell the following story to the Dalai Lama during a *Seeds of Compassion* Conference.

I love to repeat the story because it's a profound example of brain plasticity and hope. In her book, *Roots of Empathy,* she tells the story of a visit made to a school by a baby and its parents. It was an Elementary classroom. The baby and parents came to the class once

21

a month for a school year. The kids watched the baby grow. They predicted what the baby might be doing at the next visit and learned lots of relevant material about a child's life. This is Mary's story.

There was this one boy in the class who was 14 years old even though the other kids were 12. Life hadn't been very good to him. He had seen his mom murdered when he was 4. He'd been in all kinds of foster homes.

He'd likely had all the diagnoses that I know how to give. The mom [in the Roots of Empathy program] was talking this day about temperament as she interacted with her own baby in the class. She said, you know, we wanted a snuggly baby, but you get the baby that gets sent to you and you love him as he is. Our baby loves to interact with the world. So we had to get this snuggly pack. We put him in the snuggly pack and he kicks his legs as he interacts with others.

She then asked if anyone would like to try the snuggly pack. Well, the 14 year-old said he would like to hold the baby. He came up and the mom handed him the baby. The baby snuggled right in with that boy. At the end of the class he brought the baby back and handed him to its mom. Then he turned to the *Roots of Empathy* facilitator and said, "Do you think that someone who's never been loved can learn to be a dad?" That baby and that program changed that boy's life. He felt the power of connection.

In this chapter, I've discussed neurons, synapses and the power of relationship. At the core of everything I want to convey is the power that one person can have on another person. That power is conveyed through serve and return—of listening as much as we talk to our infants, toddlers, older children and adolescents. Our capacity for serve and return is what we need to take into the work we do with our own kids and kids in our communities. Can you imagine what would happen if we pooled the power of serve and return and brought its impact to our motivation to build the ecological model of human development that was introduced at the beginning of this chapter? What an enormous difference we could make for all the kids in our communities, in our schools and in our cities.

2

Attachment in the Early Years

INTRODUCTION

I n the first chapter, I introduced the child's need for social interaction with adults that are crazy about their babies. In this chapter, I consider a universal tendency among human infants to seek comfort from the adults they know when they need protection or are in distress. The social and cultural contexts children are raised in have different expectations but this essential need remains the same. As examples, some cultures expect children to be self-sufficient, others expect them to be dependent, but an infant's need to be soothed when upset and nurtured when sick is universal.

The pathway for being soothed is established through attachment behavior between adults and infants. I will focus on attachment using a Western lens, which, in general, has the development of psychological autonomy as its child rearing aim. To be successful in Western societies, each child must develop human attributes such as higher cognitive functions, problem-solving abilities, empathy, self-awareness and an ability to manage well under stress—all of which we believe are achieved by developing personal, psychological autonomy.

Secure attachment is at the center of these human attributes. While there are many cultural variations on the desirable outcomes of parenting and child development across the world, the human need for an overall sense of felt security conveyed through attachment is universal. We accomplish attachment with children by giving them exclusive, individual attention, lots of face-to-face time and plenty of verbal stimulation.

In this chapter, I provide perspectives on an infant's need for attachment, the infant brain's readiness to experience and participate in an attachment relationship and an outline of attachment theory. By presenting these perspectives and this outline, I hope to show that, because the human brain is immature at birth and later brain development is dependent on what has gone on before, the environment is significant in shaping an infant brain. During the early years, the brain is sculpted by experience with the result that an infant's sense of secure attachment, essential for survival, has a long lasting effect on the brain functions required for success. At the end of the chapter, I address the question of what parents can do to provide secure attachment for their infants and young children.

ATTACHMENT AND THE BRAIN

A felt sense of security is built through attachment systems established between infants and adults. What does it mean to say that the human brain at birth is ready to experience and participate in attachment systems? Babies, unlike many other mammals are born completely helpless and dependent on the protection of other human beings. An infant's helplessness is a mechanism for establishing connection that develops into attachment. Helplessness is involved in the development of systems of attachment that provide for survival, thriving, and for all other forms of human development. The helpless infant is a basic part of the human condition that's observed across the world. In order to have a viable human society, systems need to be in place to ensure a baby's survival. On one side of the relationship, parents require a biological drive to care for their offspring. On the other, offspring need ways to alert adults to their needs. Among human beings, attachment is one of the systems that ensure survival and that's grounded on infant helplessness.

What are some of the conditions that allow human helplessness to function as it does in the development of attachment? During the development of human beings (Homo sapiens) the human brain encountered some changes that provided helplessness as a key to attachment, as the species adapted to these changes. The adaptations made by human beings led to changes in expression or activity of the genes' DNA. Adaptations not only led to changes but also required some compromises. Very briefly, as an example, ancient Homo Sapiens ancestors explored their environment on all fours until they began to use their hands to make and use tools. Eventually they started reaching upwards and then began walking on two legs. At this point, new experiences were available to them and these experiences built new connections among brain cells. As a consequence, the brain increased in size, particularly in the large part at the front of the brain, i.e., the prefrontal cortex.

This evolutionary progress created a physical challenge. The brain was becoming larger but as females stood upright the pelvis became narrower and shallower creating a dilemma as they tried to deliver an infant's large head. The evolutionary trade off was to deliver the baby prematurely while the head was still small enough to fit the birth canal. As a consequence, the continuation of brain development happened outside the womb. This phenomenon, called secondary altriciality, means that the infant emerges at birth in a state of helplessness due to having 1/3 of the brain size of a mature adult. Neuroscience has made great strides in the recent years. Various ways of imaging the brain have been developed that offer more accessibility to the study of the infant brain. There's a clearer understanding of how brain development affects the development of behavior. A newborn's immature brain means that all the major structures and neurons (brain cells) are in place but many more connections need to be formed. Babies can't provide these connections for themselves. They rely on their caregivers to care, protect, nurture, co-regulate and soothe them. Babies need to be able to emit signals and caregivers need to receive these signals. This infant to other system creates ways that signals can be addressed as a caring adult protects the baby. Unlike an older child who can run away when distressed, an infant is immobile and greatly dependent on others. The drive to survive contributes to the ongoing processes of brain development.

To understand attachment, it's important to know how the immature brain works and how it develops. A key concept to this understanding is that when babies are born they have billions of brain cells (neurons) needed for growth, yet, as mentioned in chapter one, a brain (head) weighs only about 1/3 of what it will weigh when the child is an adult. The growth in the first three years isn't due to an increase in neurons (brain cells) but rather to a massive growth and pruning among the connections between the neurons (synapses) and the supporting cells and networks that connect them to each other. As we shall see, much of the brain growth based on these connections is sculpted by the baby's experience.

The brain matures in *utero* in a predictable way. Yet it can be modified by environmental influences such as lack of nutrition e.g., folic acid and also by toxins such as alcohol and other substances. It's also impacted by maternal stress. In the 1960s, Paul MacLean suggested a simplified version of the evolution of brain development and its structure, which he called the triune brain.[1] One analogy is that the brain is like an old city with a long history. I always imagine

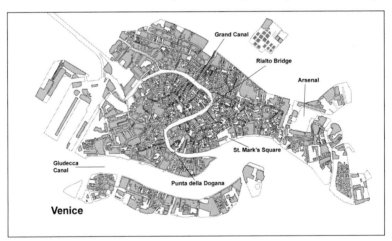

Venice when I consider this analogy. That city has its old sections where, in ancient times, the activities required for human survival took place. That part of Venice is like the oldest part of the brain, referred to as the reptilian brain. Venice also has newer sections that developed around those older ones, which in the human brain is called the Limbic area. Lastly, Venice has modern sections, as we know the city now, which were often built on the foundations of other parts of the old city. In the human brain, this newer part is called the Neocortex.

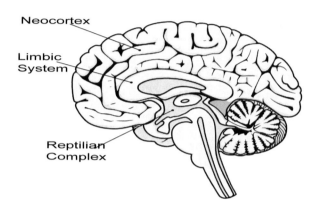

The **reptilian** brain is the oldest part and it consists of the brainstem and the cerebellum. It's present in all species from reptiles and upwards to more complex mammals and primates and is responsible for basic physiologic functions such as heart rate, body temperature, breathing and balance. Clearly, this area needs to be fully functioning in a newborn. Premature infants often require external support for these functions because the brain has not fully "wired up" i.e., made the necessary neuronal connections for these to be working.

The **limbic**/emotion brain evolved next in mammals and consists of structures, or groups of brain cells, which include the hippocampus, amygdala and hypothalamus. In human beings, emotions derive from this area. Memories of experiences, pleasant and unpleasant, are recorded here. It also houses our threat appraisal and response system, which includes fight, flight or freeze options. This threat response system is, according to some researchers, the reason we have survived as a species.[2] We needed an instantaneous drive from

27

the threat system to get us running from predators or we would have been eaten and become extinct. Babies have very few connections between their limbic system and the cortex of the brain.

Yet, eventually, in the connections between limbic systems and the cortex, access to self-regulation and soothing cognitive strategies develop. Because they're as yet under-developed in infants, physiological needs cause them distress. If something goes wrong for them, their system goes on high alert and they cry. But babies learn to regulate these overwhelming distress signals over time and make connections with other brain networks, as they're being co-regulated by another person, i.e., their primary caregiver.

These early developing sensory and perceptual pathways are crucial for learning how to read the environment, understand language, respond to faces and learn to express emotion. For the first few months, babies aren't well developed in these social skills. They eat, sleep or cry. But the way caregivers respond to their primitive needs sets the stage for the infant's soon to unfold interest in social interaction. By about 6 months of age they have built foundational pathways and begin to show obvious preference for primary caregivers. In Western society, we tend to see stranger wariness and separation anxiety begin to show themselves at this point in an infant's life.

From the perspective of a developing brain, as I talk with parents, I urge them never to ignore an infant's cry. Let me say it again: DO NOT let infants cry it out. When babies cry, they need something. If they're distressed the limbic system is ON. At this point in their development, they don't have neuronal links to higher parts of the brain, which they require in order to manipulate adults. When they cry, they need to be soothed. When babies cry their distress activates neuronal pathways in the limbic system, which develop to protect any human being from threat.

Infants have no control over these pathways. Distress activates the stress response and initiates a cascade of interactions in the body. First, there's the release of fast acting adrenalin, which increases the baby's heart rate, breathing, and initiates physiological responses, such as dilated pupils and less blood flow to the tummy. There are also signals sent to release cortisol, one of the body's stress hormones. Cortisol has many functions, one of which prepares the body for a response to injury.

To turn off this stress response, the brain requires systems and signals to convey that the threat is gone. In adults, this comfort is supplied in part by our established memories and pathways, but infants need adults to turn it off through the action of soothing them. High levels of cortisol are known to damage the brain. Longitudinal observational studies have shown that babies who are soothed when distressed will cry less. In attachment language, they become securely attached. They develop internal, mental working models to convey that the world is safe. As a consequence of relying on these mental models, the limbic alarm system is alerted less often. The **neocortex/thinking** brain evolved in primates with (arguably) its culmination being seen in an adult human brain. In the brain, there are two hemispheres responsible for the development of human language, abstract thought, imagination and consciousness. The prefrontal cortex, at the front of the brain just behind the forehead, is the last to develop. In fact there is now convincing evidence that this area of the brain is under construction all the way into early adulthood, until about 25 years old or later.[3] Slow brain development explains much of an adolescent's behavior: on one hand, the positive, wonderful creativity they demonstrate and on the other, the challenging risk-taking, thrill-seeking behavior that gets a lot of attention from adults.[4]

From the time a child is born there are brain cells in all the brain sections described above. The brain continues to grow in a hierarchical fashion: i.e., lower pathways such as sensory pathways, e.g., sight and sound, develop before more complex systems such as language and reasoning. The order and timing of development is genetically programmed but the strength of the connections made in the infant brain is affected by experience.[5] What happens early in life affects later development. This is a very important concept. After birth, the brain is experience-dependant. It can be sculpted and altered by experience because the environment affects gene expression or activity.

There's no longer a debate about what's more important nature or nurture, genes or the environment. There's general agreement among researchers that it's genes interacting with the environment that shapes the developing brain. When adults are sensitive to a baby's needs and soothe the baby that interaction activates neuronal pathways that lead to internal soothing by the infants themselves. Not attending to the baby consistently (no one is perfect and can do it all the time) leads to increased cortisol in the body and more activation of stress pathways. As a result of a lack of soothing and responsive interactions, babies are more restless, irritable and poorly regulated.

In addition to the relationship between brain development and attachment, social interactions between infants and caregivers offer other benefits as well. Initially, there's a massive overproduction of synapses because babies need to be able to adapt to the environment in which they're born.[6] For example, when babies are born they have the potential to speak any of the multiple languages on the globe. As I mentioned with my own Scottish experience, in the first 6-7 months, as they hear sounds from the specific language in their surrounding, their brain notes these sounds and brain synapses fire based on them. By one year of age, the capacity to recognize all the nuances of languages has been overruled by language sounds that get repeated over and over in the baby's environment. What gets heard gets wired into pathways; what doesn't get heard gets pruned away. As a result, their family language is the one that gets the most firings. During this experience, the earlier synapses get pruned away.[7] Infant experience is something like hearing and learning all the words to a play and then finally performing only one part of it.

Through experience, pathways that get used over and over are strengthened. The ones that go unused get eliminated.[8] The implications for attachment are very significant in the development of the child's abilities. For example, foundations for managing stress are established in very young children. As pathways are built through repetition and over time, they enable children to manage emotions well, eventually to think rationally under pressure and calm down without relying on angry outbursts or attacks of anxiety. All these pathways are built in a hierarchical fashion through the development of secure attachments.[9]

ATTACHMENT THEORY: BOWLBY AND AINSWORTH

In the latter half of the twentieth century, a British psychoanalytically trained psychiatrist and researcher John Bowlby and Canadian researcher Mary Ainsworth[10] developed what they called attachment theory based on their observations. They proposed that, in order to thrive emotionally and physically, babies require consistent, close and caring adult caregivers. If a baby becomes upset, distressed or sick, in order for the infant to survive, she or he requires responses from the environment that offer protection and care. The response of a caregiver might be predictable and calming or unpredictable and frightening. Research into human behavior suggests that when babies' needs are sensitively and predictably met, they develop a secure attachment. Secure attachment is more likely to lead to healthy exploration and development and to a higher likelihood of better psychological health. If these needs are not sensitively and predictably met, the infant's development can take a different and more problematic course.

Before I go too much further a word to the wise: As parents, we can't possibly prevent our children from experiencing future unhappiness or difficult challenges. As a mother of five I know this only too well. However, by developing secure attachments, our children will be better prepared for dealing with these challenges and disappointments. The knowledge we now have about brain development and experiences that build brain pathways, strongly supports the idea that secure attachment can help children deal with stress, manage their emotions and develop higher order functions and empathy.

Based on careful observation and clinical practice, Bowlby and Ainsworth developed attachment theory long before the workings of the brain could be imaged in the ways we now have available. Bowlby summarized the value of attachment in the following way:

An individual who has been fortunate in having grown up in an ordinary good home with ordinarily affectionate parents has always known people from whom he can seek support, comfort,

31

and protection....So deeply established are his expectations and so repeatedly have they been confirmed that, as an adult, he finds it difficult to imagine any other kind of world....For many more [children] the likelihood that a caretaking figure would respond in a supportive and protective way has been at best hazardous and at worst nil [so that]...through their eyes the world is seen as comfortless and unpredictable; and they respond either by shrinking from it or by doing battle with it.[11]

Bowlby made his summary after working with behaviors he observed and interpreted based on the prevailing psychological theories at the time. The notion of attachment took him in a different direction from many of his colleagues and also from his teachers.

Bowlby, trained at The British Psychoanalytic Institute with Melanie Klein but he couldn't agree with her hypothesis "that children's emotional problems are almost entirely due to fantasies generated from internal conflict between aggressive and libidinal drives rather than to events in the external world."[12] His life experience told him otherwise. As a student volunteer in a school for maladjusted children, he was struck by the frequent history of maternal neglect among the children. Later in postgraduate work at the London Child Guidance Clinics, he meticulously reviewed the case notes of 44 young boys who were similar in their lack of affection and their history of stealing. As he studied these similar histories of maternal deprivation and separation he was able to theorize and link their symptoms to these early histories.

In another context, in 1952, the reaction of children separated from their mothers for lengths of days was exquisitely filmed by James and Joyce Robertson.[13] The film showed the children's reaction in stages ranging from protest, to despair to detachment. As an example, one child, John aged 17 months, was admitted to a residential nursery, as was the custom of the day, while his mother was admitted elsewhere for 9 days to have her second baby. John first showed protest and tried to get attention from the nurses. But there were frequent staff changes. Caring for the emotional needs of a child was not seen as necessary. After a few days, he refused to eat and would cry inconsolably. His sleep became disturbed. Eventually he withdrew, he became less interested in the nurses or his father when he came to visit. When his mother eventually came back he ignored her and wouldn't be comforted by her.

The films of John and other children revealed the pattern of protest to despair to detachment that was so powerful, this research eventually changed the way hospitals in the UK care for children.[14] Bowlby asserted that "the infant and young child should experience a warm, intimate, and continuous relationship with his mother (or permanent mother substitute) in which both find satisfaction and enjoyment."[15]

Mary Ainsworth worked with Bowlby and contributed significantly to the theory of attachment by classifying attachment patterns and by describing the quality of those attachments. She had observed infant-mother interactions over a 9-month period in Uganda. She also was part of an extremely thorough Baltimore observational study of 26 families. She studied these families before a child was born into them and then up until the time that the child was 13 months old. What struck her were the different ways that infants expressed their distress and also the varied ways that mothers responded to that stress. As she considered what she was seeing, Bowlby's theoretical framework made the most sense of her observations. She identified three patterns in the Ugandan babies. These patterns were the following:

- Securely Attached: Infants who cried little and safely explored their environments in the presence of their mothers were named securely attached. Their mothers were more sensitively attuned to their babies and could give a fuller narrative and offer ideas about the infant's behavior.

- Insecurely Attached: Babies who cried more, were more difficult to soothe, appeared more anxious and demonstrated less exploratory behavior. Their mothers on observation and interview were less predictably responsive to their infants and didn't seem to interpret the baby's cues well.

- Not yet Attached: Infants who didn't show any preferential or specific attention to their own mothers.

In the Baltimore setting, Ainsworth made observations and developed a lab test to assess these attachment patterns. She called the lab test the Strange Situation. With the test, she was able to link early, minutely detailed home-based observations of maternal-child interaction to infant behavior in a laboratory setting. Her observations were made with mothers and infants. Researchers also now look at father-child attachment patterns.

THE STRANGE SITUATION PARADIGM

In the Strange Situation, 8 carefully constructed scenes unfold over a 20-minute time period. The scenes are designed to gradually increase the stress babies might experience. The interactions and reactions are observed and coded behind a two-way mirror.

- Scene 1: An experimenter leaves the parent, most often the mother and the baby in the experiment room to play.
- Scene 2: Mother sits and allows the child to explore the room on her or his own allowing for observations to see if the child is feeling secure enough to explore the environment, with the parent providing a secure base.
- Scene 3: A stranger enters the room and speaks with the mother. At this stage, observers are looking for the presence or absence of stranger anxiety.
- Scene 4: The parent leaves the room and the stranger stays. The stranger can offer the baby comfort if needed. Again separation anxiety is recorded.
- Scene 5: Reunion in which the mother comes back, greets the baby and offers comfort if needed. The stranger leaves. This is the key observation time as the babies' reactions to the reunion are the most telling.
- Scene 6: Parent leaves the room again, leaving the baby alone in the room. Separation anxiety again is coded.
- Scene 7: The stranger returns and offers comfort to the baby. Observers are looking for stranger anxiety and to see if the

stranger can soothe the baby.

- Scene 8: Reunion and mother returns, greets the baby and offers soothing. The baby is allowed to go back to play and explore. This again is a crucial observation time as observers are coding babies' reactions in this final reunion.

What's most important in the Strange Situation is how the infants respond when mothers return. Children became upset when mother left but some infants weren't soothed when mother came back. In this research summary, Ainsworth and her colleagues classified the children's behavior into 3 attachment categories of attachment behavior:

- Secure
- Insecure Anxious
- Insecure Avoidant

Securely attached infants were seen to explore the room using their mothers as a secure base. They would check back with her and share toys. With secure attachment, as mothers returned in the first and the second reunion, the child sought bodily contact with her and was soothed by her return. Once the reunion was established, the child moved about to explore and play in the room, quite soon after her return.

Key to Ainsworth's observations and theory is the hours of home-based interaction that she compared with the lab setting behavior during the Strange Situation. Because she made at-home observations before she observed mothers and infants during the Strange Situation, she could compare the home based patterns of social interaction between infants and caregivers with those of the Strange Situation.

If we reflect on her research from our current perspective, Ainsworth documented brain-building activities for these children and made pretty accurate predictions on what children would expect from the environment. With current brain research to back her, she might have been able to assess how likely their limbic system would be activated through their experiences and how easily they would be soothed. She might also have realized how their stress reactivity would be fired up and then return to a baseline. Given observational histories of children in her original study that showed a securely attached pattern, she could show they had experienced predictable, sensitive care giving with warm adult responsiveness when these infants offered cues as to their needs. This predictable, warm pattern had been their experience from their earliest months. About 60-70 percent of infants studied were classified as Secure by Ainsworth. Further, meta-analysis of many current studies continue to confirm her distribution.[16]

In Ainsworth's research, she observed some infants who weren't soothed when their mothers returned. She classified this group as Insecure. In this category, several sets of behaviors were observed. When mothers returned, some children seemed resistant to her efforts to comfort them. They would continue to cry and push away from their mothers when they were picked up. Sometimes they hit their mothers. In general, they didn't relax into their mother's arms. They seemed ambivalent—wanting closeness but also being bothered by the mother's attention. In these cases, there was a pattern in the observational history of their earlier years that was typified by parental inconsistency. When these children were distressed, the parental response was unpredictable. Mothers of children in this group were observed often to mismatch their response to the child's need. Ainsworth summarized that 10-15% of children were in this Insecure category. When carrying out similar studies, another researcher, Van IJzendoorn also classified 10-15% of his research group in the Insecure category.

A third group of children that Ainsworth observed seemed not to care that the mother returned. They tended to avoid her. These children had earlier histories of very poor interactions with their mothers. For example, they were predominantly ignored when seeking comfort. These mothers were more pre-occupied with their own needs and weren't sensitive to their children's needs. In looking at her data, it was almost as if the children had learned to think "there's no help here, why bother."[17] However, more recent studies have shown these toddlers aren't indifferent. They have elevated physiological stress indicators and an increased amount of cortisol in their systems. While they may appear indifferent, their limbic systems are firing. In Ainsworth's research, 20-25% of children fitted into this category.[18]

In addition, there was a puzzling group of children who initially didn't fit the schema very well. They were infants who were known to have experienced maltreatment. In fact, they had experienced frightening events at the hands of their caregivers. In her initial attempts, Ainsworth found them to be unclassifiable. They appeared dazed, frozen at times and confused. It might look as if they were approaching the parent on reunion only to stop inches away from her. At times, they might flop on the ground. In more recent research, Mary Main and Judith Solomon established a fourth category they call Disorganized.[19] In this category, there's a mix of behaviors that don't come through in any co-ordinated or systematic way. These children had a history of being frightened by the very people they needed to turn to for soothing.

Dr Alan Sroufe, a psychologist from Minnesota and another key name in attachment theory, authored The Minnesota Longitudinal Study.[20] This study shows that infants in the first three categories have developed strategies to deal with emotional distress so that they can maintain proximity with the parent. They have developed neural pathways and connections to help them deal with stressful situations. Rather than eliminating the stress, they developed some agency in managing it. However, children with Disorganized attachment are believed to lack any such strategy, which is the reason for the name given to this category. Their responses are disorganized. In this group of children, there are no organizing networks to assist in dealing with overwhelming situations and the stress systems that a feeling of being overwhelmed will turn on.

In the follow up of his longitudinal study, these children have the most damaging pathology and mental health issues.[21] As a result, many researchers now look at Borderline Personality Disorder, which is a severe disorder of affect-regulation, as an attachment based disorder.[22] These findings lead us to bring the science of attachment and neuro-science together to explore what happens when parental sensitivity in the first year is less than ideal. The hypothesis is that stress in the parent/child relationship, manifested through attachment behavior, can have the same physiological impact as other forms of toxic stress.

In her research, Ainsworth concluded that parental sensitivity in the first year is the precursor of attachment security. From a neuroscientific perspective, relational environments sculpt the brain for better or worse in the early years. The stress created by intense poverty, mal-treatment and neglect within a child's environment, can wreak havoc on the developing brain. This damage affects the reactivity of the stress system and the development of higher order functions such as self-regulation and empathy. Disorganized attachment also contributes to toxic stress.

In the process of ordinary social engagement, it's attachment and responsive caregiving that matters.[23] Secure attachment, attuned and sensitive care giving, from all known measures, lead toward better outcomes for children. In healthy serve and return interactions, children create a set of mental models that depict the self and the others within these social interactions. These are internal, working models based on a child's repeated interactions with significant others.[24] Children who are securely attached are more likely to have adaptive capabilities and a good equilibrium of self-regulation.[25] At the other extreme, children who experienced severe neglect, maltreatment and frightening behavior from their caregivers were more likely to have a disorganized attachment that has serious psychological consequences.[26] What do we know about the middle group, those who are insecurely attached? It's important to remember that the categorization isn't a diagnosis. It's a description of observable behaviors. As an example, a child can be securely attached to one parent and insecurely attached to the other. Research shows that if the environmental context changes, children with insecure attachment can begin to exhibit more secure attachments and the behavior that goes along with secure attachment. This observation has been shown in the Bucharest Adoption studies.[27] But even in situations in which children aren't as severely deprived (as they were in that study), changes in attachment can be seen if the parent-child interaction becomes more attuned.[28]

I'd like to say a bit more about the program I mentioned in chapter one, *Roots of Empathy*. It is a wonderful program developed by my dear friend and colleague Mary Gordon. It has a ton of research and is now evidence based. But more importantly from my perspective is how it teaches children in the elementary and preschool years about attachment, empathy, temperament and so many other crucial human attributes.

A baby and parent visit the classroom once a month for the entire school year , but the visit is preceded and followed up with a Roots of Empathy facilitator who helps the children learn. By predicting and observing what the baby is doing and becoming, the children can see LOVE writ large in the interaction with the parent, but they also learn, through the expert facilitation of the ROE program, about their own feelings and the feeling of others. The children learn about their own temperament by observing the children in every single lesson. I had the pleasure of observing the program in Toronto along with Dr. Dan Siegel and I was so impressed , as he also was, with the insight of the group of Grade 8 students we spoke with about the program. When the students were asked what they wished for the baby, one young African Canadian boy said he hoped the baby could grow up in a world where the colour of his skin did not determine where he could go in life. We were touched and humbled by the wisdom of this young 13 year old. The program, with its emphasis on reflecting on the baby and parent relationship and experiences, allowed conversation and reflection on the boy's own feelings and frustrations in a safe, secure environment. By the way,

Key research findings show that Roots of Empathy children perceive a more positive classroom environment by the end of the program (e.g. increased sense of classroom belonging and peer acceptance). Root of Empathy children also exhibit:

- An increase in pro-social behaviour (e.g. sharing, helping and including).
- A decrease in Aggression. For example, applied to all the children that will participate in Roots of Empathy, on average it is expected that the program will reduce the number of children fighting by approximately 50%. This is particularly

significant given that children in the comparison classrooms sho incrreases in aggression across the school year.
- An increase in social and emotional understanding.
- An increase in knowledge of parenting.
- An increase in empathy.[29]

WHAT'S A PARENT TO DO?

The simple answer is very nicely laid out in Claire Lerner and Amy Laura Dombro's book *Bringing up Baby*, which is published by Zero to Three.[30] In their book, Lerner and Dombro provide parental guidelines for making good decisions in the first three years of a child's life. What follows is a summary of their recommended approach to the building of secure attachments between infants and their parents.

1. Become self aware by asking yourself the following questions:
- Who is the parent I want to be?
- What is really important to me as a parent?
- What are my attitudes about parenting?
- What do I bring from my own childhood?
- What pushes my buttons?
- What is my temperament?
- What is the goodness of fit between me and my child and me and my partner?

2. Tune in to your child
Every behavior has a reason. What does this behavior mean to the child?

3. Make Sensitive and effective decisions
Manage your own emotional responses to your child's behavior.

4. If you can reflect about your dreams of parenting, examine your own childhood to see where some of your attitudes and views may come from. Seeing where behavior is coming from helps to not respond reactively. As one example, upon reflection, a parent might think "Maybe that meltdown in the grocery store happened because my child is tired, not because I've screwed up as a parent."

This encouraging list of plausible questions and personal responses that parents can learn to ask and to make when they're with their children builds the foundation in the young for developing their capacity to self-regulate and to care about other people, as well as caring for themselves.

CONCLUSION

But how does this list apply to parents who start out with significant disadvantages due to their own childhood experiences? Let me share one scenario with you to respond to that question. Morgan was three years old when I first saw him. He and his single parent mum Anna were referred by his pediatrician for an assessment of his out of control behavior. He had been demitted from three child-care centres and routinely got up in the middle of the night and pulled apart all the stuff in his room as well as in the kitchen. He was more than a handful. Anna was seriously worried she might hit him. She didn't want to do this because she had been frequently beaten as a child. She had promised herself when she got pregnant that she would never do this.

When they came to my office, we dealt with first things first. She was living in a dangerously old apartment and was afraid to let Morgan play outside because of broken bottles and syringes. She often didn't have enough food to eat and frequently worried about paying the rent. As a result, living with a child who trashed the kitchen was much more than just an inconvenience. Together, we were able to connect her with social services and investigate safer housing situations. Gaining access to finances made a great difference to this family. Finding a child-care centre was crucial as well because Anna needed to be in school or working to get

41

assistance. We found a centre with a broad understanding of children who have challenging behaviors.

The early history was not unpredictable. Anna described herself as a strong-willed teenage mum who was determined she was going to make a success of being a parent. Initially her focus was almost exclusively on herself and doing the right thing. She tried to teach Morgan how to behave properly. She thought that included letting him cry himself to sleep. She also put him on a rigid schedule of bottle-feeding. If he felt distressed, she wouldn't change the schedule. She refused assistance from public health nurses. When he started child-care and was having difficulties with other children, she thought that the centres were singling him out because she was a teenage mum. She constantly spoke about how the system, including her ex-partner, were 'screwing her over'. She wasn't getting very much sleep. As I probed, I discovered that she was quite depressed.

She had lots of books and toys for Morgan because she wanted him to be happy and smart but Morgan rarely settled down to any one activity. In a structured play observation she was quite intrusive and the tidy-up section was a disaster. Morgan climbed on top of the bookshelves rather than tiding them up. It was a scene they obviously had played out many times before. He showed no concern when his mum left the room and ignored her on her return.

It would have been easy to make a diagnosis of a multitude of things, but I felt it was imperative to really understand this parent-child dyad in their context before slapping on any labels or drugs!

After a few sessions, having helped with some of the pressing life concerns, Anna began to trust me and was able to share some of her fears about being worthy enough to look after Morgan. She was terrified he would be taken away, just as she had been from her parents. When we talked finally about what might be going on in Morgan's head—that he might be scared and overwhelmed—it was as if a light bulb went off! She was able to see the world through his eyes. At first, she started talking about how it reminded her of the way she felt as a child. Eventually, with time, she was able to be curious about his behavior and delight in his lovely singing voice. She came to see how her behavior had been very scary for him. In his destructive behavior, he was doing the only thing he knew how to do in order to protect himself.

Over the course of many months, things improved dramatically for them. As mum learned to regulate herself, as well as feel more in control of her own world, she was better able to read Morgan's cues. Rather than thinking he was doing things to make her mad, she realized his behavior meant something to him. She needed to understand it. She was able to meet Morgan's emotional needs and help him to develop self-regulation. He was able to attend day-care full time and flourish there. When big life changes occurred, they rattled the ship a bit. For example, when Anna started school full time, his behavior got worse. But because of what she had learned about them both, she was able to see it through.

Their story is one of a young boy who protests the absence of his mother because she was initially unavailable to him. But it's a story of tremendous courage and perseverance in a young mum who wouldn't give up. Her own life history changed due to her willingness and ability to create positive experiences with her young son. They became well connected. He got her back. She became his secure base. As a result, he could explore and return to her in times of distress.

In this chapter, I discussed attachment theory and connected the research to the capacity a child can achieve for building satisfying relationships with caregivers as well as with the world at large. Differences between secure attachment and patterns that are less than ideal help to understand the social interactions of disadvantaged children that may, on the surface, seem to some people to be just bad behavior. Attachment theories help to convey how hard it is for many children to get along with other people and to care about them if they have not been securely attached during intimate relations with people who care for them. When children are securely attached during the early years, they have the developed capacity to be sensitive to and aware of the needs of other people, based on the hopeful personal experiences they enjoyed during their early years. Jaak Panksepp conveys these dynamics beautifully when he says that

The quality of childcare has lifelong consequences for mental health. Children whose emotional feelings are cherished and respected, even their angry outbursts, shall live more happily than those whose early passions are denied. Both excessive distress and tender loving care leave lasting marks on the emotional circuits, and mentalities of developing brains.[31]

The role of parents in the development of a child's ability to care for themselves and to care about others is central. As parents learn to be present to the young, as teachers attend to learners in the classroom, a child's ability and willingness to regulate themselves and to care for others develops as they experience everyday life. Even in simple day-to-day interactions, we're teaching children to be good citizens and to live well with other people.

The Social Brain: Serve and Return

INTRODUCTION

While health benefits of caring for the young continue to be my concern, the focus for this chapter is on the development of civility as an important aspect of the well-being of the young so their future skills include caring for others. Stress, mentioned in the previous chapters, is important in this research. Science researchers look at brain pathways and stress pathways and consider how the immune system gets set up early in life. They hope to discover how a healthy system might develop so it can last a lifetime. By bringing many fields of study together, implications and connections can be made.

In this chapter, I look at how the environment between a baby and caregiver initiates a cascade of interactions that have the potential to support civility, that is, a child who cares about the welfare of others. As South American educator, Paulo Freire believed strongly, humankind's vocation is best understood as becoming someone "who acts upon and transforms the world, and in so doing, moves toward ever new possibilities of fuller and richer lives individually and collectively."[1]

Human beings are wired to connect and it is this capacity that forms the basis of Freire's belief about humanity's vocation. But the importance of building relationships and connections with our children from infancy isn't always promoted as much as, say, helping them to develop reading skills. A good friend of mine once described overhearing a lift line conversation between a mother and her adult son at a mountain ski hill. As he was getting off the lift and heading away, the mother asked her son where he was going. He replied he had to go because he was babysitting his kids (her grandchildren). My friend wanted to jump off the lift to tell him he needed to be doing a lot more than babysitting! She wanted to say, "You're the dad. You don't get to babysit unless you pay yourself. Your role as dad is massively important. You're building your kids brains, including how they will feel about themselves and other adults. This isn't just babysitting!"

Children thrive when the adults in their lives care deeply about them. The capacity to let people know they're important is one of the things I'll always remember about Dr Dan Offord. When with him, you always felt he was really listening to you, actually attuning to you as you spoke. As his colleague, during our social interactions, I experienced a sense of well-being because I "*felt* felt." I had a felt sense of being heard through his attention to me, just as a child feels when a parent welcomes her to climb up on his lap so she's able to completely relax and convey what's on her mind. That sense of connection to significant adults is a requirement for healthy human development. Why? We're a social species. We require human contact and connection, right from the start.

I long to see the day when all children have at least one adult whose eyes light up when they see the child enter the room. "Connect with me" is a signal little children send out as a frequent request to adults in their lives. The ability and willingness to respond to them in return is essential to the felt sense of connection that's at the heart of all human relationships. This movement back and forth between adult and child is the serve and return of healthy social interaction. It's a two-way contact that's most important in a child's development. If you can have that back and forth, expressed with delight and awe in the children themselves, they will thrive.

A CHILD'S TEMPERAMENT AND THE ROLE OF SERVE AND RETURN

Now what does it take to have one's eyes light up as a child comes near you? Anyone who has more than one child knows that they come into the world with very different ways of interacting because they have different temperaments. Some are easy to figure out. Some are pretty hard. It's easy to have your eyes light up when everything is going smoothly. It's harder if you're deprived of sleep and can't figure out what's making your baby cry so much!

I have five great kids so I know this really well! When we had our first baby we were super anxious, of course, but he was pretty easy to figure out. We could quickly tell what his cries meant. He was very responsive to our back and forth (serve and return) smiling and cooing! He hardly ever cried. We thought we were wonderful parents. Then 18 months later, along came our daughter. First of all, she came out looking like Winston Churchill. The music in the background was the Emperor Concerto. A warning? From birth, parenting her was very different. She was hard to figure out. She cried a lot unless I was holding her. She didn't whimper—it was 'a bring down the walls of Jericho' kind of cry. When she was a baby it took my husband and me a lot of time to help her soothe. But her delight due to these interactions was infectious. She beamed. People passing by who saw her face would stop and comment on her expression. She felt things in a big way, even as a baby.

But we were exhausted by her high needs. We were sleep deprived, irritable and unsure of what we might be doing wrong. She continued to be intense as a toddler. She delighted in small things and that was wonderful. It was also challenging. She didn't like the feel of things such as the scratchiness of clothing tags, or the stitch lines in her socks, or having her shoes too tight. When she made her mind up about something, it was next to impossible to shift her. It was much harder to keep having my eyes light up when we differed, or to have positive back and forth interaction when what I often experienced with her was a battle!

As a little one, she was a challenge to understand. To make it more awkward, I was a doctor, a psychiatrist, doing a specialization in child psychiatry. Even with all my training, I'd never heard about temperament. I started reading everything I could find. As one example, I read books with titles such as *The Difficult Child*[2] or *The Fussy Baby book*,[3] all of which helped us understand our girl.

The book *Raising your Spirited Child* by Mary Sheedy Kurchinka[4] really resonated with us. We came to rely on it. It spoke of nine different types of characteristics babies seem to be born with, e.g., intensity of emotional reactions, persistence, sensitivity and reactions to new things. We learned our girl was spirited. She was more intense, persistent and sensitive than was our son. We came to understand that we needed to work on the goodness of fit between us. We came to realize the wonder that she was and stop wishing she was less intense. We no longer tried to mould her into what we wanted her to be.

My daughter's intensity was good training for a child psychiatrist. She didn't like change. She never took a bottle. She started to walk and then ran. She started to talk and then talked in sentences. Her developmental path was very different from our first child. Luckily we were well supported. I come from a big family and got all kinds of advice. Some was good. Some was bad. A few people insisted that I just let her cry and that it was okay to let a baby cry it out. They even thought it was good for her lungs. This is one bit of advice I didn't take. Even then, we knew we had to soothe her when she cried and pick her up—that a baby should never be left to cry it out. How can a parent convey to a child that she or he is safe and loved if you leave them when they need comfort? We knew we couldn't follow those books that said let babies cry. We couldn't justify that reaction in our own hearts. As parents, my husband and I read a lot of books and learned a lot of strategies.

Spirited children can present challenges for parents. It's common for many parents to feel their spirited kids are doing things on purpose—to get them angry or manipulate them. What it came down to with our daughter was a sensitivity issue. She wasn't trying to make us late for a family dinner by having a temper tantrum if she didn't have on the right socks. She was highly sensitive to the feel of things and hadn't yet learned how to manage that sensitivity. It was our job to help her regulate her sensitivity by helping her recognize that the socks made her feel itchy and then help her get a pair of socks that didn't have that impact on her. When we handled the situation that way, it was a relief for everyone. Because of that early experience, in my clinical career, I've recommended Kurchinka's book on the spirited child many, many times.

Why do I emphasize temperament when talking about the early years in connection with a focus on helping children care about other people? It's because we must consider individual characteristics of each child wherever we work with them, whether at home, school, a sports team, at church, synagogue, temple or in the community at large. We need to think of each child as unique with much to offer. In communities, caring about the early years requires addressing how to support each and every child. We need to consider the individual needs of each family. So often children who have high vulnerability also have parents with high vulnerability. As with the principal I described in an earlier chapter, to be effective, we ask questions: What do I know about this behavior? This family? This situation? Too often we believe it's easier to think we can interpret behavior based on our current understanding and try to manage it from our own perspective, rather than genuinely listening to and observing what's going on for and in that child or family.

Having the habit of asking the question 'What do I know about this?' helps when trying to figure out other peoples' behavior. When I was a resident in medical training, Offord pointed out to me that sometimes educators or doctors have great ideas for how to help children and families but they get confused and frustrated if families don't take advantage of opportunities they set up for them. For example, a teacher might think of having all kinds of fun things for a family to do in school. Then, if families don't turn up, they wonder what's wrong with parents.

What teachers need to ask is "What do I know about this?" If they ask that critically reflective question, they might realize that many parents have no more desire to walk into a school than they have to walk into a dentist's office. These are parents who felt school was awful. For them, it was a place where they felt put down or worse. If teachers want to be effective in helping children and families, it's necessary to ask critically reflective questions at

49

individual and societal levels. This questioning helps to understand complex issues such as temperament. That understanding makes a huge difference in how we work, not just with children, but also with each other.

THE BIRTH AND GROWTH OF SELF-REGULATION AND CARING FOR OTHERS

How do we view children and the influences of childhood on them? Our views of individual and social interaction impacts the way we nurture, educate and support children. Do we want them to grow up to be self-reliant, exploratory, content and able to meet challenges? If we do, how we think of them affects how we interact with them. Do we think, for example, that kids are empty vessels that we mould for success? Do we imagine we can fill them up with information so they're able to get into the right pre-schools, schools and colleges? A young Korean patient of mine called this parenting approach "stuffing the duck."

Adults who rely on this approach may believe childhood behavior and accomplishments should reflect well on them so they can appear to be successful parents. This way of thinking shapes our approach to discipline, education, socialization and skill development. In its extreme, it's an approach that's seriously questioned, for example, in South Korea. Children there report extreme unhappiness and feel suicidal under the pressure it creates for them. Another well researched and oft-cited study from the Organization for Economic Co-Operation and Development (OECD),[5] notes that South Korea has the highest youth suicide rate in the 34 countries that inform their research;[6] scholastic pressures are a frequently cited cause of youth unhappiness.

Could we take another view, one that doesn't see kids as empty vessels to be stuffed? Might we see kids as competent, capable and resourceful when they're given the opportunity? Do we see them as able to interact well with others and capable of resolving their problems if they receive appropriate support?

I suggest we reconsider our view of children and childhood. If we think of kids as capable, and think of parenting and educating them in terms of supporting them as they use their innate curiosity, love of learning, drive to grow and empathy toward others, we interact differently with them. If we take the second approach, we're able to create an environment in which they learn and where they demonstrate self-regulation. What do I mean by self-regulation? It's an ability to be boss of one's own attention, emotion and behavior at an appropriate level for one's age and culture. It means being able to deal with unexpected changes that you didn't necessarily want, like your classmate taking your favorite toy at school. In a 2 year old, for example, we wouldn't expect a whole lot of self-regulation but by the start of school, at 4 or 5 years old, we expect children to be able to control their attention, emotion and behavior at an appropriate level.

What might self-regulation look like? Suppose a 5 year old, let's call him Jimmy, is playing at school and another child comes up and takes his toy. Jimmy has good impulse control so he doesn't hit out at the other child. Instead he regulates his annoyance and calls out to an adult and says to the interloper, "Don't take that. It's mine." A model child might even say, "Why don't we take turns," but that would be your sister-in-law's kid. In contrast, another child who lacks these skills, let's call him Ryan, might hit out at the child who's trying to take away the toy. The simple civil act Jimmy carries out expresses self-regulation. His response uncovers layers of development I want to investigate further. A child who's capable of civility has had positive relationships and likely has been well supported and nurtured during pre-school years.

A third child, let's call him Jerry, may have a similar experience at school, someone takes away his toy, but Jerry has a developmental disorder that interferes with the development of the skills of civility Jimmy already has. It's essential for teachers to understand Jerry's world but what about Ryan? He not there yet. It's unlikely he's benefitted from consistent nurturing parenting that Jimmy has experienced. Or, he may never have been exposed to children his own age and hasn't developed these skills at this point in his life— which doesn't mean he can't develop them.

Rather than judging Ryan, it's important to ask the question: What do I know about him? If he comes from a family or a community where there's high toxic stress all the time, adults may not have been able to spend time with him to help him develop language and self-control over his impulses. If he's living in a situation of neglect, his brain may be constantly on high alert or on guard—constantly warning him that something bad is going to happen. This kind of toxic and constant stress influences how Ryan's brain develops and, consequently, how he acts at school. If a child pushes against him as he enters the classroom, a faster and stronger signal is sent to the threat sensor or fight/flight centre of his brain. Unlike children from non-toxic stress homes, whose 'watch out for danger' centers in the brain haven't been so hyper-acutely tuned, Ryan may interpret the push as an aggressive event that could be harmful. What does he do? He hits back.

BECOMING SELF-REGULATED

Recognizing and managing emotion, stress and learning self-regulation are key to a child's healthy development. I want to say more about self-regulation. Here's one example. When we're sitting attentively focused and listening to someone speak, and taking it in, we're demonstrating self-regulation. The evidence that we're self-regulated is that we're giving our attention to the speaker. We focus intention and behavior on that task. We're not jumping up and down or running around the aisles. In self-regulation, impulsive behavior is inhibited. We're emotionally in control. This is what self-regulation looks like. Now it's easier to be self-regulated if we're interested in the topic and it's harder if the person isn't a good speaker, or the topic is of little interest. Under those conditions, our mind wanders off and we start making grocery lists. We wonder where the woman in the seat ahead of us got the beautiful scarf she's wearing. When we have no interest in the speaker, we're easily distracted. We might begin to feel restless but we inhibit that sense of wanting to leave by shifting around and moving. We look as if we're self-regulated in our posture and perhaps our gaze behavior but in terms of our attention, we're not. In this situation, we're unlikely to take in much new learning.

Even if some people in the audience have terrible personal problems going on, or big life issues that are pressing in on them, with self-regulation, they keep their emotions in check. Road rage is an example of the absence of self-regulation. It arises if a driver doesn't recognize his or her emotions or if people don't process them effectively. In road rage, people just react.

In learning to be self-regulated, we first need to be regulated by others. In this way we learn to safely experience our own emotions, recognize these emotions and develop ways of dealing with them. A baby that's routinely soothed when she cries will cry less. Why? Because, as alarming sensations such as *I'm hungry* are repeatedly soothed, the offending stimulus (hunger) fires fewer alarms in her brain. The child's brain comes to associate being comforted by her caregiver and the experience of being soothed. She gradually learns to soothe herself. Her distress at being hungry is extinguished or at least significantly lessened. She also learns that she can have an impact on her environment.

Children and babies can develop strategies for self-regulation very early, although we must acknowledge that some do so more easily than others. Recall that temperament is a factor for many children. As they develop more self-regulation and a sense of security, the easier it is for children to be joyous explorers. When we help children achieve self-regulation, it doesn't mean we're inhibiting them—we're helping them develop pathways for success.

THE SCHOOL READINESS TRAP

How do children learn self-regulation? As one might imagine, that learning is many-layered but for the most part, children learn self-regulation in daily back and forth interactions with the adults in their lives. Initially, babies become regulated by being regulated by others and in that way, over time, through relationship, learn to self-regulate. Children also learn to regulate themselves through the community and the cultural expectations of their group. As an example, if a community sees it as rude for children to get food before their elders receive food, children will learn that rule through many interactions in the community over time.

I expect most people in the Western world want children to arrive at school eager and ready to learn and to have already developed some of the rudimentary skills they require to do well in that situation, such as being able to communicate. There's a trap however that has developed in the whole school readiness movement. Dan Offord and scientists like him who developed instruments such as the Early Development Instrument (EDI) describe and measure all the domains needed for success in school. These domains include the following:

- Physical health and well-being
- Social competence
- Emotional maturity
- Language and cognitive development
- Communication skills and general knowledge

Too frequently, people equate school readiness with developing children's text-based literacy and numeracy skills, at times, at the expense of social/emotional literacy skills development.

Even if children read and write they will have trouble if they can't get along with others. A better predictor of school success is social and emotional competence and their excitement about learning. These are stronger indicators than a high Intelligence Quotient (IQ) by itself. But do we see parents and educators focusing on opportunities for children to play and explore the world of relationships, even though there's good evidence that this is how they learn best.[7] Unfortunately teachers and parents are caught in the trap—one that I have coined "the tyranny of cognitive seduction." The trap has us thinking that literacy and numeracy are the most important aspects of early years development and primary markers for success at school. They are important and should be fostered, but not at the expense of play. Children learn through play. Brains are built through play. It's how children acquire knowledge and insight about the world.

In Ontario, where I carry out most of my psychiatric practice, colleagues working in childcare have been getting increased pressure from parents to spend more time preparing kids for school by having them do text-based literacy and numeracy drills, what I tend to think of as drill and kill. Arming themselves with research and support from the Council of Ministers of Education in Canada (CMEC), childcare workers still try to persuade parents that having kids learn the problem-solving skills of how to get along with other people is as necessary a set of skills to acquire as is practice in numeracy and text-based literacy.

There are communities across the country where the EDI shows large vulnerability.[8] In these areas, many children score low numbers on one or more of the five domains bulleted above, as well as in general knowledge. In some wealthier communities vulnerability is evident in children who read and write but have lower scores (are vulnerable) in social competence and emotional maturity. Even though these communities and families are well off, their children can't get along with the others. This is of great concern because it may represent a lack of development in empathy.

It's most likely that the second group has economic and cultural advantages over those in poorer communities and is better able to seize opportunities that come their way later in life. But here's another problem: if their scores on getting along with others are low, how will these children impact the development of civility when they're involved as adults? If they have little empathy, we're all in trouble. We need to pay attention to developing the whole child in both types of socio-economic settings. Children learn through all five domains: physical, social, emotional, cognitive and communicative. These competencies aren't acquired in isolation from one another: they're acquired with other people. I often say love builds brains. My focus is on developing the whole child. The way to address vulnerabilities isn't to single out and pathologize one of the five areas noted above. The way forward is to bring them all up together.

Is bullying an absence of healthy relationships?

Like many people, I'm increasingly worried about reports of bullying at school. It seems to start very early and can last and cause damage throughout a lifetime. In Hamilton in 1992, I was part of a research survey that looked at needs and gaps in services with about 3300 children in childcare. Many of the teachers in the survey described children who had aggressive behaviors and noted a need for support in order to deal with them. When we interviewed the teachers, we found it wasn't only physical aggression that caused a problem but also name calling, racial slurs, exclusion and relational aggression—all of which were present in a sizeable number of children. For example, relational aggression in 3 year-olds was alive and well. What that survey told us wasn't that they had to bring in programs to teach children about nice ways to speak, but that the childcare community and parents had to build civility within the community so that everybody belonged and everyone had a sense of purpose. There is a wonderful group of Canadian researchers who study bullying. They have seen that relationships are at the heart of the matter. Their network is named Promoting Relations to Eliminate Violence (Prevnet).

Are we creating a sense of belonging in our childcare centers, play schools, library programs and at home? If a person has a sense of belonging, the stress hormone levels go down. Just think about your own experience. Suppose you're working with a team of people and there's someone who's really toxic. Do you feel like going to work? Do more people get sick in that environment? Is there more absenteeism? If you sense your contribution isn't valued, how do you feel? How about if you're with someone who makes it clear that your work is appreciated, don't you feel more like participating? Stressful relationships affect the immune system's functioning. We know that if people are in a situation where they feel valued and respected and are given a flu shot, they have less of a reaction to it[9] If people are in lousy relationships and they have a cold, it will last longer. Immune systems are affected by psychological well-being. As we will see, a sense of belonging has implications for a child's experience of the world.

A declaration of interdependence

A sense of belonging has a major impact on child development. Developing a secure sense of belonging is one of the primary tasks of childhood, but a child can't be successful on her own. Currently, there are kids who are vulnerable to predators on the Internet. This isn't because IT and technology have come in and taken over our kids. It's because society has changed. We haven't kept the family at the heart of what's most important to a young person. Families are now under tremendous pressure to keep up. Work no longer ends when you leave the workplace; emails and texts continue, even in the middle of the night because we work in a global context.

Young families feel this pressure even more, as evidenced in the work of Canadian researcher Dr Paul Kershaw. He developed the expression "Generation Squeeze". In his view, we haven't strengthened the interdependence among family members. How many families have or can have family dinners during the week? How many families are able to make sure they have time just to be with their kids? Are parents feeling so much pressure to make sure their kids don't lose out that they busy themselves being chauffeurs to ballet lessons and sports' practices? Parents have become managers of their kids' time rather than people that spend face-to-face time with their children. Too often, it looks as if we believe the most important thing is to cram children full of activity and things because they're empty vessels waiting to be filled. They need the skills, we say. We believe that in this competitive world, they need an edge up. But the edge up for children is time spent with family. The edge up is being together building relationships. The edge up is learning to resolve conflict. If we ask ourselves how much time we spend correcting and directing our children, and how much we connect with them, I think most of us will find we spend much more time correcting and less time connecting. This is a challenge and a problem.

How are the Children?

If we ask how children are doing, the reality is, apart from the EDI, we don't have an indicator of how all children are doing. We

57

live in a society that simply doesn't know this. How many kids are in child welfare across the country? The data isn't available. We know how many people have heart attacks. We know how many people are on particular drugs, but not how many children are in the child welfare system across Canada.

What's the percentage of kids who have mental health problems? Dan Offord carried out the Ontario Child Health Survey (OCHS) in 1984. That study showed that in Ontario 1 in 5 kids, aged 4-17 had mental health problems.[10] Has this percentage changed? It's taken 30 years to get money to do the study again, in 2015. Up to then, it wasn't a priority. Governments seem to have dollars to bail out big business. But do we have the will to bail out our children? I think part of the reason we don't have the will is that we think childhood is a happy, protected time. We love our kids. We believe that, mostly, they turn out okay.

The unfortunate reality is that in a recent Toronto survey of kids from grades 7 to grade 12, almost 60% said they were experiencing overwhelming distress.[11] Overwhelming anxiety isn't good for the brain. It isn't good for problem solving. Our kids are the canary in the mineshaft in a society that's not paying enough attention to what makes civility possible. At its core, civility is about learning how to care about other people and yourself in relationship to them and realizing how to demonstrate interdependence with them.

Why do people who care about interdependence worry when they hear about bullying? One of the reasons is that it gives us a picture of whether kids are learning to be empathetic. Are they learning to care about others? Thankfully, in Ontario, we're now talking about student well-being strategies and educational engagement through the lens of their well-being rather than bullying prevention. Our youth justice system is talking about relational custody and using strengths-based counseling.[12] Why? Because what we've been doing for so long hasn't improved the life chances of children and youth. According to much of the research, as in the Toronto example, the situation is getting worse. What's the mechanism behind some of these changes? Changes in approach are based on brain research.

THE POWER OF WORDS

Brains are built by experience. If it's good experience, the architecture that's formed is solid. If it's negative experience, that also builds the brain. Brain plasticity has a dark side. A baby can't discern if an experience is beneficial or not. It's simply changed by the experience. Take for example, language development. In an important study, carried out by the American psychologists Betty Hart and Todd Risley,[13] they gathered data on the number and significance of spoken language in the early years. Hart and Risley devised a method for sampling the actual number of words that young children heard. They studied a group of 42 families over several years and counted up the number of words children heard during that period of time. They also looked at the children's vocabulary development. These families were grouped in welfare, working-class and professional home categories.

What they found was that the number of words kids heard was very different based on whether they were living in a poorer family or in a well-to-do family. They observed that, on average, kids living in poorer families heard about 13 million words in the first 3 years of life—that sounds like a lot. When you consider 13 million words, imagine those dendrites and neurons that are taking in information and sending out signals. The more often the stimulation comes in, and comes in over and over again, the bigger the brain's pathways. But with 13 million words coming in, how big is the highway compared to kids in well-off families who heard, on average, 43 million words in the early years? How big will brain pathways be if a child has heard 43 million words in the first 3 years of life? Right from the start, in those children, there's already a 30 million-word gap between the two groups.

That gap is more than twice the number of words poorer children experienced in the first 3 years. Children in professionals' homes were exposed to, on average, more than fifteen hundred more words per hour than children in welfare homes. Over one year, that amounted to a difference of nearly 8 million words, which, by age 4, amounted to a total gap of 32 million words. They also found a substantial gap in tone and complexity of the words used.

As they crunched the numbers, they discovered a direct correlation between the intensity of these early verbal experiences and later achievement.[14]

Does the number of words a child hears really make a difference? When researchers looked at kids in the study to see how many words they had, they couldn't be certain of any differences at 16 months of age because expressive language is just developing at that point. Differences showed up at 24 months. Children who heard more words had more language. By the time they start school (in Ontario kids start school at three years eight months) some kids have 500 words and others have 1200, 1300 or 1500 words.

What difference does it make if children access more words when they arrive at school? These children have more options. Suppose a child approaches another who has access to 500 words only. If a conflict arises, such as an argument over a toy, the child with 500 words will have fewer tools in his tool kit as he reacts to the first child. Generally, it will be the fists. If children have 1200 or 1300 words, they have access, not only to more words; they've had all kinds of experiences to help integrate signals in the brain.

Over time there has been criticism directed at Hart and Risley's study so I want to include additional current information. It's important to note that in more recent studies, it wasn't just being poor that left children with fewer words. Some of the kids from a poorer family had 1200, 1500, even 1600 words. Why? These kids had moms and dads who talked to them, read to them and listened to them so that the back and forth movement between adults and children was maintained. Some of the kids with rich parents had only 500 words. Why? Both parents worked. They hired caregivers who weren't speaking to these children in their own language, or perhaps, in any language at all.

Another study was carried out to replicate the Hart & Risley study.[15] These researchers looked at 19-month old children in poorer families in certain areas of the United States. During a 10-hour period, they put a little microphone on each child and listened to the spoken language these children experienced. They didn't count TV watching. Nor do videogames count in terms of holding the brain's attention for language. They counted face-to-face language experience. What they recorded in those 10-hour periods was a massive variation in the number of words a child heard. When they calculated the number of words per hour, some heard 67 words in a 60-minute period, which is a language experience that includes fewer words than someone will hear in a 30-second television commercial. Other children in the research heard 1200 words in that one-hour period.

The number of words children hear isn't just a poverty issue. There are fantastic parents who rear kids in their own bedrooms while living in poverty and actually parent better than some wealthy families. Positive language experience is about parenting. It's motivated by a concern for the well-being of children in the present and the future. But I'm not just talking about talking. Good language experience that builds healthy brain pathways throughout the early years is about talking to your baby, reading to your baby, and listening to what your baby says in return. It's about picking up a baby's cues and having the back and forth interaction, the serve and return that builds those big highways in the brain.

When do we first see empathy?

In addition to developing big brain highways based on rich experiences of words, the empathy that a child develops through the back and forth experiences of warm, nurturing and responsive parenting helps a child learn the important social skills of becoming someone who cares about other people and the environment. If parents want their children to learn empathy, they spend time watching, listening and becoming co-researchers with them in the world when they are still very young.

Empathy is learned in relationships. Yet we're living in a society in which there's more parental isolation than we've had in the past. We're losing our parenting DNA. Adults aren't passing down ordinary practices that happened in a village or extended family. What does that mean for all of us during this present moment? The children's treatment centre where I work developed a video called *Heads up and Ready to Roll*. The video teaches parents that it's good to put a baby on their tummy so the baby can have his or her head up as they learn to roll over. In my experience, this practice was common in the past. Parents didn't need a video. They'd seen aunts and uncles teach their babies how to roll over.

What does empathy look like? I was recently in a meeting and was told about young parents who are desperate for information. They're talking and talking to their babies, but aren't listening to them. To depict empathy, I frequently show a video clip of research that was carried out by Felix Warneken and Michael Tomasello[16] in their research on altruistic behavior in the early years. In one section of the video, a toddler who's about 15-18 months old is standing beside his mother who's seated in a chair in the corner of a room. She's watching the behavior of a stranger, an adult male. The man is standing in front of a closed cabinet, trying to put a few toys into it. He attempts to put them into the cabinet by softly banging them against its closed door. He carries out the action twice. The mother remains seated in the chair and watches the man who can't put away his toys. After a moment of observing the man's action, the toddler leaves his mother's side and goes over to open the cabinet for the man. He then looks up at the stranger and moves out of his way to let the man put his toys away.

This brief clip eloquently captures the child's social nature. The small boy 'read the mind' of a stranger. The toddler hadn't been in the room before and hadn't viewed that particular dilemma before, yet understood what the man was trying to do. He put himself in the mind of the other. We call this empathy. The researcher didn't cue the little boy or ask anyone for help. His mother didn't instruct him. He just knew what the man wanted to accomplish. He also looked up at the stranger to let him know that he could try again to put away his toys.

How did the toddler learn to do that? Was it a fancy program called Empathy-r-Us? No. The key is that the toddler already knew how to do it. He didn't learn empathy through a program. He learned it through thousands of interactions with loving adults that predictably responded to his needs. During these social experiences, they conveyed to him that it was alright to have these encounters and they would help him if he got stuck. The little boy in the video appears well attached to his mother and seems to feel safe enough to venture away from her side to assist another person. Babies learn to read social cues by having their own cues read and responded to by those who care for them.

The power of serve and return is massive. We learn empathy though humane caring. A child can learn to care for others in high-quality programs for moms and tots but the most important ethos is in daily interactions each child has with people in his or her most intimate environment. As a result, we have to think of how to help families provide support for children during the early years? In addition, how can we encourage intergenerational connections among families so that healthy parenting practices are passed on? It still takes a village to raise a child. Village conditions impact all children within the sphere of their social influence.

THE IMPACT OF STRESS ON THE BRAIN

A final key concept in realizing the importance of early years experiences on serve and return, and the development of concern for others, is the impact of stress on the developing brain. When speaking about the early years, I frequently use a video clip produced by psychologist Ed Tronick that he calls the *Still Face Experiment*.[17] In the video, a mother faces her little one and plays with the baby. At one moment, the mother turns away and then faces the baby again with a still face (completely unresponsive). She shows no signs of engagement no matter what her baby does. At first, the baby tries to engage her mom. She points, smiles, gestures and then starts to protest until she's screeching. Because the mom doesn't respond, the baby becomes more and more distressed. She looks away, cries and even loses body posture by flopping forward in her baby chair. Then, mother returns to interacting with the baby. All is well. Imagine if children experienced a Still Face every day. What would happen? They would try and try but stress hormones would constantly, chronically be turned on. Eventually they would stop trying, but their stress levels would remain very high.

In the experiment, the baby experienced intense but passing stress. Based on much research, we now know what causes a human stress system to be activated by engaging several systems in the brain. The Harvard Centre on the Developing Child has wonderful resources on the topic of stress in children's lives. In their work, they've demonstrated different levels and types of stress. First of all, there's positive stress. Not all stress is bad. Some stress motivates people to get things done. There's also tolerable stress, for example, if someone who's close becomes ill or dies. Illness and death are difficult to deal with, but nurturing and supportive relationships help people manage. In contrast, toxic stress is worrisome and damaging. Toxic stress exists in a human system itself. It's systemic stress that's experienced repeatedly and is unbuffered by healthy human relationships. Toxic stress is what children living in neglect and maltreatment experience every day.

In the *Still Face* video the little baby falls apart behaviorally. The child can't hold herself together. The experiment lasts two minutes. During that time, mom doesn't respond in the usual way. The baby's gestures and cries have all been learned to get mom's attention. But they're not working. The back and forth reciprocity she has come to expect is failing. Imagine the impact on the brain if toxic stress is continuous. The areas of the brain that are particularly vulnerable to high levels of stress hormones are those responsible for new memory and learning. Toxic stress affects areas of the brain that help with problem solving, thinking through to the consequences of actions, remembering and managing emotion. In other words, toxic stress impacts the very areas of the brain that allow a child to develop empathy and caring for others.

Do we know enough about the relationship between stress, the brain and the human stress system? Montreal researcher Sonia Lupien and Harvard researcher Robert Sapolsky write about the complicated stress system in a way that makes it accessible. Sapolsky wrote a book called *Why Zebras Don't Get Ulcers*.[18] They don't get ulcers because, as they eat their food, the process of munching is stress relieving. The only time a zebra gets stressed is if a lion is around chasing or ripping a zebra apart. Human beings however are wonderfully creative. We can get stressed just by thinking about things. Lupien looked at reasons people experience stress and situations that turn on stress system hormones. To explain the human stress system, she uses the acronym NUTS to stand for Novel, Unpredictable, Threat to the ego and Sense of loss of control.

If we look at her model and consider what makes us feel stress, we can apply it to many experiences. Suppose we say its time pressure that stresses us out. But what is it about too little time or a looming deadline that's stressful? What is it that makes time feel stressful? Do we feel stressed, even if we're doing something difficult, if we've done it many times before? Again, if we're feeling stressed, we can ask ourselves: Is it novel? Is it unpredictable? Is it a threat to the ego? Does thinking about it create a sense that I might lose control? One example from my own experience as a professor in medical school might help. I was teaching a class of 400 students and asked them to imagine their own graduation—a situation that would change their student status. In Ontario, July 1 is change over day when young people who were medical students the day before suddenly become doctors in a residency program. I asked them to imagine July 1. Was the thought stressful? Is it NUTS? You betcha!

The stress system is an ancient system built to keep us alive and help us perceive and discern a threat and act on it. All mammals have a stress system. Deep inside the brain is a group of neurons, called the amygdala and the hippocampus. These areas of the brain form two parts of the body's stress system. They're part of a complex, marvelous system that keeps us safe. How does it work?

To put it simply, if we see a snake we need to have a system that's fast enough to allow us to react so we're ready to run or remain on guard. When we see the snake, a superfast signal is sent to our amygdala—our fight, flight or freeze centre in the brain. We also require input from other areas of the brain to help us discern whether it's a snake or a stick. Otherwise we would be jumping in fear every time we saw a linear object on the ground. We need a survival safety system. Otherwise we might say: Oh, what's that interesting slithering thing? Is that a rattling sound I hear? We'd never survive as a species without a stress initiated survival system.

Stimuli turn on the amygdala deep in the brain. The amygdala sparks a series of signals that pass through several structures and reach the adrenals on top of the kidneys. Adrenalin is released. We're ready to run. We breathe faster and sweat. Our digestion slows as we prepare for disaster. Again, what happens if you skid on ice while driving your car? All the sensations you experience come from your adrenals in action. The experience of skidding sends a signal for the adrenals to release cortisol—a stress hormone noted earlier.

Normally, cortisol goes up in the morning and down at night. If we have a persistent stressor, the adrenals increase the release of cortisol, which in turn converts it into energy. As a result, if you're running, you can keep running. We need cortisol in stress situations but you also need the system to turn off the stress chemical tap. If the tap is always on with no way to shut down the signal our body is overwhelmed by these chemicals. High persistent levels of cortisol are bad for brain and body.

In ordinary circumstances we have another part of the system to regulate the release of cortisol; it's the hippocampus—a cluster of neurons responsible for, among other things, new learning and memory. For example, because London cab drivers need to know so many different routes in and around London, they have huge hippocampi.[19]

The Hippocampus is part of learning. It's part of the stress system, both for memory as well as for regulating cortisol levels. It has receptors that monitor how much cortisol there is around and sends a negative feedback message to stop its release. In summary, there's a balancing act in the body: the amygdala fires adrenaline and cortisol. The hippocampus figures out what's going on and says, enough cortisol and turns it off. However, the system can get primed to act too quickly and intensely. This is what happens in anxiety disorders and when kids experience toxic stress. The sad reality is that when a child's brain is forming, during the earliest years, the brain is most vulnerable to the damages of toxic stress.

CONCLUSION

Children who experience toxic stress because they live in neglect or intense poverty or experience maltreatment will have exaggerated cortisol responses. Their amygdalae seem to be easily triggered. They perceive threat and aggression in situations that may not be intended as such, but their brain energy is consumed by vigilance—for very good reasons. They're thinking: Watch out! What's going on? Is this safe? If the brain is preoccupied with these messages and busy with them, the hippocampus isn't free to learn about multiplication tables or how to get along with others.

Let's take an ordinary example. Suppose a door slams shut very suddenly. For most of us it would be a surprise or shock. Our adrenaline would go up. But then we would say, "Oh yes, it's really windy. That's what happened." But for those who experience toxic, persistent stress, every time a door slammed in the past they knew mom was coming in to beat them. What would their brains do? The thermometer for stress responses—how it gets turned on and how fast it goes up and stays up—is rigged early in life. We know that high persistent levels of cortisol can damage the brain, cause fibromyalgia and many other medical conditions. It also damages the child's ability to learn.

One idea about how this happens is that early childhood experiences set a person's stress reactivity—which affects how the body reacts to a stressor and recovers from that stressor. So one can imagine that if, in early childhood, someone's stress reactivity system gets tuned to respond in the extreme and persistently, there are different consequences than if one's reactions are not as intense and recovery is rapid.

The impact of high persistent cortisol levels may adversely affect the brain and the immune system. As a child psychiatrist, my response to these adverse affects is to find ways to explain how the brain works to help the young understand the process so they become agents in their well-being and recovery. I try to make things simple. I explain to them that when I heard about the stress system, the amygdala made me think of a porcupine. I have a wonderful porcupine puppet to show them. When a porcupine senses danger it prickles up to protect itself. In the brain, the porcupine amygdala starts a cascade of signals leading to a release of adrenaline and cortisol. The porcupine sends a signal down through the stress system pathways: it tells the body to release adrenaline, release cortisol. It's not safe here.

I tell young people that the amygdala has a friend called the hippocampus. To explain how these two parts of the brain work together, I use a hippopotamus puppet to represent the hippocampus. I hold up the hippo and porcupine puppets and show a child how they interact under favorable conditions. The hippo is responsible for new learning and memory so when the porcupine gets upset (releasing adrenalin and cortisol) the hippo can call on its memory to calm down the porcupine and say that there's no danger here (stop releasing cortisol).

Problems start if the porcupine is firing over and over again. If the porcupine isn't receiving calming messages from the hippo, it continues to bombard the brain. What happens under these conditions is that the hippo gets overwhelmed, tired, worn out and seems to 'go to sleep'. At this point, we see cell death in the hippocampus and other areas of the brain, including the prefrontal cortex, which is also part of the brain that's essential for learning. If these pathways are set by toxic stress, they have a long reach into a child's future by having impacts on health, behavior and educational attainment when the child becomes an adult.

This chapter explores the importance of the social brain and our deep drive to connect with others. I also discuss what really matters in a child's early years if they are to be successful at school and in life. I explore how developing a child's vocabulary, their exposure to words, helps them with the skills of self-regulation, which is the best predictor of school success. We've also discussed the huge role that the social brain plays in human interaction in terms of building relationships and developing empathy, or concern for others, that's at the heart of civility.

I also look at how the environment between a baby and a caregiver initiates a cascade of interactions that have the potential to build concern for the welfare of others. While health benefits of caring for the young continue to be my concern, the focus for this chapter was on developing civility as an important aspect of the well-being of the young so that their future skills include caring for others. Stress, mentioned in the first chapter, is important in this research.

Science researchers look at brain pathways and stress pathways and ask how the immune system gets set up early in life with the hope of discovering how that system might develop so it can move in the direction of a child's growth towards health.

LOVE BUILDS BRAINS

4

Resilience and Recovery

INTRODUCTION

I n the previous chapter, I talked about the social brain, the impact of stress and what we need to do as community to put children on a solid pathway to health. This chapter looks at resilience. Teachers and parents have become quite aware of the role resilience plays in a child's life. Resilience refers to someone's ability to bounce back from difficult, even traumatic, experiences.[1] Many of us have asked why it is that some children rebound while others seem to be caught in trauma that has rocked their world. There are many factors that contribute to recovery and this chapter is going to examine resilience, because it's one of those factors.

One of the key concepts I discuss in the chapter moves from thinking about individual characteristics to viewing the effects of the environment and the resources in it that support resilient responses. In describing resilience from this systemic approach, the chapter looks at responses children make to trauma and loss by looking at a whole world experience that shapes and informs those responses.

Using several case studies, I outline the nature of resilience and pick out its role in recovery to make the point that resilience, i.e., doing well in spite of adversity, is an outcome of a set of inter-related components in a child's life. I propose that resilience relies for its development on relationships, both those that precede the crisis and those that are made available during and after the crisis. As mentioned in earlier chapters, those relationships are nested in concentric circles around the child, e.g., in caring families, supportive communities, hospitable school cultures and civil society in general. The following two scenarios give a picture of the differences between children that bounce back from adversity and those who seem continually caught up in a sphere of influence that trauma has on their future development.

TWO CASE STUDIES

- Case Study #1: Two girls woke up to another morning of shouting between their parents who were arguing about their older brother because he had not come home again the previous night. Each parent was working at two jobs, trying to climb their way out of the poverty of an inner city subsidized housing project. Anna, scowled, as she put on the same clothes she wore yesterday, and worried about what the kids at school would say about her. The other, Jenna, was already thinking of an art project her teacher assigned. She didn't notice her mismatched socks as she waltzed into the kitchen, seeming almost oblivious to the tension that was thick in the room.

- Case Study #2: Two boys, John and Ryan, dozed in the back seat after an intense weekend at a basketball tournament when suddenly the van spun out of control and crashed into the side of the road. Three of their teammates were killed in the accident. John and Ryan were sitting together at the back. They were miraculously unhurt—or so it seemed at the outset.

  Both went back to school to resume their routine, but altered life. Counselors were available to all students, but neither of these two boys went to see them. After several months John still woke up with nightmares, his grades were dropping, he seemed to have lost interest in many of his favorite things and refused to talk about the accident. His parents, initially concerned, were increasingly frustrated that he wasn't "getting over it." Ryan, though initially very sad and frequently emotional, appeared to be back on track. He spoke of their lost friends and wanted to start a basketball scholarship in their names, which was a surprise to those who knew him since before the accident, he was seen as quite shy and retiring.

Why is it that these children, similar in some characteristics, when faced with risk and trauma, have such different psychological outcomes? Why is it that for some young people, challenge leads to growth and change, yet for others only to more suffering? Questions such as these led researchers in the 1970s to explore an observation that some children develop well under risk conditions, while others don't. These researchers believed that understanding the factors and conditions that led to better outcomes in some children and youth could help us learn how to improve the life chances of all children who encounter hazardous experiences[2] such as those that were affecting Anna, Jenna, Ryan and John.

In this chapter, I explore the concept of resilience and say that it is not a personality or inborn trait as once was thought. Resilience is a manifestation of a complex interaction of factors, both genetic and environmental, and at its heart, is a form of adaptive behavior. It is an interactive relationship between a child's biology and his or her environmental conditions and shows that neither biology nor environment alone can account for resilience. A strong belief for me is that children and youth can handle crises better if protective factors, communication skills and supportive conditions are intentionally fostered in the family and the communities that surround them.

A NEW WAY OF THINKING ABOUT ADAPTIVE BEHAVIOR

Resilience refers to doing well in spite of adversity. Researchers have pointed out that behavior associated with the term isn't simply part of someone's personality; it's not something some people are born with and others aren't. It's a type of adaptive behavior, a set of observable traits that arise when someone is faced with the difficult scenarios that Anna, Jenna, John and Ryan were experiencing. The term refers to an ability to rise above adversity and come out the better for it. People that demonstrate resilience are those that thrive in the face of trouble. Two of the children in the scenarios described above are able to adapt to difficulty in positive ways; two aren't able to do so. How are we to understand the adaptability Jenna and Ryan are expressing?

Adaptive behavior in general, which can be defined as the ability to cope with the demands of everyday life, includes self-help strategies, communication and social skills. Adaptive behavior has for a long time fascinated researchers, clinicians and parents alike. Until the 1970s, the study of typical human development and the study of abnormalities in psychological development (psychopathology) predominantly formed into two separate disciplines. The merging of these two perspectives led to the field of developmental psychopathology (DP). As these two discourses were linked, resilience research benefited from their marriage, because, as a form of adaptive behavior, resilience requires that someone is exposed both to an adverse event or conditions, and demonstrates an outcome in which the person does better than would have been expected. For example Jenna's and Ryan's exposure to risk was similar to Anna's and John's but the outcomes differed. What is it about Jenna and Ryan and their interaction with the system within which they lived, that led to differing outcomes, i.e., to their positive pattern of recovery?

As scientists examined the descriptors, underlying processes and conditions that led to positive responses in young people such as Jenna and Ryan, the field of resilience research unfolded. The exploration was greatly influenced by Bronfenbrenner's ecological systems theory, depicted in chapter one, that held to the core idea "that human individuals are living systems continually interacting with the contexts in which their lives are unfolding, including family, peer groups, schools and larger systems."[3]

The pre-eminent scholar and child psychiatrist Sir Michael Rutter, also posits that resilience research started by recognizing the huge individual variation in people's responses to the same risk experiences. As an example, some children who lived with parents who had schizophrenia didn't fare well while their siblings did. Rutter suggested that if we could understand "the mechanisms underlying that variation [it would] cast light on the causal processes and, by so doing, [would] have implications for the intervention strategies with respect to both prevention and treatment"[4] of children and youth that are undergoing significant stress. In other words, if we can figure out why Jenna and Ryan handle these challenges well, we may be able to understand and to help Anna and John?

In the past, people looked at how conditions in the environment affected the individual. For example, researchers asked about the effects on a developing child of environmental conditions such as poverty, single parenthood, dangerous neighborhoods and parental schizophrenia. It was as if these conditions were determining how children would turn out. In contrast, the idea of resilience that interests me moves from paying primary attention to external risks and looks at the interaction between those external risks and a person's response to them. When we see resilience in this way, the personhood of the individual moves from a passive to an active role.

In one way, resilience researchers turned their field glasses around and looked through the other end. They focused not on the far object, i.e., the environment in which a child struggled, but looked close-up, at internal processes of the child, the object near to hand. For example, Anna and Jenna were exposed to the same conditions of external risk. Both experienced living in poverty and shared the same parents whose educational attainment didn't improve during the girls' early years. Yet they responded differently. What are the factors that led to their different adaptations? Is a healthier response an outcome of birth order, temperament, differences in their exposure to abuse, their intelligence, having preferred status in an important arena, or, is it simply that one of the girls got better genes for adaptive behavior? Jenna's behavior constitutes a better way of adapting to her situation since she accepted mismatched socks and didn't worry what people would say about her. Her behavior is a positive adaptation because she was able to think about an art project that she looked forward to as a positive way to express her talent.

It's important to clarify that resilience is a term used in many contexts and is easily confused with other concepts, such as competence, coping, positive mental health, or even resiliency. Coping and adapting describe behavior that's a response to stress. These strategies don't imply that the behavior is positive or successful. We can cope with stressors by simply going through the motions of our day-to-day rituals, as one example. Resilience refers to behavior that is a constructive, positive adaptation to stressful situations.

Resilience is also different from resiliency, which is a characteristic or ability to return to a previous level of functioning after a stressful experience. Some people have said that it's a better descriptor of rubber bands than it is of people. Resilience, based on my first-hand knowledge as a psychiatrist, as well as on the research, refers to being transformed and altered by an experience of adversity so that one isn't the same as one was before it happened. The person with resilience doesn't return to a former state of functioning, but is actually better off. This idea of resilience describes individuals who don't simply cope but actually recover and demonstrate they're moving on with life in a positive way.

THE CHARACTERISTICS OF RESILIENCE

Individuals such as Mother Teresa, Pope Jean Paul II, Bill Clinton or Oprah Winfrey, to name some exemplars, are people who have faced significant adversity and demonstrated resilience. They had difficult early life experiences and not only overcame adversity but became great, in at least some capacity. In the past, we may have thought they were invulnerable, superhuman, somehow inoculated against the conditions of their childhood. Such thinking was reflected in the 1970s by articles like one that was in the Washington Post, March 1976, which stated: "Trouble: A bubble to these kids," a headline implying that some children could simple burst the bubble of adversity around them and move on.[5] This view of children and adversity was followed by the myth of the 'golden child.' This was a child who stood in the midst of despair, yet remained gleaming and unscathed. The problem with this view of childhood and youth is that it promotes the idea that, not only were the resilient children special, but that resilience is a quality given only to a few.

These attitudes suggest that somehow children who bounce back from difficulty have been untouched or unaffected by those experiences or that they have superhuman traits that make them invulnerable to difficulty. As a result, people tended to think that resilience was an inherent quality of an individual—some people have it, some people don't. This isn't only a false idea; it minimizes the effort and success of young people who overcome adversity. The Latin term invulnerable means 'not to wound' and intimates that one is incapable of being hurt or is immune to attack. It's essential to understand that resilient people have been attacked, felt the wound, were affected by adverse events, but have overcome the attack. What is it about them that allowed them not only to survive, but to thrive? The answer may come as a surprise, since it lies in what they are able to rally to their aid.

Resilience doesn't come from rare and special qualities, but from the everyday magic of ordinary, normal human resources in the minds, brains and bodies of children, as well as in their families, relationships and communities.[6] The ongoing study of resilience has revealed that the adaptive behavior connected to it arises from interactions within and between individuals and their environment. As American psychology researcher Ann Masten discovered, what began as a quest to understand what was seen as extraordinary achievement (in the individuals named above) eventually came to reveal the power of ordinary experience. The characteristics of resilience are ordinary internal capacities within a child, externally within a family and also in the communities that surround a child.[7]

Characteristics within the child

Masten's work was informed by a longitudinal study, Project Competence, which followed 205 children and families from the 1970s to the present. The study continues with over 90% of its initial population still participating (many years later). As she looked back over data collected on these children, she observed that young adults who demonstrated resilience in their twenties had shown the following characteristics in childhood, such as:

- Good intellectual and attention skills
- Agreeable personality in childhood
- Achievement motivation and conscientiousness
- Lower stress reactivity
- Parenting quality in childhood and adolescence
- Positive self-concept
- Competence in childhood in terms of conduct academically and socially

Some might think these characteristics are inborn but most are manifestations of interactions between biology and the environment.

For example, the development of attention skills in most children requires attentive care giving in infancy and also nurturing, warm responsiveness as adults set limits in toddlerhood. Children learn to inhibit their impulsiveness and begin to focus their attention during experiences in the family, at school, or in social settings as people help them by co-regulating with them.[8] We want to keep in mind that there are some children who are biologically differently wired and may have more hyper activity. But even these children can fare better in the presence of a nurturing, co-regulating environment. In co-regulating environments, a positive self-concept comes from the experience of doing well and being acknowledged for that accomplishment. In contrast, if children are bombarded with messages of what they're constantly doing wrong, they develop self-concepts that are negative and self-defeating.

So what is it about Jenna that makes her resilient? On the surface, we could read her story and decide that she just doesn't get it—that she isn't paying attention to what's going on in her household, and further, that her sister actually has a better grip on reality. However, according to resilience research, Jenna has a different outlook, one of optimism. She appears to have a more agreeable personality. Is that because she is temperamentally less intense so she can let things go? Is she easier to parent and subsequently receives less negative attention? We can notice that she has lower stress reactivity. Things don't stress her as much as they do her sister. When events are stressful, she's able to get back to a pre-stress state more quickly. We all know people who can't let go of issues and get stuck and even make themselves sick. The ability to leave issues aside requires the self-reflective ability to say: "I can deal with this later." This response develops as someone has positive experiences of successfully dealing with challenges.

Anna, on the other hand, is stuck in a negative outlook. She hasn't been able to see beyond the moment that's 'stressing her out'. Perhaps as the older of the two girls, she has had more responsibility placed on her shoulders, which has left her feeling resentful. Perhaps she has a temperament that dislikes change. She may be slow to warm up and may give out less warmth during social interactions so that her family members feel less secure in her love for them. She may be prickly in new situations. Due to the over-riding stress of her family's poverty, her parents may be unable to find a way to help her identify her negative emotions and to mature by reflecting upon them.

Jenna has a sense of purpose and can focus her attention on her interests and exclude distractions. She's likely aware of conditions in her family, yet she focuses on what can be in her world (an art project) rather than on what's absent in her environment (matching socks). Perhaps she epitomizes an African proverb that I came across that says, "It's not what you call me, but what I answer to that names me". Anna, however, is caught up in thinking about what she doesn't have.

But resilience is more than optimism. Jenna has faced the difficulties and has continued in an intentional way to be hopeful. It's not that she's oblivious to her circumstances—something else is going on. Masten concluded that she and her colleagues

> learned that youth who overcome childhood adversity and con-
> tinue on to adult success have more protections and resources in
> their lives than their peers who do not fare as well. We observed
> 'late bloomers' whose lives took a dramatic turn for the better

in the transition to adulthood, suggesting that new resources, opportunities, and supports converge in this window to promote positive change.[9]

Another group of researchers under the direction of Harvard University professor Stuart Hauser addressed the processes that underlie resilience. They interviewed 67 teens who had been significantly enough disturbed as teenagers to be admitted to a locked unit in a psychiatric facility. The book, *Out of the Woods* (2006) tells the stories of 4 of these youth who haven't only survived, but are thriving. Sadly, only 9 of the 67 young people were doing well. Many continue to lead very troubled lives. By looking at their narratives from the time of their admission to the facility at age 15 until adulthood, Hauser's group were able to delineate three characteristics that are crucial to resilience; they are

• Personal agency and a concern to overcome adversity
• A self-reflective style
• A commitment to relationships.[10]

In Hauser's terms, Jenna and Ryan had a sense of agency—a sense that what they do matters and a belief that they could intervene successfully in their own lives. They believed they could make a difference even when their optimism was challenged. Rather than becoming emotionally beaten down by the loss of his friends, Ryan wanted to make meaning out of their deaths by creating a scholarship in their names. He had a sense that he could make a difference. He may very well have had a family that understood that his reticence (when he had expressed this reluctance to talk about the accident) stemmed from being an introvert and not avoidance. Over time, they may have successfully communicated that they accepted him as he was and may have been available to provide support whenever he asked for it.

In contrast, John's behavior suggests that he was feeling isolated and lost. He didn't seek out others as a means of comfort or reach out for assistance. There could be many reasons for his actions. One may be that he still felt too vulnerable and hurt. Another could be that his reaction is like that of some children whose parents can't meet their emotional needs when they are upset, distressed or ill. Attachment theory proposes that when children have predictable adults in their life that respond to their emotional needs, they face stressors (stress inducing events) in a better way.[11] If caregivers avoid responding when children need them, or are unpredictable in their responsiveness, the young develop a working model or worldview that tells them people aren't reliable. This can lead children to give up and focus the blame for their difficulties outside of themselves, rather than looking for ways to be agents of change in their own circumstances, by using their own talent.

Masten and Hauser discovered that competence and developmental tasks at one age are effective forecasters of good future development. That is, resilience tends to endure. Yet they also learned that late resilience is possible. Many thriving young people didn't demonstrate resilience as they struggled through earlier hardships, but they did so eventually. This is a profound lesson and brings parents, teachers and counselors much hope. One of the key factors seems to be that the young person is open to the messages that they're doing well and someone is there for them. Resilient children are those that can tell the story of their own life—they reflect on their experience. They stand back from the difficulty and impact their own life story in positive ways.

Characteristics within the family

A crucial factor appeared in the lives of children who showed resilience: it was the presence of a secure base, a safe harbor; that is, adults who were available and present for them. Children and youth that demonstrate resilience had one or more adults who loved and believed in them and remained connected to them in order to provide consistent emotional support. Grandparents, uncles, aunts, friends and teachers shone the magic of connectedness on these children and encouraged resilience in their lives. Models of family functioning described by Olson, Russell and Sprenkle (1989) identify three characteristics central to healthy families, which are:

- Cohesion, which facilitates togetherness
- Adaptability, which balances flexibility and stability
- Clear, open, consistent communications

Research studies demonstrate that healthy families solve problems with cooperation, creative brainstorming, and openness to others' ideas,[13] which is a point of research that's very similar to the processes described by Hauser.

If families feel they can make a difference in a difficult situation and exert positive control over some aspects of it, they reach better outcomes. In addition, having the ability to reach out to others for support appears to be a characteristic of resilience, both in individuals and in families. This reaching out includes maintaining ties to institutions and social groups. Schuster and others found that 90% of Americans surveyed immediately after the 9-11 attacks reported turning to prayer, religion or spirituality in an effort to cope.[14]

In terms of family dynamics, resilient families are less reactive, they can say 'this too shall pass' and employ creative brainstorming when difficulties arise.

Characteristics within the neighborhood

The well-being of a family is impacted by its neighborhood too. In the community at large, resilience is strengthened among neighbors when they get along and work together (cohesion), adaptability as well as open and consistent communication. Felton Earls is the lead researcher in a multi-year, multi-million dollar study called the The Project on Human Development in Chicago Neighborhoods. He studied the impact of the city's neighborhoods on human development. He co-authored a pivotal paper in 1997 that appeared in Science in which the authors proposed, "that the differential ability of neighborhoods to realize the common values of residents and maintain effective social controls is a major source of neighborhood variation in violence."[15]

As part of their research goals, they hoped that a notion they termed 'collective efficacy" would become a buzzword among social scientists and policy makers. Collective efficacy is a form of social cohesion among neighbors in which they understand that they're all willing to intervene on behalf of the common good. At the heart of collective efficacy there is trust, reciprocity and a willingness among people to look out for one another. Earls also notes that cities that sow community gardens may reap a harvest not only of kale and tomatoes, but healthier children and safer neighborhoods.[16]

Froma Walsh, from the University of Chicago, also studied traumatic loss and gave a compelling argument for expanding the focus from individual symptom-focused intervention, to an approach that "taps strengths and resources in relational networks to foster healing and posttraumatic growth.[17]As with individuals and families, when a neighborhood believes in its collective efficacy in resolving its own difficulties, it acts out the characteristics that we see in resilience.

The work of the Canadian scientist, Dr. Michael Ungar, has changed my own view and how I approach resilience. Heleads the Nova Scotia based Resilience Research Centre, and is a prolific author, including a regular blog for *Psychology Today*,[18] and gifted speaker and is the Canada Research Chair in child, family and community resilience. His website has many wonderful free resources, including tools for assessing resilience and what worksin designing programs that build reslience.

He defines resilience this way:

> In the context of exposure to significant adversity, resilience is both the capacity of individuals to navigate their way to the psychological, social, cultural, and physical resources that sustain their well-being, and their capacity individually and collectively to negotiate for these resources to be provided in culturally meaningful ways.[19]

Resilience very clearly is not just about personal atributes or characteristics of the individual but rather is about the ability to figure out how to get what you need to be able to get through tough times. Ungar's resarch supports nine things that all children need to be resilient:[20]

- Structure
- Consequences
- Parent-child connections
- Lots and lots of strong relationships
- A powerful identity
- A sens of control
- A sense of belonging, spirituality andlife purpose
- Rights and responsibilities

Once again we see the power of connection and relationships. When kids are in supportive relations at home and in the community and have an identity as a caring thoughtful, hopeful individual, their well-being is improved and their contribution to a civic society is made possible.

EPIGENETICS

In chapter one, I introduced the idea of epigenetics. Now I want to say more about it as we consider a person's ability to recover from difficult life circumstances and the role other people play in that recovery. Our developing understanding of biology and genetics strengthens the idea that good neighbors make a difference. To make this case about resilience, we need to have some understanding of the role of genetics in human development. There's a continuing debate in scientific literature about whether a 'resilience gene' exists. One of the most exciting areas of research currently is the study of epigenetics. Genetics is the study of DNA-based inherited characteristics that are present in any and every organism. Epigenetics is a special branch of this science that looks at factors that affect gene functioning without changing the actual DNA.

As one example, imagine a computer in which DNA or the genome (the complete set of 23 chromosomes) is the hardware. Epigenetics is the software that tells the genome how and when to work, as well as how hard to work. Some researchers explain epigenetics by using a simile of words and stories. For them, DNA is like the words of a story, but the story line is ever changing through the frequency and timing of particular words that a storyteller uses. The ebb and flow, this movement of the storyline, is what scientists call the epigenome[21] Epigenetics is a branch of research that's concerned with the relationship between genes and environment (genetics times environment), as well as with their interactions. It's fair to say that genetics and epigenetics are the next great frontier of science.

As part of this early epigenetic research, The Dunedin Study is a large longitudinal study from New Zealand that's providing groundbreaking evidence of genetic/environmental interaction. Researchers know that people are born with variations in their genes depending on their parents' contribution. We get one set of genes from each parent. A gene often comes in two varieties of the gene (such as a gene for eye color that makes eyes brown or blue). An individual can have two copies of the gene of the same variety (brown-brown or blue-blue), or two copies of a different variety (brown-blue). When looking at serotonin, a neurotransmitter in the brain known to be involved in depression some differences appear. Researchers found that people receive serotonin transporter genes from their parents that have either two short alleles (think of arms of their DNA, like the blue-blue above), two long alleles (like brown-brown), or one long and one short allele (blue-brown).

In the case of the serotonin transporter gene, there's a relationship between the length of alleles and a tendency toward depression. But what the researchers discovered is, unlike eye color in which these genes produce actual differences in eye color, the mere presence of these alleles isn't enough to cause depression. Rather, in people who have both the presence of two short alleles (making them vulnerable to depression) those who also experience maltreatment in childhood are the ones who had high levels of depression.[22] The depression needed both the gene variation (alleles) and the negative experience in order for depression to manifest.

There are similar findings with the gene that regulates another neurotransmitter, MAOI, which is seen to be low in people with anti-social or conduct problems. Yet low levels alone don't lead to difficulty in social interaction. However, if children have both low levels of these transmitters and they also experience maltreatment in childhood, their problems soar.[23] Sir Michael Rutter also concluded his research with findings that strengthen the theory that there isn't one single universally applicable resilience trait.[24] From the perspective of biology and environment, resilience is an outcome of the interaction of genetic makeup and environmental effects. This is why, when neighborhoods act together and believe their collective actions can have significant effects on their quality of life, they strengthen resilience in their communities.

CONCLUSION

Resilience research offers hope to children and youth as well as to parents, teachers and counselors. But how does research help adults foster resilience in the young? Evidence in the research suggests that what matters is a basic sense of connection to others through attachment and social support. The oft-used African proverb 'It takes a village to raise a child' truly is the heart of resilience. But we also need to recognize that sometimes 'It takes a child to raise a village'. Children can be examples of resilience and can teach us how to recover from loss in a way that makes all of us more human. If parents are supported in their attempts to be emotionally responsive and available to their children and focus on the development of social relatedness with them and with other community members, they will enhance the role of empathy throughout childhood and into young adulthood.

When empathy develops, the pathways for empathy and resilience work together. Too often parents are challenged to focus their attention on making children behave well, rather than emphasizing a desire that they should grow up to be people that can love well. If we accomplish that goal, other factors come along with it. Children become more able to regulate emotion, arousal and behavior. If they are given opportunities to learn and experience effectiveness, they develop what is called self-efficacy, which is a sense that 'I can do it.' Self-efficacy is a fundamental attitude in civil life, if and when it's paired with a child that knows how to be open to other people and to love them. Civility is having a sense that what you do matters.

The four young people in the opening scenarios can now be viewed through the lens of resilience. They have access to varying levels of internal strength in terms of attention, ability to regulate their emotions, ability to relate to others and hope for the future. Does this mean that Anna and John are doomed? Not at all! Resilience research tells us that they're demonstrating a greater need for supportive environments, for people in their lives who can help them construct a new narrative, a new meaningful story around which to live their lives. People can come around Anna and John. These people can focus on what they do well, believe in them and see their futures hopefully by supporting their capacity to increase their own internal strength.

Hope is perhaps the greatest internal characteristic of resilience. In addition to having hope, we need to learn how to ask for help. Humor is important to resilience as an adaptive response. In addition, viewing oneself and other people in terms of strengths not weakness is important. Finally, having some kind of meaning in life—which doesn't necessarily mean having formal religion, but does mean having a large enough story to live within so that the young can feel connected to the world. Ultimately, a sense of connectedness lies at the heart of resilience.[25]

This chapter shifts our view from a focus on the individual interpretation of human experience to one that offers a systemic approach to the lives of children. The concept of resilience helps make that shift more visible. The knowledge gained through resilience research may inform and inspire adults who care for children. The possibility of recovering from loss is a human potential. As Confucius said, our greatest glory is not in never falling, but in rising every time we fall.

5

Connection is the Key

INTRODUCTION

I n this chapter, I look at a few of the impacts on North American education in the last half of the twentieth century. I've been a children's psychiatrist for more than 30 years and for a number of years I was a special advisor to the Premier of Ontario and advised the Ministry of Education. How governments think about children and education is a primary concern for me. I'm also aware of what people in government try to accomplish for children and education. For example, are you aware of *The Brain Story*,[1] which was developed in Alberta by the Alberta Family Wellness Initiative? It's a cartoon-like overview of how the brain works that's accessible to children and adults. What I do is translate knowledge, particularly about brain research and make it accessible to teachers, parents and people in government. As a result of my work, I'm aware that we need to be thinking about teaching our children very differently. A primary mantra for me is to say that connecting with children comes before correcting or directing them. My purpose in this chapter is to say that relationship and learning are so intertwined we need to ask ourselves often whether we're connecting with kids, or, are we simply correcting and directing them.

If you assess your own parenting and teaching practices, what's your ratio of connection to direction or correction? To make it harder for us, some of the impacts on education during the last century have tended to emphasize correcting and directing, rather than putting the role of connection where it belongs—as the key to helping children benefit from education.

WHAT'S IT LIKE TO CONNECT?

What do I mean by connection? What would it be like if I was an adult who connects so well with children that kids come to know for sure that what they do and who they are matters to me very much? The following story has a number of elements I pick up and develop throughout the chapter.

A Story

A friend of mine, also a researcher, came to visit me and told me this story. She flew from Vancouver to Toronto so we could collaborate. We both do research on a felt sense of connection. Just before she got on the plane, she noticed a family that was travelling together, grandparents, siblings and their children. As she sat in her seat on the aisle, she saw one of the young women from that family seated in the aisle across from her, on her right, one row ahead. As the flight began, she heard several babies crying. After an hour or so, only one of them was still crying. It was about 90 minutes into the flight so she looked around to see where this little one was sitting.

She was startled to realize that the infant was sitting in a car seat beside the young woman from the extended family she first noticed in the airport. As she continued to observe her, she realized that, up to this point, she hadn't seen any behavior in the young woman to indicate there was a baby beside her. So my friend thought that a woman in that row on the other side of the baby must be its mother.

She observed that young woman also. The woman on the other side didn't touch or look at the baby but looked every so often at the young woman in the aisle seat. My friend was confused. Then she noticed that the infant was reaching its hands up to the young woman who was across from her. Every few minutes, the baby was looking towards this young woman, reaching up and crying. From my friend's perspective, the baby seemed upset. She noticed that the young woman was looking at her phone most of the time and seldom looked at the infant. When she did look at the baby (9 or 10 months old perhaps) it was for very short times, with no eye contact. At that point, my friend leaned forward to ask the young woman if she might ask her a question. The young woman replied that yes, she could. My friend asked,

"Can you tell me what theory you're using as you sit with your baby?"

This bright, self-aware young woman was very clear about her theory. She replied that her theory was that the baby was most comfortable sitting in his car seat and would fall asleep soon. My friend then told her that she researched children's experience, and that, as she looked at the infant, she thought the baby was asking for her. The young mom looked at her baby. In a few minutes she undid the straps and picked up her child. She held the baby close. My friend noticed that she appeared awkward at first but after 10 or 15 minutes, the baby settled down and fell asleep in his mother's arms. After a while, the mom put him back in his car seat where he slept for the rest of the flight.

This story helps to consider what it means to connect with children and to think about the way our theories of the child influence how we respond to them. As you read this chapter, I'd like you to remember that the way we think about a child shapes the way we feel about a child and leads to the way we act toward a child, as the airplane story conveys.

As mentioned, the focus for the chapter is connection. I learned about connection from my teacher Dr Dan Offord, who I mentioned in an earlier chapter. As our teacher, he was able to make us *feel felt*. A feeling of being felt by one's parent or teacher—of being seen, heard, acknowledged and known—matters to the child's ability to learn. This is particularly true for children who are at higher risk. Being with children in this sense is more important than having the latest toys, latest methods, latest strategies—it's more important than the smoothness of your lesson or the significance of what you want them to learn.

Once again, content matters, but how you get it to children and how you 'get' or understand them is at least, if not more central to their ability to realize learning is interesting to them. It's the quality of the relationship that children remember, not the content. The issue for learners is how you made them feel. I have a dream that every child will have at least one person in their life whose eyes light up when they enter the room. Every time I walked into the room with Dan, I *felt felt* by him. I had a real sense of him appreciating me. I work with many childcare workers (in the daycare/childcare world). They tell me it's kids who are hard to work with, the kids who use your sleeve instead of tissues when they have a runny nose, that are never ever sick! They're always there. They're in the room every single day! My dream is that these are the kids will have adults whose eyes to light up as they walk into the room.

PROGRESS NOT PERFECTION

So how can we create a better world? I take the neuroscience of brain research and try to understand it really well in order to act as a translator of it. I'm a knowledge translator so that my readers can take it and use it well with their kids. I want this book to help maintain an adult's excitement about the science of making a difference in children's lives.

I also have my own experience with my 5 children. As their mother, my mantra is progress not perfection. As we consider our desire to make the world a better place, it's important to be generous to ourselves. As I think about my 5 children, one lesson they taught me is to be aware of temperament. This is because each one has a radically different temperament, as I said in chapter three.

Temperament refers to traits such as persistence, sensitivity and intensity. As I said, our first child was easy. When our second child came along, she cried constantly if I wasn't holding her. She had to be held all the time. I recall my mother saying to me, "I know about this attachment stuff Jean, but what about crazy glue?" If you consider the learning environment you establish at home or in your classroom, do you attend to the role that temperament plays in a child's life? Understanding temperament improved our daughter's experience as well as our experience of her.

The same is true in the school classroom. Do you ask yourself what it is that engages each child's attention? Kids come into your classroom with very different temperaments. As teachers consider a strategy that's promoted by people who shape curriculum and classroom practice, it's important to develop different ways to introduce that element to your kids. We know that, at birth, kids come out differently. As a consequence, we need to think about the overall strategies we're asked to use in terms of different ways children learn. As one example, how can we find ways to engage children so they can learn self-regulation?

Back to my own experience with our second child—one book I read called babies like my daughter 'mother killers'. If you have a highly sensitive, spirited child, they're going to have more challenges integrating into a full day of learning. If you don't understand that, you'll end up with what we have in Ontario right now—many, many children who aren't meeting school expectations. These children haven't learned to self-regulate. They can't manage a full day of learning because they haven't learned to manage their emotions and impulses effectively. As those who work with children, we can ask ourselves questions that help to focus on essential kindergarten competencies so we recognize what children need help with as they enter and remain in the school setting. A most basic need that each child has as they enter kindergarten is the need to belong. If you don't belong, you can't learn. If a child feels they don't belong, they experience unwelcome stress.

We must learn to see that stress behavior is not misbehavior. One assumption that helps us make this move is to believe that *kids will do well if they can*—rather than thinking that kids will do well if they want to do well. We need to be thinking about the whole child. We need to ask about the essential competencies needed to produce success. In a wonderful book, *Becoming Brilliant*[2] the authors, who are now the playful learning gurus, trace back to how we got to where we are at the present moment in our beliefs and practices at school. They ask the question: When did education become all about 'stuffing the duck'? When did our curriculum become all about getting content and inserting it into children? Our friends in France see it differently. For them, 'stuffing the duck' produces *foi gras*, which is delicious, but that's not what I'm talking about. I'm talking about stuffing content into our kids.

If we take children's love of learning into account, it's necessary to understand how temperament is a key component in their development.[3] For my part, we didn't learn about it in medical school and teachers aren't learning about it in their educational programming. But temperament matters. Sensitive, high-spirited children will have more challenges as they try to integrate into a full day of learning. In Ontario, we have a million 4 and 5 year olds in a full day of learning. Of these children, lots of them have great difficulty integrating. It's not because they need their nap. It's that they haven't developed the ability to self-regulate. As a result, expectations are too high for them. It's not that they aren't ready for kindergarten; kindergarten isn't ready for them.

What are we doing to help them succeed? In many schools, very early, we're labeling and suspending these children. We also have them on a modified school day. What we need to do is to ask a different question: What are essential competencies for Early Childhood Educators and teachers so they can meet the needs of all the children in their classrooms?

Again, let me emphasize that if you have little ones in your classroom whose engines run on high, you have to recognize that the way they act is stress behavior not misbehavior. We have to think from a mental model that tells us that kids will do well if they can— not from the model that says kids will do well if they want to. We have tended to see the human will as central and so we've thought we just have to incentivize children so that they will access learning in the classroom. That very belief fails to see learning as interesting in itself. It fails to acknowledge the necessary competencies a child needs to fit well into a learning environment. The approach I recommend proposes that children will do well if they have the skills to do well in the schoolroom setting. Skills include: stress management and coping, identification and management of emotion, positive motivation and perseverance, healthy relationship skills, self-awareness and sense of identity, critical and creative thinking and executive functioning.

Learning those skills begins with connection. If children feel that no one is with them, no one cares for them, they can't learn. As we emphasize social and emotional development, they learn better. At an earlier point in our educational history, we relied on IQ. But a better predictor of success is a child's social and emotional learning. In one research project, a group of kindergarten teachers filled out a set of questions focused on how their learners got along at school, how interested they were in others and their ability to show empathy. Researchers checked back on these children 15 years later.[4] They discovered the best predictor of future success was among children who, in kindergarten, could share with others, get along well with others and could show empathy. It wasn't IQ that provided for their success. It was social and emotional competence. What does this mean for what we must do in the early years?

Connection is the key to future success so that kids can develop social and emotional competencies characteristic of children who share with others, get along well with them and show empathy. What do we need to start doing and what do we need to stop doing to help children acquire these skills? Our strategies must begin by connecting with the child. The competencies develop through meaningful connection with adults who parent and teach children.

THE TYRANNY OF COGNITIVE SEDUCTION

Kindergarten should be about developing emotional and social competencies through play. Since the brain's architecture is sculpted by experience until about 8 years old, early learning should be about democracy, collaboration, citizenship, creativity and critical thinking. The way children are taught these competencies is through play-based, inquiry driven learning. Once again, children need to read by grade three because after that they read to learn. Without reading skill, learning is difficult. But from kindergarten to grade 3, they need to acquire other competencies that allow them to succeed in school and in life.

In *Becoming Brilliant*, the authors assess some of the impacts on North American education that they believe shape how we do things at school. They cite the impact of the Russian success with Sputnik (1957) as one source for the influence of what I call the tyranny of cognitive seduction. Because the Russians were successful in putting a man in space and Americans were slower at it, educators bought into a belief that literacy and numeracy are all important. While they matter, we haven't yet realized they aren't the only important competencies.

With the success of Sputnik, people began asking whether our kids were getting the right sort of education and decided that the Russian kids must have a better one. Then along came President Bush with the "no child left behind" program. As a result, if a child didn't succeed, we labeled or expelled them. The reaction was to establish core principles and high stakes testing—both of which potentially diminish creativity and the love of learning.

I'm not saying that cognitive development, literacy, and numeracy don't matter. There's no question children need to be reading by grade 3. Unfortunately, people took that to mean they should start learning to read before grade 3. As a result, kids in kindergarten had to focus on what we might call *schoolification* rather than the freedom to play. Kindergarten teachers gave away their sand centers and turned to reading as a way to prepare children for school experience itself. They lost focus on the love of learning and creative exploration of a learning environment. When are children's brains ready to read? The brain's capacity is at 7 years old. The trouble is that many children who come to school and can read and write, can't get along with each other.

I agree that learning to read is important. In some parts of the United States, the decision on how many jail cells to build is based on the number of children who aren't reading well in grade 4.[5]

But this statistic is not a predictor; it's a marker. If children aren't reading well, it's due to many other conditions in which they live that shape their experience. Children need to have a sense of purpose, belonging and meaning. If those are missing, life doesn't go well. They also need to enjoy creativity and develop critical thinking skills. How might these aspects of learning be incorporated into our classrooms to support the love of learning?

In creating the love of learning, we need to expose children to literacy from birth, even in utero. How do we do that? We read to children. We listen to them. As one example, in Cree culture, an Elder told me about the belief that each child has a story to tell. Take time to hear those stories. There are some guiding principles to recapture. Just as First Nations people groups teach us, we need to be thinking about the whole child and the competencies of the whole child. These competencies include more than the ability to read, do math and write; they include whether children can get along with others and care for their environment.

Too frequently, we forget about play! And, it's all about relationships. Teachers are in the business of human development. We need a revolution that says if we address children's emotional and social development, they learn better. Kids need to be great scholars and enjoy the well-being that includes hope, purpose and a sense of belonging.

In the First 2000 Days project,[6] researchers looked at social and emotional development in children. As a result of their research, we can say that kindergarten should be about learning the skills of democracy, citizenship and critical thinking through play-based, inquiry-driven learning. In addition, the First Nations Continuum of Wellness Framework[7] looks at the meaning a child develops, the ability to give to others, a strong sense of identity and of belonging as well as an overall sense of well-being. Children can acquire these skills when we address their social and emotional development.

But what occurs at school to undermine a child's well-being? What sense of belonging is there for a child who's in the Turtle reading group instead of the Rabbit group? One little girl I often talk about refused to go back to school after the school break because she was in the Turtle group. Why do we insist on comparing children instead of looking at what each one brings in terms of their gifts and talents. In First Nations' belief, children are the sacred ones, the heart of the nation. We should be thinking about how to rear each child into the good life—which involves each one being able to accept and value who they are.

WHAT'S YOUR VIEW OF THE CHILD?

It's not difficult, if you go to many toy stores, to see that the number of educational toys outweighs the number of play toys. In fact, millions of educational toys outstrip the number of play toys. If we believe children must develop their IQ in order to succeed in life, and we think that happens if they're exposed to 'education' early, we'll buy educational toys. Recall that earlier I said, the way we think about the child shapes the way we feel about the child and leads to how we act toward the child. How we think is essential to keep in mind.

What is your view of the child? Some options presented in the chapter so far include seeing children as the sacred ones, the heart of the nation. In the well-known *Reggio Emilia Program,*[8] started in an Italian town by that name, children are seen as competent and their learning environment is also their teacher. They're seen as the possessors of a hundred languages. There are many teachers who see children as a source of inspiration. In the story at the outset of the chapter, a young mom believed her baby would be best off in his car seat where he would eventually fall asleep without direct eye contact or involvement from her. She was certainly very patient in her belief.

What do you see as your job as a parent or teacher? Some kindergarten teachers say their job is to prepare kids for grade one. I know of one young mom who went to the school to hear about her son's learning journey. When she met with the teacher, she was told that this teacher saw her job as making sure he had his number and letter sense. Unfortunately, she was told, the boy liked to play with the wooden blocks and was always busy building something. What the teacher meant was that 5 year olds need to focus on numbers and letters. Though this boy loved to work with blocks and building, which meant he has spatial intelligence, his gift and interests were not valued by his teacher. In contrast to that teacher, many hold the belief that children have much to teach them and they have much to share with kids. When a child is in the classroom with one of these teachers, engagement is possible, because, in their classrooms, there'll always be something in the room that each child loves to explore.

One feature of brain research that's important to consider as we think about our view of the child, is that what we pay attention to is what gets built up in the brain. An aspect that interferes with a child's ability to connect effectively with others is anxiety. There's a reported increase in children's anxiety. If I think about it, and ask what causes anxiety, I can't help wondering about the self-esteem movement in the last century that dominated North America school cultures. The self-esteem movement worries me. In our current contexts, children's games no longer have winners and losers. Everyone gets a trophy. Children are sheltered from the idea of losing. Children get stickers and awards just for showing up.

As I was growing up and we played musical chairs, we took away a chair! If you try to play that game now and take away a chair, someone will say—oh but then a child won't have a chair to sit on. Hey! That's how the game works! If you don't get a chair you have to figure out how to cope with that. We've created a world in which we want children to be so safe they have no opportunity to learn what to do if they don't have a chair to sit on. I've observed many children put their heads on their desks and just give up when something goes wrong.

We focused on self-esteem instead of self-efficacy. Self-efficacy is about knowing what to do if something goes wrong. It's a feeling of belonging (even if you don't have a chair) and being strong and competent. There were so many beliefs about the child built into the self-esteem movement and they need to be reconsidered. Are children strong and competent, as the *Reggio Emilia* approach views them? Are they fragile and need constant protection from any sense that there's anything for them to learn about how to cope with life and how to get along with other people? In my view, children need to learn what to do when they fail. During play, children have an opportunity to learn what to do if things don't go well.

So much of what we thought in the last century has pushed play out of the classroom, even in kindergarten. We haven't been letting children learn about who they are—we've been focused on what we want them to be. In some interactions I have as a child advocate, I've realized that it's School Board Trustees that may be pushing play out of schools. They believe that numeracy and literacy offer the best and most important content to learn. Once again, our view of the child impacts how we feel about them and how we act towards them.

Another source of anxiety in children is one I worry about. When I see parents on their devices, paying attention to their phones even though their children are trying to connect with them, I'm concerned. How many have a rule that you can't bring a device to the dinner table? Devices are wonderful ways to acquire content but they don't help us to develop wisdom. Socially, the focus on our devices is dangerous. We know that what builds the architecture of the brain is sculpted by experiences children have up until 8 years of age. What if, from the time a child is born until the time she's 8 years old, she's mostly experienced parents who focus on the links they have with their devices, rather than connecting with her?

One view of the child that's emerging through brain research is that babies are born to connect. Babies at two days old are able to imitate a parent who is sticking out his tongue. What is the evolutionary point of the baby's ability to do this? What does it accomplish? It draws the parent toward the infant. The social brain of an infant is hyper connected to their caregivers, who can be parents or grandparents.

Why do I care about all this stuff? Children need to connect at school. What we've learned about the brain in the last two decades is that an infant brain at birth is about 1 pound (infantile brain) and about 3 pounds (almost adult sized) by the age of 5. The experiences adults create for them build the child's brain. Experiences children have in their early years literally turn on brain cells. In the past 10 or 15 years, we've learned a lot about the brain. As neurons wire up together they create wonderful networks and pathways. Neurons that fire up together wire up together.

100

We used to think that intelligence was relatively fixed at birth. But now we know that experiences sculpt the brain. The brain is not only a product of our genes; it's a product of genes plus experience. As one example, in Canada, we're learning a lot about what happened to First Nations peoples in Residential schools. What's now being studied is the inter-generational transmission of trauma—the atrocities we put First Nations children, parents and grandparents through—and we're trying to see whether it changed the expression of their DNA. We know that trauma changes the level of activity in someone's DNA.[9] So, when young people die in First Nations communities, we must consider whether it's due to inter-generational transmission of trauma. Do we believe that their deaths are due to poor life choices? Or, are we open to the possibility that the deaths of young First Nations people are due to the effects of a long history of experience and the effects of that history on their genes.

WIRED TO CONNECT

Children are wired to connect. I have to confess that sometimes it's hard for me as I'm out and about with other people to watch parents interact with their children. I have a soft heart for children. The other day while waiting for a plane, I watched a mom interact with her two children, one was four and the other was six years old. Her negative interaction with the children made the situation they were in much worse. As I looked at her, I first thought, oh, couldn't she do differently? As I watched her for a while, I thought again, and felt sorry for her, wondering if she knew how to do it differently. As she scolded the boys for every move they made, the worst-case scenario occurred: People started looking at her and judging her. I felt sorry for her and for myself too, to be honest, as I thought about what the next four hours on a plane was going to be like.

If the mom had had support, and if she knew that waiting would be difficult for little ones, would she have brought crayons, toys or books to help them wait? If she thought of herself, not as a behavioral manager, but as an emotional coach for these little boys, if she thought about how to help them manage their boredom in that environment, would it have gone differently? What were these two boys learning in that airport about themselves and about adults?

What's the point of a baby's ability to connect? Babies are born learning. When my son had just had his first child I have a video of the two of them. The baby is locked into his daddy's face. The social brain is locked onto the parent's brain. My son is talking to his baby and sticking out his tongue. The baby watches his dad. And then, his little tongue sticks out, just like daddy. He's less than a week old. Nancy Jones is an Ojibwa elder. In the first year of life, she says, we keep the baby close to our bodies all the time. The baby is connected to us through that first year of life. Our First Nations peoples developed snuggly packs before the rest of us thought of them.

Another outcome of connecting with babies is the development of language. In many provinces, there are geographical areas where children have heard 30 million words less than other children. What happens in the lives of those children? Researcher Ann Fernald[10] looked at the language children experience among people who are poor. She observed a range of language experience in that income category. The range within the poverty category was as wide as in the population as a whole. Financial wealth is not a guarantee of language wealth. In wealthier families, children may not have a large number of words if their caregivers are people who have little access to English language themselves. Language experiences build interconnections within the brain. The more words a child has, the more quickly they learn at school.

When children have plentiful connections in the brain, they come with access to a large number of words and can handle a new sentence such as: "Here is the kitty on the couch." If they know 'kitty' and they know "is the" and "on the" they only have to pick up the word couch. Because there is usually a picture to go along with the sentence, the image helps them with the meaning of the word couch. If a child doesn't know the words noted above, then the sentence is lost to them. They are stopped by trying to figure out "is the" "on the" even if they know the word "kitty." Many parents who live in extreme stress due to poverty can't afford the time it takes to spend talking with and reading to their children. However, again, economic poverty itself doesn't determine a child's language poverty. In Fernald's research, she found many low income moms and dads who speak and read to their children and in general provide their little ones with good language access by connecting with them while they're together.

What we need is a kind of coalition effort in which communities find out what experiences children have had before they ever arrive at kindergarten. As Fraser Mustard[11] reported, the young brain is ready for experiences of hearing and seeing. The child needs the stimulus coming in at just the right time so that the brain cells can get ready for seeing and hearing. Teachers must observe the individual needs of each of their children. It may seem odd, but the greatest numbers of kids who aren't ready for school are from the middle class.

This may seem contradictory, but it's based on the solid research work of the late Dr. Clyde Hertzman at the University of British Columbia. He used the Early Development Instrument (EDI), which is an instrument that measures readiness for school, to look at the entire population of children in British Columbia by geographic region. As he looked at the population level, i.e., every child in B.C., he was able to identify that the greatest number of children who aren't ready for school are from the middle class. When he divided the B.C. population into 5 income brackets from lowest to highest (each bracket is called a quintile), he observed that the highest percentage of children who aren't ready for kindergarten are from the lower income group. He also saw that the greatest overall number of vulnerable children is from the middle class. Many programs target their interventions towards the lowest income group. But just targeting the lower income group is going to miss the majority of children who need support.

Is it ever too late for a child? Dr. Bruce Perry tells of a child who was raised in a crate because his caregiver only knew how to raise dogs. Luckily, with intervention that little boy who originally could not speak or walk, learned to do so. Perry is a U.S. child psychiatrist who specializes in trauma. Is it ever too late for a child? What I've learned in 30 years is that what I think affects both what I feel and what I do. So, I ask myself what I'm thinking about the child that I'm with. How will that thinking impact what I do and what I believe the child can do. My theory is that, based on brain research, the brain is plastic throughout life. It's never too late.

TWO CONCEPTS: PLAY AND STRESS

Earlier in the chapter I proposed a view of the child that I want to say more about. I said that stress behavior is not misbehavior. What does stress behavior look like and what can parents and teachers do to respond to it by connecting with the child before they correct or direct the behavior? How can we teach children so that their stress levels are manageable? Further, how does stress affect the brain?

Recall that the early childhood brain learns best through play. Scientific research is clear about that. How can play help when a child is experiencing unwelcome stress? First let's focus on stress and the brain. As described in chapter three, stress fires up the amygdala[12] in the brain. When children have continuous and toxic stress and continue to experience that stress at school—or because of school—their brains act as if they're encountering a threat, such as a bear. Their stress system is activated, but the degree and duration of activation varies, depending on the stressor.

The Harvard Center on the developing child has a wonderful set of resources, including one about stress and the brain. They raise awareness that all stress is not equal. There are very good and positive effects of stress; for example, stress gets us activated to prepare for a race, an exam or a speech. This is positive stress. These researchers also describe tolerable stress, in which the stress system is activated but the effects of it are buffered by having people around—relationships help to manage stress. Because it's buffered, it's referred to as tolerable stress. Stress that's worrisome is called toxic stress, in which there is an experience of ongoing stress without any buffering by relationships.

We need to be better able to identify when stress is becoming toxic for children. We can identify certain situations where it's most likely to occur, such as conditions of maltreatment, bullying, neglect, parental addictions or severe mental health problems. It's more challenging to identify toxic stress outside of these conditions, but evidence suggests that it exists.

As young people are asked about their perception of stress in their lives, many are reporting high levels of anxiety. What's less clear is how anxiety is impacting their stress system. Many in the field are concerned, including me, about two matters: Do we have an epidemic of true anxiety disorders in the child and youth population? Or, have we given the young definitions of anxiety and stress, which they then think they have? One worry is that, along with these definitions, we haven't given them the normalizing messages about stress or the tools to manage anxiety—which is a normal part of growth and development. So I have to ask, have we helped them understand the functions of positive and tolerable stress, and informed them about what they need to have access to when they experience stress?

How is toxic stress different from positive and tolerable stress? Under toxic stress, as the amygdala fires up, the hippocampus (which supports new learning and memory) experiences prolonged activation, which in the long term can cause cell death. Under the condition of toxic stress, the brain goes on high alert. Other areas responsible for new learning (prefrontal cortex) don't function as well if the brain is worried about survival. In chapter three, I call this condition porcupine brain—the child's brain and behavior become prickly. Just when the child needs others the most—the child pushes people away. What will help? What's the solution to porcupine brain? The solution is relationship, relationship, relationship!

CONCLUSION

Children arrive at school excited to learn and wired to connect. If things go well, and their relationships are positive, they can learn and thrive. However, there are many experiences that might interfere with their freedom to thrive. What this chapter has explored is how essential it is to be reflective about our views of the child. If, as parents or teachers, we view the child as an empty vessel, rather than as someone who is resourceful and able to contribute to their own learning and development, we'll set up a very different relationship with them.

Research is showing that children who have better self-regulation as they enter kindergarten—better able to get along with others, be empathetic and manage their emotions—are more successful in school and in life. With better self-regulation, the child can access better relationships with other people. This means that when they're exposed to stressful situations, they're able to access others to help them buffer their stress. This is why a focus on social and emotional development is essential in the early years of life and of education.

It concerns me to observe what I've described as the tyranny of cognitive seduction in school settings, which some people call *schoolification*. When we focus on cognitive development, at the expense of play and social and emotional development, there will be many children who can't meet these intellectual demands because they're just not ready yet. How these children demonstrate their lack of readiness is often through behavior. As described in other chapters, and thinking again of the view of the child, it's important to think of these behaviors, not as misbehaviors, but as stress behaviors. When we intentionally connect with children and build relationship with them, it buffers their stress and we're able to reframe and help them learn and grow. As pointed out in the chapter, one of my mantras is connect before you correct or direct.

In addition, the brain is plastic throughout life. If we can modify the stress, the child can begin to learn, especially through play. The child can learn what to do if things are scary and if something goes wrong. And remember, if children have one person whose eyes light up as they enter the room, their capacity for self-regulation and learning through play is enhanced.

Yet, when we talk about the challenges of kindergarten, are we asking the right questions? I recall meeting a 5-year-old named Mohammad in a kindergarten classroom. The teacher led them through an exploration of *The Mind Up* curriculum, which is based on current brain research and helps children acquire skills such as self-regulation and a positive mindset for school and life.[13]

The class was learning about the amygdala, neurons and how to develop calming techniques. The teacher had a vase of water on a table and added food coloring to it. When she asked the children what they saw and why it was happening, Mohammad immediately jumped into an explanation of light refraction and described how the retina works. The teacher brilliantly acknowledged his input by saying, "Yes, Mohammad has a lot of background information, doesn't he? What else to people see?"

When I spoke with the teacher afterward, she told me that Mohammad had already been in 3 other kindergarten classes but had been asked to leave because of his disruptive behavior. In this classroom, it seemed to me, he was experiencing tremendous success. He was acknowledged as having a lovely brain. But the play-based and inquiry-led learning approach allowed him to explore the environment so he was able to work with others on projects. In the previous kindergartens, his behaviors were described as misbehavior and teachers saw him as interfering with their lesson. In my view, his behaviors were clearly stress behaviors.

So, there was a significant mismatch between his previous learning environments and the one I observed. In this class, he was thriving. It's true that he needs to learn self-regulation, but the learning environment needs to be more helpful to him. So, if we want children to do well, we must reframe the question. If we have only been asking, is this child ready for kindergarten, we must now ask, is kindergarten ready for this child.

6

Infant and Preschool Mental Health: The Power of Relationships

INTRODUCTION

The focus for this chapter is infant and preschool mental health. In chapter one, I looked at the typical healthy development of young children. In this chapter, I look at situations in which there are more difficulties and challenges with typical development. Mental health is an area that's close to my heart. As I consider the early years and issues surrounding mental health, I've titled this chapter the power of relationships. Why do I say the power of relationships? It's because I know that love builds brains. Let me say that again: love builds brains. In the early years, it's the power of relationship that sets the foundation for later brain development. When I'm speaking about the importance of relationships, I'm referring to face-to-face interactions—they're the absolute heart of the matter. As the Harvard Centre on the Developing Child says, relationships are the nutrient of the brain.[1] When I emphasize the power of relationships, and think about infant and early childhood mental health, I want people to know we're really thinking about more than the beautiful relationship between infant and parent or between infant and caregiver. The power of relationship is about more than the connections among all the people who are crazy about these babies. We also need to think about relationships we build with each other in the infant medical health field, as well as among communities and families and between policymakers and researchers. When I talk about the power of relationships, I really would like to be able to think of everyone involved as a network connecting all of those who affect and effect children's lives.

Why do I describe those involved with children as part of a network? I have a dream, one my readers have heard already, that every child will have at least one adult whose eyes light up as the child enters the room. The other dream I have is that children who have more struggles in life will have their eyes light up as they enter a room because there's a special person there. I long to see a day when, in every room children enter, there's someone who sees them for the great potential they have and who knows them for who they are.

I think of my own grandchildren when I have these dreams. When I speak to groups of people, I'm obliged to tell my audience whether someone is sponsoring me. First of all, I'm in infant and early childhood Mental Health and there isn't any money out there. So no. No one is sponsoring me. If I have sponsors, it's my own children and grandchildren, because I want the world to be a place where people's eyes light up when they see my beautiful grandchildren. And I want that for all other kids as well—ones I don't even know.

THE TEACHINGS OF THE ELDERS

I made reference in an earlier chapter to the insights of Tom Porter, a Mohawk elder. As a children's advocate, I've been touched by First Nations' teachings. In Indigenous cultures, as I've said, children are the sacred ones. They're the heart of the nation. Can you imagine what Canada would be like if our North Star belief (a belief that orients us to our direction in life) was that children are the sacred ones, so that everything we do, every policy we make, was focused on how those actions and policies will influence the next seven generations? Can we actually stop and think about the possibility of thinking about our very youngest citizens in all of the decisions we make?

Another idea Tom Porter taught me is that his people don't describe children as having special needs. They describe them as having special rights. Just that minor change in language has great implications. Using the term special needs automatically implies there's something wrong or something missing in a child. It forces us to use a deficit lens. Whereas, if we say they have special rights, we realize we have an absolute obligation to them. That obligation starts with listening to them. As Tom talks about it, when we think of children as having special rights, we have to stop and think about the beautiful story they've been sent to tell us. That's the teaching of the Elders.

Can you imagine if we really thought that all children are born ready to learn right from the start? What would be different if we could see them as capable and competent, right from the very beginning? But you know it doesn't start off well for all babies. What we're now learning in terms of infant and early mental health is that more than half of all mental health problems at age 26 were diagnosed already in childhood and adolescence.[2] We see a moderate amount of money being spent on older children, as we absolutely should, but what about the early years?

DEFINING THE ISSUE

When the mental health Commission was looking at how Canada spends its dollars, they realized that mental health was the orphan of the health system. They also saw that, within the health care system, the mental health of children was the orphans' orphan. What about our preschoolers and young children? It turns out that they aren't even considered.

As we think about the early years, and ask ourselves what can go wrong, a whole lot of the work many of us in the field have to do is to convince people to pay attention to this age group. In Ontario, in 2014, I was invited to bring together a group of authors to look at the evidence we have on children less than 6 years of age and problems they experience in social and emotional development. We wrote a paper called *Supporting Ontario's Youngest Minds*, which investigated the mental health of children under 6 years of age. It's available at the website Center of Excellence and is available in English and French.[3] What did we discover? One realization was that issues are hard to measure because there's so little information. There are a lot of studies that look at the prevalence of mental health problems but they don't start until children are at least 4 years of age. So we know that from 4 years to 17 years of age, the prevalence of mental health problems is high. For this age group, a commonly used figure is that 20% of children suffer from mental health issues. As we were working together to write that report, we had to do a lot of digging to find information for the less than 4 years age group. There are some very good international studies that identify the number of kids under 6 with significant challenges in their social and emotional development. This number is about 18%. In other studies, it's as high as 26%. Even with these percentages, as I talk to many paediatricians and bring up my concerns, they react by saying, "Infant mental health, what is that?"

So we have a very big challenge in convincing many people that mental health problems can start early and can last a long time. In fact, many don't go away. The Ontario researchers that worked with me on the Supporting Young Minds project were involved in writing a further paper[4] that looked at 3 to 6 year olds. Why does this matter? In Ontario, we now have full-day learning for 4 and 5 year olds. This is the first time in that province that almost all children are now in a full day of school. If school settings are play based and fun, they provide an ideal context for children, including those with challenges. Play based learning brings a sense of belonging and well-being to children. The curriculum is a deep, rich, joyous experience, as it should be.[5] During the shift to include all children in a daylong program, many kids showed up with major behaviour challenges, particularly with significant self-regulation difficulties. We're fortunate that we now have a measurement tool called the Early Development Instrument (EDI). In the spring of each year, when they've known the children in their classes for a few months, all kindergarten teachers fill out a 105-item checklist on each child. The checklist asks about physical, social, emotional, linguistic and communication development. But it's not a diagnostic test because the statistics are gathered and researchers aggregate all the numbers so that they can look at populations of children. What this aggregate data is telling Canadians is that we're failing up to 32% of our children across the country before they even arrive at school.

What do these numbers mean? When we look at the aggregate numbers, 32% of all Canadian children don't have the skills they need to do well in school. Given these aggregate numbers, the Offord Centre (that developed the EDI) can now assert that when children arrive at school without the requisite skills to do well, they are vulnerable and tend to stay vulnerable. The Offord Centre has followed many children from Kindergarten to Grade 3 and 4 in order to come to this conclusion.[6] When I hear people talk about how kids today can read and write but can't get along with others, I want to shout, do you realize how devastating this is for their future success and well being? People don't seem to realize how serious these difficulties are for children—for the rest of their lives. Unfortunately, the government in Ontario changed after these reports came out and there has been little if any action on moving forward with the implications of this research.

In terms of mental health in the early years, I had a wonderful reporter call me up once. She told me she was reading reports from California that pointed out how 4 year olds can talk, they can read and write, but they can't play together. I responded to her by talking about what I call the tyranny of cognitive seduction. In the world of early education, we have for far too many years privileged certain ways of knowing. They typically are literacy and numeracy. Of course, both matter very much. The problem is that people don't get the right balance among several ways of knowing, and don't include social and emotional skill development along with literacy and numeracy. Children develop various areas of skill acquisition, including social, emotional, physical, linguistic and cognitive skills, but they learn them all together as a whole experience. You can't privilege one above the others and provide a holistic learning environment. Social and emotional skills are as important as the other skills. There's excellent research to say that children who

113

develop social and emotional skills do well later on because they know how to get along with other people.[7] The following chart offers an overview of how many organizations, individuals or groups impact child development:

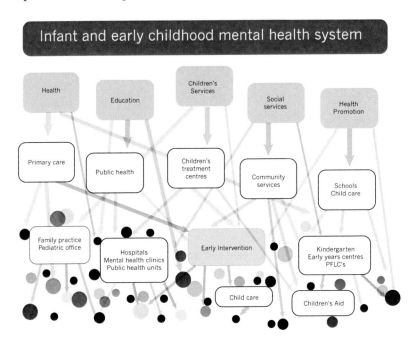

EXAMINING THE SYSTEM

Earlier I said that I want to think about everyone who's involved in working with children in the early years as forming part of a network. Yet, as we look at the current situation, as represented in the diagram, we've got many, many hands involved in the lives of children under 6 years of age. As examples, there's Public Health, Primary Care, schools, Children's Services, Social Services and all kinds of other people, all of whom touch children's lives, but they do so from the silos they work in. There's a lot of silence between these silos. There's some communication and collaboration but what happens if you've got a mom, dad or partner who has mental health issues. If you approach one of these silos, you may hear someone say that, we're very sorry but our funding doesn't cover mental health for children and for adults at the same time or in the same place.

As we look at the chart and reflect on the the multiple influences on a child the present situation seems chaotic. That picture will be familiar to many across the globe when it comes to infant and early childhood mental health. Those of us in that Ontario research group I mentioned earlier were compelled to look in Canada and internationally to see who's building the best model for supporting young children. As we asked ourselves how we might go about looking for an effective model, we had to talk about our approach. We realized that, if we continued to work from these silos or assume that we could treat each individual or family on their own, we could see that the task would be impossible. We would never have enough people to treat everyone one at a time.

Population Strategy for Child and Youth Mental Health[8]

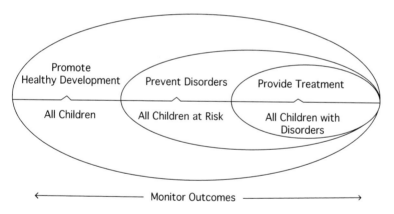

The evidence suggested that we needed to think about promoting the healthy development of all children. If we were going to make a difference, we needed a big public health approach to situations children encounter. We had to ask ourselves whose job and passion it is to inform parents about the importance of their relationship to babies so that brain development is encouraged. We sought healthy promotion of brain development for all children, but we knew it's also important to recognize there are some children who are more at risk, due to life circumstances or conditions at birth. We needed to have early identification practices that were effective and could screen children to find those who have more significant challenges. We also needed high-quality, evidence-based treatment programs once we did find them. Both the children and their families need these programs. There's no such thing as a baby just by herself or himself. There's always a baby along with the adult or adults in their lives.

I continue to be part of a group of concerned individuals who work for children's well being. We sometimes ask ourselves how big the problem is that faces us. The most pressing problem is that children with serious mental health issues often can't manage to stay in school. Early childhood mental health problems sometimes show up as problems of behaviour. These behaviours may be thought of as aggression, non-compliance or self-injury. There are studies to show that preschoolers in pre-kindergarten are being expelled at a rate that's more than 3 times that of their older peers in the grades from kindergarten to grade 12 combined.[9] In the U.S., little ones in pre-kindergarten are being suspended and expelled from school. Research also looks at whether these children have had some really hard things happen to them before they arrive at school—situations that create what we call adverse experiences.

THE ADVERSE CHILDHOOD EXPERIENCES STUDY

The research that concerns the well being of this group of children is called the Adverse Childhood Experience study (ACEs).[10] It was an adult health study to look at 17,000 people and consider their health outcomes. As part of the study, which involved completing many questionnaires, one section asked 10 questions about early experiences. These questions asked whether participants had experienced neglect, abuse or family dysfunction before they were 18 years of age. What researchers found was that the more ACES someone experienced (adverse childhood experiences), the more likely people are to be sick as adults, the more likely they are to have trouble finding employment and the more likely they are to have emotional problems. ACES accumulate over time. The higher the number of adverse experiences, the worse the situation becomes for a person. There's another study that looked at social and emotional development in kindergarten and looked at participants later in life. That study advised that we look at social and emotional learning in the early years.[11] As I travel across the country, speaking in many places, I hear and observe that something's happening with preschoolers. Kindergarten teachers tell me that more of their children are hyperactive. More of them are bored. More children don't' seem to be able to play well together. It's alarming that in one Ontario study, called the Ontario Child Health Survey, researchers looked at thousands of kids and compared their results with data from 1983. As they compared the two sets of data, one from 1983 and one from 2014, what do you think they uncovered? The data showed that the kindergarten teachers I spoke with were right. Research revealed that there has been a significant increase in levels of hyperactivity in the 4 years to 11 years age group. In 1983 the rate in males was 10% and in 2014 it was 16.2%. In females it increased from 3.3% to 5.7% over that same period of time.[12]

The Ontario Child Health Study is an example of research that didn't get re-funded for over 30 years, even though the original research had a profound international impact. The initial study put child mental health epidemiology on the map. When data from 1983 and 2014 were compared, the results are surprising. As one example, even though the numbers for diagnosed anxiety disorder had not gone up between 1983 and 2014, there were an overwhelmingly high number of people who perceived anxiety (i.e., believe they're in distress and need help) in the 2014 data as compared with 1983. While the actual disorder diagnosis hadn't gone up, the perception of difficulty increased. There's something happening that's starting early. What should be our response? What's the thing we need to be doing? We need to support young families so they can raise their children in ways that get them the help they need.

A DEFINITION OF INFANT MENTAL HEALTH

The research data show that many young children aren't moving along a track that will allow them to be successful or happy during their lifetimes. We've been talking about the research that's been carried out with the age group 4 -11 years. Let's talk about infant mental health by looking at the 0 to 3 years age group. I've got my own research group, my own gorgeous three-year-old grandson, twin boys who are 22 months and little girl, who is 3 months old. They've got a super geek grandmother. Nana is always watching and figuring out what's going on between their behaviour and their brains. I want to capture all that's going on as they develop. Because of my knowledge, I can actually see their brain development right in front of my eyes. But what's the task of babies and toddlers and preschoolers under 6? Well, it's really all about learning how to build relationships and connections.

Zero to Three is a very important U.S. based advocacy and education group. Many countries and Canadian provinces have adopted their definition of infant and early childhood mental health. This group states that infant and early childhood mental health is the developing capacity of the child to

- Form close adult and peer relationships
- Experience, manage and express a full range of emotions
- Explore the environment and learn

I suggest that their description of this capacity is in essence describing healthy social and emotional development. They also say that a child's capacity to do all this happens in the context of family, community and culture.[13] When thinking about infants, it's interesting to think about the following concepts. Human babies are born so prematurely in terms of brain development that some people think of the first year of life as holding a baby in an external womb. Imagine that thought. When you hear the teaching of some First Nations' cultures, they have thought this way for a long time. As one example, they have the teaching of the Tikinagan or the cradleboard. Little ones are placed in the cradleboard so that

118

they're fully protected and also fully engaged in the activities of the community as they're carried along. When we listen to the voice of these elders, we recognize the need to be protecting our youngest families and supporting them.

Babies need to form close and secure relationships with the meaningful adults in their lives. This is called attachment, which I described in chapter two. Through attachment the child learns that the world is a safe and secure place to be—the message they gain is—I'm secure. Children who are securely attached feel safe enough to be able to go out into the world and explore. They also know that when they're sick, distressed or upset, there's someone there to look out for and to look after them. They can come home to a secure base.

However, if you have a little one who has a significant language development issue, what happens if they don't understand the word world around them? They may be reading emotion but not understanding fully within themselves what that emotion is because they don't have the language for it. Without that understanding, they may develop anxiety and not want to reach out into the world. If a child has no acute observers in his or her life in a mother, father or other adult who can pick up that a little one is feeling anxiety, the child may not be able to attach securely. Little ones need to develop attachment relationships that are predictable and secure so they are free to learn how to experience, manage and express a full range of emotion.

Now that we're grandparents, we have lots of toys and books at our house. All of it is in the living room. That room looks like a playhouse. It's a wonderful space. But what did the twins decide one Sunday? Even with all those toys, they wanted to have the same item at the same time. They chose my little measuring tape from my knitting bag. You know the ones, when you push the button it goes swish. The whole length of tape gets sucked right in. They loved it. First of all, we played a game. Silly Nana. I pulled it out and made a sound as it went in—I said doodly doodly doodly. They both wanted it. So what was I supposed to do? I looked for another tape measure. There wasn't another one. So I suggested, why don't we try taking turns and maybe we could use a timer.

Hello Jean, you might say to me. Those children aren't 2 years old yet. You're thinking of using a timer with them? I know, I know. It's a little above them developmentally, but I thought, let's see what happens. My daughter was there as well and she suggested a plan. She said, we'll put on an alarm and call it the big noise. Then I said, when the big noise goes—let's all do the big noise. By that time, one grandson was already saying aloud, when we hear the big noise, it's time to give the toy to my brother. Isn't that a wonderful plan? Scientifically proven. Not.

But you know, the marvellous thing was that we introduced it one week and when I was down at their house a few days later they were doing it successfully with each other. Geek Nana is thinking to herself, what's happening in those brains? So I've got this picture in my mind of how you learn to experience, manage and express emotion. The picture captures the fact that deep in our brain we have what's called the Reptilian Brain, an old brain; on top of that reptilian area, we have a limbic brain. Children learn to manage their limbic brain (emotional brain) though experience, by loving, nurturing and co-regulating with the adults that love them. That loving co-regulation helps with the connection to the thinking brain or the prefrontal cortex.

Dan Siegel, an American psychiatrist, uses a hand model to describe the brain. He uses his hand to say the palm of the hand represents the most primitive part of the brain, the midbrain and brainstem. Next he invites us to look at our thumb and bend it into our palm, this represents the limbic or emotional system. Lastly, he invites us to fold our fingers over the folded thumb and this represents the cortex with the knuckles being right at the prefrontal cortex. The thinking part of the brain is the last area to develop. It's under construction until at least 25 years of age. But these little toddlers are learning how to experience their emotions, i.e., their limbic brain. They're learning to use their words to connect with other people and other experiences so they can bring that limbic brain under self-regulation along with their thinking brain. They're learning how to experience, manage and express their emotions.

Most of the time children are challenged to manage their emotions and spend a lot of time flipping their lids, which Siegel describes by flipping his fingers in the air. When they're upset like this, it's their emotional brain in the driver's seat not their thinking brain. So they have a meltdown. When we see children who have self-regulation difficulties in the early years, the behaviours we see have to do with being unable to manage and express emotion and behaviour. Children don't learn to manage emotion on their own; they need help from others. We call this the co-regulation that happens in the context of family, community and culture. Children's mental health is based on healthy social and emotional development within those concentric circles that surround a baby and that offer healthy interaction.

So what does a young child need? He or she needs a developing brain in good working order that has appropriate environmental stimulation. The most important environmental stimulation is not flashcards or Baby Einstein or baby Britney or who knows what program is coming next. Their development is formed by the back and forth, the serve and return, of face-to-face social interaction with people who care deeply about them.

So we care a lot about the brain. In Alberta, with all the work that the Palix Foundation and the Alberta Family Wellness Initiative is doing in the field, people in that province are educating many adults about why they must care about the brain. The big science story today is that the brain is not just about genes; it's about the interaction between experience and genes. We now know that intelligence is not a fixed trait. You aren't just a product of your genes. You are a product of all of the environmental influences that are expressions of the daily drip-drip-drip of everyday life.

It's face-to-face time that babies need most for the developing brain. In addition, we know that we need to pay very close attention to attachment. We know there's a huge impact of trauma on the developing brain that influences how all the brain's pathways connect. But, and this is the good news story, we also know that you can come from a family where, as a young child, you were exposed to many adverse childhood experiences but also to positive emotional connections with adults who cared about you. As adults protect the young, even those who experienced difficult family environments, their brains have a better chance for a satisfying life.

IMPACTS ON THE BRAIN

I had finished reading a paper on an infant's ability to imitate others within the first weeks of life just before my son had his first newborn. I asked him to see what might happen when he had the baby's attention if he stuck out his tongue. We wondered if the baby would imitate that action. I have a video of their interaction. It's amazing to see how a baby this little, who doesn't even have awareness of having a face, will respond to his dad's face by sticking out his tongue.

This insight into a baby's potential is the work of Andrew Meltzoff[14] and others at the University of Washington. What we know is that the brain gets built by serve and return interactions. We also recognize that children experience interactions that aren't positive, such as neglect or maltreatment. Unfortunately, these interactions also build connections in the brain. These negative experiences may be due to maternal or paternal depression or due to severe life situations such as poverty or addiction. We know that what's happening is the children and infants may not have the sense of belonging, of feeling safe, of feeling felt that we want them to have so they can feel safe and secure. When we think about the impact of negative interaction, we have to think about toxic stress.

When I think about what the science tells us about toxic stress, I reference work from the Harvard Centre for the Developing Child. What they state is that some forms of stress are good. If we didn't have stress we wouldn't be performing at our best. The stress that's most damaging to mental health is toxic stress, which is the prolonged activation of the stress system in the absence of protective relationships. I often see the evidence of toxic stress in kids in our child welfare system. However, I also worry about the level of stress being experienced by our little ones who are in childcare or school where the academic expectations are developmentally inappropriate. In some situations, they're being unduly pressured.

The demands of the full day at school as well as academic pressure can lead to high stress and even behaviour problems. I recently heard a story about a little girl who didn't want to go back to school after March break. The problem she told her mom was that she knew she wasn't in the top reading group. She's 4 years of age. The stress that was created for her was so high that she didn't return to school and her mom couldn't buffer that stress any other way than to keep her home.

A concept I find fascinating, and applicable to that little girl's problem, is what's called *Schoolification*,[15] which is the unrealistic shifting of academic expectations from grade school to kindergarten and preschool. What we need to see happening is what my colleague Jane Bertrand and the Ontario based Lawson Foundation talk about—*Playification*.[16] We need playification in our pre-kindergarten and kindergarten programs. Why? Children learn best through play. The evidence is irrefutable. With *Schoolification*, we create high levels of stress for many little ones.

The problem we see with kids is that, if a stressor is there all the time, what we see in their behaviour is irritability, poor memory, difficulty focusing, and with critical thinking, we see anxiety and fear. What we observe from the impact of high levels of stress, when it's not buffered by positive relationships, can look like, and be interpreted as, attention deficit disorder (ADHD). In addition, I question how many children are being mis-labelled with hyperactivity. Is it possible their behaviour is stress behaviour, not misbehaviour and not ADHD or hyperactivity?

We need to be examining the stress in children's lives because it affects their physical and developmental regulation in terms of sleep and appetite as well. I concern I have is when aggressive, impulsive behaviours are observed and people turn to checklists and under-analyze the conditions that may be contributing to the behaviour. Sometimes the context for the behaviour is not analyzed and exploration with the family is left out. It's essential to sit with family and teacher to understand a child's dilemmas. The urgency to intervene as early as possible is related to the concept of toxic stress. We need to be building up the protective factors that give parents the support and access to resources that they need.

As communities, are we coming together to figure out what to do about the adverse childhood experiences many children face? If professionals who are involved with children want to respond to their needs, we have to overcome the chaos factor that's depicted in the *Infant and early childhood mental health system* diagram ealier in the chapter, and the tendency to operate within silos. We need to work more collaboratively. For example, what's the role of primary care physicians and paediatric physicians in the early years? An action of the Canadian Paediatric Society has been to develop and release a position statement called Relationships Matter: How clinicians can support positive parenting.[17] A key recommendation is to have paediatricians and primary care doctors pay attention to relational health.

Relational health refers to more than how tall or how much language a child has; it's also about their social and emotional development. The good news is that we have knowledge about what can help infants, toddlers and their families. In Alberta, the need for addressing social and emotional development in childcare is being addressed using the Pyramid Model.[18] This model involves going into childcare settings and coaching teachers on social and emotional development. Another valued program called *Beyond Behaviour Management* is used in some Ontario kindergarten programs. That program looks at many of the elements that are essential for social and emotional development. These elements include the following:

- Attachment
- Collaboration
- Adaptability
- Self-Regulation
- Belonging
- Contribution[19]

CLINICAL INTERVENTIONS

I want to touch briefly on just a few interventions that require extensive training for families who are experiencing significant challenges with their littlest ones. In Alberta, a friend and colleague, Dr Carole Anne Hapchyn is a child psychiatrist. She's looking at a promising model called the *Neuro Relational Framework* (NRF). The model was developed by Dr Connie lillas, who is a colleague in California, and it's also being used in other programs in Alberta. This model starts by looking at stressors that create toxic stress in a child's life. It looks to find what can be done to engage the child in interaction. It also emphasizes that, when working with infants, toddlers and preschoolers, we need to engage them at the emotional level as well as engage their five senses. NRF brings interaction right down to the child's neural pathways and helps parents become educated about these neural pathways and also helps them understand their child's behaviour more fully.[20] The NRF model works by helping adults learn how to read a baby's cues, and make sense of the environmental and relationships that have an influence on the baby. Through the model, there can develop a beautiful synchrony between babies' needs and the parents' understanding of their infant and, as a result, responsiveness between them can occur.

Another program of intervention is called *Circle of Security*. This is a parent-based intervention that very respectfully helps parents learn about attachment and so they can build attachment with their little ones. It focuses on creating a secure base for an infant. In the program, there's recognition of the child's thoughts and needs. The approach in this intervention from the infant's perspective can be expressed in the following way: a child thinks/feels something like: "I need you to support my exploration but man oh man do I ever need you to welcome me back when I'm needing protection and comfort."

Circle of security is a wonderful program with evidence to show that it can help a family if there's an attachment issue. Another program that was developed in Toronto is called *Watch Wait and Wonder*. This is an infant-led approach for working with infants and their families. In the Watch, Wait, and Wonder psychotherapy, we help the parent and infant discover for themselves a new way of relating to one another and we aim to prevent a repetition of inter-generational transmission of insecure attachment patterns.[21]

CONCLUSION

The idea I want to leave my readers with at the end of this chapter, is that my hope and goal is for improved parent-child interaction and relationship. I want a child to feel that their favourite place is inside a parent's hug. What we're learning is that we need to pay attention to our littlest ones. We need to be creating for them and for their parents, experiences in which they can be recognized as having rights in their own terms—in terms of their personhood. Any approach that provides these secure experiences comes with the knowledge that we need resources to support children and parents, whoever they are.

I learned a story on Vancouver Island. A grandfather was telling children a story that talks about two wolves that fight a battle within us. One of the wolves is evil, angry and jealous. It's battling inside our heads with a wolf that's good, a wolf that's joyous, kind and loving. One of the little ones in the circle who was listening intently to the grandfather, asked the grandfather, "Which one will win?" The grandfather looked at him and said, "It depends on which wolf you feed."

In this chapter, my underlying concern is to ask which wolf we're feeding in our youngest children in Canada. All those people who work with children need to pool their resources. These resources include our coalitions, our energy and our passion to work for the benefit of our littlest ones. These resources also include our very presence, through our face-to-face encounters with the young. Children need the support that allows them to have their eyes light as they enter a room because there are adults in the room that offer them with what they need most—their full attention. In addition, when there are significant challenges in relationships with little ones, we need to recognize our behaviour and the interventions we provide during the early years is essential. We have evidence based and promising practices that make a difference in little ones' lives as well as the families that support them. To make these positive changes, we must recognize the truth that, not only do many young children *have* mental health issues, but also that intervening as early as possible has long lasting impacts and these interventions can create significant differences for generations to come.

7

The Adolescent Brain
Under Construction

INTRODUCTION

I n the previous chapter, I focused on the mental health of infants and pre-school children. As mentioned, this period in a child's life is a key time for face-to-face social interactions that build the brain. In these daily acts of connecting with little ones, adults convey their love for them and, as a consequence, the young feel felt; they feel seen, heard and understood. In this chapter, I want to move on to another crucial period in the life of the brain, which is adolescence. This is another very important time for social and emotional development, as well as for the many other competencies that are necessary for developing life skills and for human thriving.

A strong feeling I've had throughout my work is best described as a sense of being in the middle of a very swift stream along with children and families with so many challenges rushing past me. I'm standing in the middle of the water, madly trying to capture one or two of them, as fast as I can, to reach out and help them. One of my mentors, the late Dr Paul Steinauer, a Toronto-based child psychiatrist, pointed out that it's necessary for at least some child psychiatrists to move upstream. We need to figure out why our kids are falling in the water in the first place.[1] So I decided I was going to dedicate my life to doing more upstream work. One of the things I discovered that helped a great deal is brain plasticity. As I learned more about the importance of the brain, I found a lot of research that was dense and hard to get through. I wanted very much to find ways to translate that knowledge into more accessible ideas. I wanted more people to understand this important research. Now I work with teachers, parents and many others. When it comes to teachers, I want them to think of themselves as human developers. It's important to think about more than academics. We need to think about the well-being of children and youth. I use a metaphor of double-stranded DNA when thinking of working with youth and children. One strand is academic achievement, the other strand is well-being. The glue that holds the two strands together is relationship.

At the heart of the work I do as a speaker and child advocate is the issue of relationship. How do parents and their children connect with each other? How do they understand each other? How well do they take each other's point of view into account? How well can they stand in the shoes of the other? When I talk about relationships, I'm referring to the power of connection between people, but also to our relationship with ourselves. What's our relationship to our own thoughts about ourselves? In chapter two, in a section called *What's a Parent to Do*, I outline some important questions parents can ask themselves. These questions are significant again as your children become adolescents. It's essential to consider what you believe is important to you as you walk with your adolescent through these years.

The purpose of this chapter is to outline changes that have been discovered in the developing adolescent brain. I want to underscore the magnificence of this period of time, when adolescents express tremendous emotional spark, social engagement, novelty-seeking and creative exploration. Dan Siegel refers to these aspects as the essence of adolescence.[2] I want to emphasize how important parents are to adolescents during this amazing time of life.

At the beginning of the previous chapter, I asked the question of who's supporting the family as they care for children during the early years. I must ask this question again. Where are the supports and influences on the family from the community, region and country, as parents care for teens? As we ask about supports and influence, we also need to think of geographical, ethnocentric, religious, other associations that families see as important, such as sport teams or camps—all of which offer potential support and influence. As we think of nested relationships that surround youth, people ask me all the time what one area I would spend money on to get the biggest bang for a buck. The reality is that we have all these concentric circles surrounding the family. It's hard to say where we would get the biggest bang for our dollars. But I'm sure we should focus on the relationship children have with their parents and people who are significant in their lives—if that doesn't happen to be parents. If we invest as much as we can in those core relationships, as a guiding principle, we'll make a big difference for children.

The role of government is also significant in providing, or not providing, support. The group of people who advocate for children and work directly with them have thought for a long time that children are not on the radar of most governments. When you stop and think about it, one issue is that children and youth don't vote. So, who listens to their voice? As adults have more and more stress on them, they need more of us to ask how we can bring communities together to support parents, children and youth.

In order for youth and parents to have good relationships, they also need support from the community; the community needs support from the government, and the government needs the support of the population. All of this support is necessary if we want to have a healthy, well-functioning, financially viable country. But let's return to what we can do and what we can understand about adolescents.

In this chapter, I talk about adolescence in a general way. I'm not describing psychiatric disorders, as one example. It's a general chapter about typical adolescent development, as well as some of the challenges adults face as they try to accompany their youth. The first question adults often ask is this one: Why do they do the things they do? We ask this question when we see teenagers take outrageous risks and can't understand why they do it. If you consider some of the risk-taking behaviour young people carry out—skateboarding along a cement abutment, jumping out of a plane, taking drugs,

131

involving themselves in risky sexual situations—we look at them and say they just don't realize what they're doing. From an adult point of view, they aren't thinking about what they're doing. However, the reality is that they are thinking, but they're thinking about something different than the adults who watch them. A young man who jumps out of a plane, knows the risk but is focused on more than risk? What do you think? He's focused on the thrill of what he's doing or wanting to do.

Trying to understand the adolescent brain is very different from what I was taught in medical school in 1981. At that time, people thought risk-taking adolescent behaviour was due to hormones and puberty. In the past decade or so, research is discovering that changes are happening in their brains that affect adolescent development. We can see those changes by looking at their behaviour, but now, with neuro-imaging, we can get brain images that picture these changes. As we look at the brain, we can see differences taking place.

Before we talk about neuro-imaging and what we can now see as we reflect on adolescent behaviour, something that's really important to me is the way we frame our interpretation of their behaviour. Since so much is going on in the brain, I have some strong inclinations—one of which is to insist that all behaviours have a reason. This is true even for little ones who are having a temper tantrum at 2 years old. There's a reason why they're having that temper tantrum. The reason they're having that meltdown may be because they're super stressed. Since they can't express themselves, they can't tell anyone they're hungry because they don't have the words or the capacity to stop and say so. They don't know how to say, "Oh Mommy dearest, my heart is breaking because you left me to go and talk to that woman about the teenage brain and you weren't at home with me"—or some such thing.

EVERY BEHAVIOUR HAS A REASON

Behaviours have a reason. And all behaviour happens in a context. As adults, we need to be detectives. We need to discover the reasons for behaviour and its context, if we hope to help children and youth.

Over the course of my work, I've been influenced by the work of Dr. Ross Greene, a U.S. based psychologist. He's the one who I first heard say that kids will do well if they can. This belief is really important as we work with youth. Kids will do well if they can. There isn't a single child I've seen who wanted to be at the end of her or his rope. If they could have gotten out of the troubling behaviour, they would have done so.

Many adults have a mindset that says, "Well kid, you got yourself into this mess. If I give you enough rewards (or punishment), you'll get yourself out of it." But when you stop and think about what that implies, we're assuming that a young person's behaviour has to do primarily with the will, a point I made in an earlier chapter. The implication is that if an adolescent just works hard enough, they're going to snap out of the behaviour, just like that! But what I know, from 30 years as a child psychiatrist, is that many kids don't need to work harder, they need to work differently. They don't have the skills required to snap out of it. There are two ideas to keep in mind when an adult realizes they have the mindset referred to above: first, all behaviour has a reason and second, all behaviour happens in a context. There's a reason for what's happening and there's a situation that has arisen that led to it. Troubling behaviour is an indication that a young person hasn't been able to come up with a strategy to just snap out of it.

The idea that all behaviour has a reason is also based on the work of my Canadian friend, Stephen de Groot. His view is that all behaviour contains operating needs and goals.[4] We do something for a reason. That reason is often to meet a need or reach a goal. For example, someone might have the operating need to make a difference and then creates the goal of working in an organization such as iHuman in Edmonton Alberta.[5] Suppose we visit this adolescent drop-in centre that focuses on engaging street kids in the Arts. iHuman's purpose is to help youth learn important life skills. As staff members talk about working with the youth, one issue that comes up is conflict, particularly social conflict in that space. If you work at a place like this, one staff member might say, you're well advised to consider your own needs and the goals that drive how you interact with the youth. That is, a staff member might say, "I love these kids so much. I want them to grow and have a satisfying life. I'd do anything for them. I know that can't happen unless there are people whose eyes light up as they enter the room. So every day, my eyes will light up as each kid comes in the building."

What iHuman staff members have learned is that love is complex. Many of the kids have lived with adults who forced inappropriate 'love' on them. People who said they loved them—dropped them when things weren't easy. In response to the issue of what it means for staff to love the youth, this staff group focuses, not on love, but on the humanity of each one of the youth. It's a core value for them to respect and support the humanity of everyone who enters the building.

As a result, many aspects of staff interactions take on a different focus. That core value, though it took effort to establish it, is a new way to think about staff/youth interaction, as well as the individual needs and goals of each staff member. As a result, the value shifts attention away from coming to work at iHuman in order to love and to save the kids. These youth don't need a saviour; they need to develop trust and the emotional/social skills that will allow them to have a successful, satisfying life. If staff goals and needs are in conflict with what youth actually need, reflecting on the core value of the humanity of each youth who enters is at least a place to start in clarifying why each staff person is at the centre.[6] As I write this book, I'm very aware that there can be conflict between adult needs and goals as people spend time with adolescents. As one example, an adult might think something like, "This is what I need to do. I need to make a difference." As a consultant, I talk to teachers and parents who seem to give up and emotionally exit a relationship with a young person because the conflict between their own goals and needs is at a breaking point. Someone who needs to make a difference but isn't seeing that difference in a kid's life may think something like the following: "You know, I really care about kids who have challenges. I try really hard to give them all the support I know how to give, but they don't take it. They don't accept it. They don't change their behaviour."

When I'm with teachers and parents who are thinking this way, I sit with them and say, "Well, what would it take for you to understand or recognize that these kids aren't ready to accept the goodness you're trying to offer them? What would it take for you to accept that maybe they're coming from a very different place than you are?" Sometimes, I engage with adults to discover what they understand about the reasons for the kids' behaviour that's causing them so much distress. Remember, all action has a reason. How might we discover what motivates the behaviour of youth we work with? Let's talk about adolescent behaviour more directly. It's really important to think about the biological reasons for behaviour, as well as the psychological reasons. Adolescents have biological drives. In adolescence, there's a biological drive to be with peers. It has a huge effect on the young. A book I mentioned earlier by Dan Siegel, *Brainstorm*, talks about why we have a biological need in adolescence to connect with people our own age.[7] When you think about it, the survival of the human race depends on these connections. If kids had just stayed quietly in the cave with Mom and Dad, they'd never have gone out across the plains to meet other groups of girls and boys. They would never have procreated. We wouldn't have the wonderful billions of people we have on the earth. We're here because of the physiological drive to connect with one's age group.

There are other biological drives and changes that are going on during this time period as well.

In the past, people thought of adolescents as mini-adults. Because they're tall, people thought they were ready for life, ready to be adults. It was as if teens were adults in waiting. But there are numerous changes happening within an adolescent body. While these changes are occurring, a young person needs to find ways to be comfortable in their own skin. Trying to find this comfort takes place in the context of very important peer relationships. Youth have to figure out what group is in, what group is out, and also how to behave and fit in with what's happening.

At early adolescence, 12 or 13 years of age, all this adjustment is still fairly simple. As a teen gets older, life gets more complicated in terms of social connections and social fit. In addition, there's a strong societal expectation that young people will manage their own thoughts, emotions and actions. Adults expect young people to be self-regulated. But self-regulation is still under construction. Kids are learning to figure out who are and who they're going to be. They have a view of themselves. They have a view of how others see them. As well, kids are capable of more abstract thinking. So the picture is complex. I use the word teenager, and teen, but adolescence isn't only a time between 13 and 18 years of age.

Adolescence starts when puberty hits, which can be at 9 or 10 and continue to 24 or 25 years of age. That whole time is adolescence. During that period, thinking areas of the brain (prefrontal cortex) are developing. That age range (9-25) is different from what used to be assigned to adolescence. In the past, it was seen as a much shorter period, marked by being a kid on one hand, when adults looked after you, to being an adult and taking on adult roles.

This long adolescence isn't the case everywhere in the world. I visited Kenya a number of years ago and observed that adolescence in that country was a very short time. Young women were married at an early age, many in their teens. Earlier in North America, the time frame was closer to 7 years, from 12 to about 18 years of age. Now, it's a huge number of years in comparison to our earlier history.

Yet the behaviour of adolescents has been described for centuries. Apparently Socrates described youth as fickle in their desires, which are as transitory as they are vehement.[8] Adolescents are excitable and full of mood swings. Even ancient cultures were aware of these patterns. Shakespeare talked about young people getting wenches with child, wronging the ancestors, stealing, fighting and having brains that are boiled. In Western tradition, for almost 2,500 years, people have been talking about this period of time.[9] Even though adolescent patterns aren't easy to live with, it's still true that what we think about adolescence affects how we feel about them and influences how we act towards them.

Let me tell two stories. One of my colleagues heard me speak on adolescence and invited me to speak to his Board members. To introduce me, he told this story. He said, "I used to drive to Tim Horton's (a popular Canadian coffee shop) and this bunch of kids used to walk right in front of me as I went through the drive-through. They annoyed me. I would scowl at them. I thought, teenagers these days are not respectable or respectful. What are they doing here? They're a pain. I felt angry. Then I would give them another scowl."

He continued. "Then I heard Jean's talk and realized that the teenagers outside Tim Horton's didn't even see me. They were busy affiliating with their buddies, while their brains are under construction. That's what Jean told me. They're developing. They're not mini-adults. So after Jean's talk, I felt really curious about what's going on with these young folk. I went to Tim's for coffee at the drive through and rolled down the window while I waited. I said, "Hey guys how are you doing?" Well those kids nearly had a heart attack because a grumpy old fart was finally trying to talk to them." My friend's story tells the truth: what we think directs how we feel and shapes how we act.

I have another story that helps to explain what I want to say about adolescent brains. A patient I had a few years ago told me about her experience when she came late to class one morning. That particular teacher told her to go right down to the office. He hated when kids were late. He believed that kids who are late don't respect the hard work of their teachers. He felt annoyed and rejected her by sending her out of the class—out the door and down to the office.

The next day she came in late again. It was a different teacher because she was on a rotation. This teacher told her to go sit in her seat at the back of the class. She sat down and promptly fell asleep. This teacher came to her after class and asked her what was going on. She said, "Well sir, my mom is really sick in hospital. My dad is spending as much time as he can with her. But our family business is running a restaurant, so after school I have to go straight to the restaurant. I'm there until closing. So I don't get to bed until 2 in the morning. That's why I'm late. That's why I fell asleep in class." This teacher was curious and asked her a question. He wondered about what was what's going on. In taking action, he reached out to her.

My point in these stories is that the behaviour of both these teachers affected the brain of that girl. How she was treated changed her biology by changing her brain wiring. When we think about adolescence, it's really important to stop and think about what we're thinking about a particular person's behaviour. It's essential to ask ourselves what we actually know about what's going on.

THE NEED FOR RELATIONSHIP IN ADOLESCENCE

When I talk about the early years, I'm very clear that social interaction with infants and young children is all about relationships. Now we're on to discussing adolescents and it's still true—what matters is relationship, relationship, relationship. It's only in the last 10 or 15 years that brain researchers have understood how important relationship is during adolescence. As the brain changes during this period of time, and develops dramatically, the way we interact with teens will impact how these experiences change their brains.

How do we know this? There's an important book called *The Brain that Changes Itself,* written by Canadian psychiatrist Norman Doidge.[10] He works in Toronto and wrote the book based on his research on international studies that explore how the brain works and repairs itself. In contrast to what he uncovered, when I was in medical school, we used to think we got our genes from mom and dad and were destined to be a certain way. Based on his work, and many others, we know brain cells get activated, quite literally, by experience; it's no longer accurate that once a brain is set, that's all there is to it.

In adolescence, experiences kids engage in literally build pathways in the brain. These pathways are networks of connections. Based on experiences, as brains develop, what isn't being used is being snipped away. So the process is best described as use-it-or-lose-it. As these pathways are built, areas of the brain connect to each other in a space between brain cells called synapses. When young people are involved in a youth group, basketball, school plays or are volunteering at a Senior Citizens' home, their brains are activated very differently than are the brains of young people who are in the basement playing Grand Theft Auto. With brain development, young people learn by doing—by having particular experiences—and, based on those experiences, for better or worse, their brains are changing.

The term we use for the brain's ability to change is called neuroplasticity. I want to talk about neuroplasticity in general, before we apply it to adolescence. Let's use an example. Suppose a man you know has a fall and hits his head hard. He has a concussion. Parts of his brain were bruised by what happened. The brain is damaged. Your friend has to recover. But what's involved in that recovery? Doidge wrote the story of one man who needed to recover all aspects of what the brain had been able to do before he was injured.

This man had been a very successful University professor who taught poetry. But he had a stroke, which left him unable to walk or talk. He went to Rehabilitation but didn't recover full function. One of his children happened to be a neuroscientist, Dr Bach-y-Rita. When his children saw him, they weren't satisfied that he had gained as much function back as might be possible. They realized they weren't going to give up on their father. They refused to leave him as he was. They knew that brains develop in a hierarchical way. That means simple things get wired up first and then more complex areas get wired up. They thought sensory modalities, hearing and seeing, would get wired up first.

The last part of the brain to get wired up is complex abstract thinking. If their Papa couldn't walk or talk, it meant they needed to target lower down in his brain and figure out how to help him. They came up with the idea that he might need to learn to crawl again. After all, that's something young children learn to do very early. So they helped him learn to crawl. Then, he got walking. They helped him with simple words first. They did all of this recovery work with him based on their understanding of how brains operate. They committed themselves to helping him. The outcome of the story is that their father got back to teaching at University. He recovered full functioning to such an extent that he died climbing a mountain.

During an autopsy, doctors discovered a hole in his brain where he had the stroke. But his recovery, with the help of his children, rewired around the dead space. He rewired around his deficit because his family members asked themselves questions about how the brain is actually constructed. It was through his children's relationship and their actions that his recovery was possible.

In addition to the learning this man's children provided, it's now evident that aerobic exercise, or lifting weights releases transmitters in the brain that help with healing and with new brain growth. Exercise releases a substance that some call Miracle Grow for the brain. Its real name is Brain Derived Neurotrophic Factor (BDNF).[11]

The more we study the brain, the more we realize it's not a fixed organ in a machine; if it's damaged, that damage isn't necessarily permanent. If you told me all of this about the brain when I graduated in 1981, I would have said it sounds like science fiction. What's different now is that we know about neuroplasticity. What can we think now? If there's damage to the brain, even based on harmful experiences, people absolutely can have better recovery from serious neurological injury than was predicted in the past.

This is very good news for me as a child psychiatrist working in psychotherapy. The brain is capable of change throughout life. When we're engaged in psychotherapy in a productive way, we're helping people rewire their brains and reconstruct how brain cells communicate with each other. Guess what the most important part of my work has been? You've heard it before: it's the power of relationships. Just like the relationship between father and children that enhanced the remarkable recovery for that University professor, we have great studies to show that it's not the kind of therapy a therapist uses. It's the therapist that he or she is that makes the difference. But if someone is not genuine with kids or young people—if you don't create a sense of trust to convey that you'll listen without judgement—you're never going to get out the first door to that relationship opportunity.

UNDER CONSTRUCTION

Adolescence is a time of growth and maturation in the brain. Dr. Jay Giedd, a U.S. neuro scientist, provided us with visual images of adolescent brain development.[12] In the images he captured, he shows a brain that has blue areas of maturation. To get these images, he studied the same brains over time and looked at these brains using an MRI machine (magnetic resonance imaging machine). As he studied these brains, what he saw changed the world for young people and changed how we view people in this age category. He saw that brains weren't finished growing when kids are in childhood. There are major structural and functional changes in the brains of children through to adolescence.

As I said, the adolescent brain is under construction until at least 25 years of age. In addition, in Western societies, the work of Arnett and Cote[13] describes a new period they named Emerging Adulthood. They call the years between 18 and 25 a time of self-focused exploration facilitated by socially sanctioned moratoriums on having to take on adult responsibilities. Many parents will recognize this time because their kids have finished College or their first University degree and are now back living in their basement!

One cultural aspect of this lengthy development is that the time when young people take on adult roles has shifted significantly. Back in the day, Marie Antoinette (the last queen of France before the French Revolution in 1789) was 19 years old when she took the throne. Alexander the Great was king of the ancient Greek kingdom of Macedon by the age of 20. He died at 33, after beginning his campaigns at 15 years old and conquering the known world of his day.

Both these leaders were taking on adult roles during what we call adolescence. Social expectations were vastly different then. We don't expect kids to take on adult roles at 14 to 19 in twenty-first century western cultures. The dissonance between what parents experienced and what we expect of youth can cause tension, to say the least. At one conference where I was presenting to family physicians, a family doctor came up to me after the session and told me he joined the Merchant Navy at 16. When he was 19, he became captain. Then he asked why his patients would never have had that experience. It's possible to think that kids are just not growing up. As parents, we might think we've failed as we observe the pattern. But society has changed dramatically. In many societies, kids are still given adult roles and opportunities. They are mentored into adulthood. They are offered apprenticeships and contribute significantly to their communities. Some people in the West are asking if we have infantilized our kids and kept them in a hothouse called high school for so very long.

As I think about western cultures and adolescence, I'm very curious about the concept of service learning and about engaging deeply in learning that supports other people? This approach to adolescence is based on good science and what Canadian educational leader Michael Fullan describes in his book, *Deep Learning: Engage the World Change the World*.[14] If young people have opportunities for deep learning that's also service learning and they engage in inquiry-based projects, these activities change their brains. If adolescents give back to others, their learning utilizes a social drive and changes their brains in terms of the way they think, act and interact with others. Laurence Steinberg, an American psychologist, also studies adolescent brains and describes brain maturation.[15] He outlines changes in the brain that have to do with becoming more specialized. What kids are busy doing in service learning is building their brains. As is true in the early years, what gets wired up and repeated over and over will become a super highway of connection in the brain.

In adolescence, it's fair to ask which parts of the brain are growing during these experiences. Networks in the brain develop in different areas at different times, which I describe later in this chapter. What we know from the science is that the emotional part of the brain, the limbic system, known to include the fight-or-flight system, is under development. This growth happens ahead of the Stop. Think. Plan. area of the brain, known as the prefrontal cortex. So on one hand, we've got a brain that says, "Hey man, I want to do it. It's so exciting (whatever that is)." On the other hand, there's an executive director that's still in training or not even hired as yet. Steinberg and others talk about this dilemma as being like having an inexperienced driver with a fast accelerator, but no brake.

While risk-taking behaviour may worry parents, adolescents have magnificent creativity. If you want a sticky problem solved, bring in a bunch of teens to think about and work through it. They aren't constricted by adult experience to declare in advance that an idea won't work. But during adolescence, with brain plasticity, the young are also more vulnerable. We don't know why the majority of adult mental health problems begin in childhood and adolescence. But one of the things people talk about is that there are all these moving parts in the brain; all this change is happening, so youth are more at risk.

KEY MESSAGES

When we talk about the adolescent brain in a general way, there are some key messages to convey: Their brains are under construction. Adolescents are under construction. There's a big myth out there that kids don't need adults when they become adolescents. This is just not true! They need more of our time and more of our attention to help them create a sense of belonging and identity. If you listen to the media, you hear all of this bad stuff about kids getting in trouble. Sometimes it sounds as if youth crime is on the rise. But it's not. It's much lower now than in earlier years. On television, we see commercials in which kids are rolling their eyes at their parents to convey they don't want to be with them. Don't believe it. Kids who have positive parents, who are there for them, who have clear boundaries, offer lots of love and have high expectations have better outcomes. The research is very, very clear about that.[16]

So what's going on in the brain? Pruning and re-modelling is it's major activity. Siegel talks about activities kids are engaged in and why we need to give them lots of opportunity. In one story I read, teachers were wondering about how to get students more engaged in school. They did a survey of grade 7 to grade 9. In the survey, kids said they didn't feel like they belong in school. In that data, fewer than 40% believed they belonged. Teachers then asked them what would make them feel like they belonged? Students talked about having more activities at school. Could we have more clubs? Are there more ways to build connections with each other? Are there ways we can have more adults who show us that they care? The kids were actually asking for experiences that help build brains.In addition to needing activities, and adults who show they care, there's a huge social issue because human beings are absolutely wired to connect. This is manifest in infancy but in adolescence it flourishes. The social brain conveys to us that affiliation, attunement and attachment to peers are all extremely important. This is not a surprise. What is a surprise is that people think it means they're less attached to adults. That's not the case. Children and young people who have strong positive social and emotional connections to significant adults have lots of attachment room to develop strong peer connections as well.

Kids who don't have those adult relationships in their lives, have less room for expansive, healthy peer relationships.

If you don't have adults in your life whose eyes light up when they see you, you've got more difficulty. As an example, you won't have a mental model about what relationships might be like. Quite often, peer relationships are a significant challenge. A young person without invested adult relationships may not know how to become a friend. The only people this adolescent can fit in with are other kids on the margins of social life. Very often we see that kids who have challenges with socialization have an attraction to kids who are outside the standard or norm and who may demonstrate challenging behaviour themselves.

Another key concept has to do with how adolescents experience and read emotion. This insight comes from the work of American psychologist Paul Ekman[17] and Deborah Yurgelun Todd,[18] a Harvard neuropsychologist. Ekman isolated muscles in the face for every human emotion. He developed an on-line program to train people to read emotion more effectively. As an example, he shows people a picture of a face expressing fear. The expression of fear is conveyed as a person uses particular muscles in the face. Using his program, it's possible to increase one's awareness of different facial expressions that convey particular feelings. If you go to his program, you see that facial expressions use specific muscles when someone is feeling an emotion. As an example, if someone is feeling disgust, they raise the nose, like they would if they smelled a bad smell. Disgust is expressed by using those particular muscles—by lifting and wrinkling the nose.

Yurgelun Todd was doing research on adolescent emotional development. As part of her research, she showed kids a picture of a facial expression. They would look at the picture and comment on what they thought the person was feeling. Often, they said the person looked really angry. She would then ask what they meant by really angry. She also started showing kids a series of pictures of different emotions.

She discovered that adolescents saw different emotions in facial expressions than most adults would see. For example, they saw anger when an adult would see fear. As she continued to research adolescent emotion, she observed that they were reading more anger, that is, they were reading hotter emotions than adults read. She was curious about this tendency and put her adolescent subjects into scanners to observe them. What did she find? She found that, compared to adults, adolescents process emotion through their super fast acting amygdala more than through their slow-acting thinking brain. When reading an emotion, adults rely on the front part of their brain—the executive functioning part of the brain.

Teens rely on the super fast reaction response of the amygdala. What does this mean? Well, very often this difference signals a communication gap between teens and parents. A breakdown of communication occurs because teens may be misinterpreting facial expressions of emotion. They may see more anger than there actually might be. Why? If they process emotion in the amygdala rather than with the thinking part of the brain, they involve their own fight or flight reactions. The amygdala tells the body to be on guard. Watch out! This part of the brain warns of impending danger. The emotional brain dominates in adolescence. This part of the human brain is firing and developing ahead of the part of the brain that tells the body to stop, plan and think about it.

I get the opportunity to speak to parents and teachers across the country. I tell them that because adolescent brains are under construction, kids are reading more emotion in their faces than they might think they're expressing. A kid may say, "Why are you so angry?" when the adult doesn't think they are angry. Kids can tell if an adult cares about them. Caring makes all the difference in the world. If more adults recognized that as well, it would make a difference. But I know it can be an uphill battle. We need more young people talking about the brain to a lot more people.

What about parents who look at a teenager's angry face and think the teen doesn't like them anymore? It's hugely important that no matter what expression or signal you think you're getting from your child, the signal you send, over and over again, is that, hey, I'm here. I accept you for who you are. Loving our families is unconditional. When things aren't going well, you don't take it personally—as much as you possibly can avoid doing. You don't bring up tough things to talk about just as you're walking out the door or just as they're leaving the house. You take time and choose your time well.

When adolescents engage in risk-taking behaviour, they pay less attention to the danger. They pay attention to the thrill of what they're doing. Siegel calls this response hyper-rational. What does a hyper-rational response imply? Before the legalization of marijuana, I had an opportunity to talk to many kids about its effects. Even with all the negative research observations about the effects of marijuana, they focused on ideas that said marijuana is not a problem. They simply ignored anything that raised concern about the effects of marijuana on the brain and body.

So what are some key messages about adolescence? To summarize, kids will do better if they can; kids are under construction; they desperately need time with adults whose eyes light up when they enter the room; peer groups matter for very good reasons; the emotional brain dominates, thrill seeking is central; and, all in all, adults need to keep in mind that what they think about teens, shapes what they feel about them and directs how they act towards them.

THE POWER OF PEERS

I talked about the issue of peer attachment as being essential for survival. Something I talk to teachers about is that we don't use this adolescent pattern of development to advantage at school. Kids learn together very well. If we give them skills for how to work together, their ability to solve problems together is one of the drivers of adolescence. Peer power is hugely important. However, I know there are negative impacts of peer power. I have a video that shows the impact of peer presence on adolescent behaviour. It's from a video program called The Brain on Trial and features American actor Allan Alda[19] In the video, there's an adolescent in an MRI scanner while he's doing a task in which he has to decide whether he will stop his car at a stoplight or go through the light. If his timing is wrong, the car crashes. The first time, when the adolescent is in the scanner, he does just as well as all adults do. In the second trial, he's told that his friends are going to be watching him. In the second scenario, he takes more risks and has more accidents during the simulation.

What this experiment shows very clearly is the effect of peers on the young man's reward sensitivity. He takes more risks to get more rewards, more thrills, if he thinks his friends are there and watching him. The irony is that his friends were not actually watching. His was told that as part of the experiment.

During adolescence, the last area to develop all its connections and networks is the prefrontal cortex, which is under construction until 25 years of age, or later. The prefrontal cortex is thought to be engaged in planning and organizing as well as in impulse inhibition. It's still under construction during adolescence. So kids have a challenge. American actor Flip Wilson used to say "the devil made me do it." The limbic system is saying, "Hey, do it now!" The underdeveloped prefrontal cortex is saying, "Hey, stop and think about it, stop and think about it." So during adolescence, there's a brain mismatch. This video shows how teens drive a car if an adult is with them and how they drive if their peers are in the car. The video is alarming. If peers are watching or are in the car, the part of the brain that says stop and think is taken over by the part that engages risk.

So what can we do about these dangers? Firstly, we can ensure that teenagers are trained to drive properly. Secondly, we can let them know about brain development and the increased risks. Thirdly, we can make sure that no matter what dilemma they find themselves in, we provide support. There are some people who say we shouldn't allow kids to be in cars with their peers and some who say they shouldn't drive until their brain matures. Both of these positions are extreme and don't take into account the other competencies young people have. The extreme reactions to adolescent dangers doesn't' take into account that the majority of adolescents don't get into trouble; they do well and make it through adolescence intact.

ADOLESCENT BRAINS AND SLEEP

For adolescents, there is also something different happening with their sleep patterns. What gives people the feeling they need to go to sleep is part of what's called a Circadian rhythm, which involves Melatonin in the body that regulates the sleep/wake cycle. In adolescence, that sleep/wake cycle gets shifted so that the need or thirst for sleep occurs later at night. Research is showing that, although teenagers may get less sleep than younger kids, they actually need more. So there is a dilemma. The sleep/wake cycle may not hit until midnight in teens but they still need 9 and 3/4 hours of sleep, which is more than children and adults need.

In general terms, we're learning so much more about the restorative power of sleep. What we're seeing is that in some school districts, School Board members have set a later start time for school. If kids come in and they're absolutely sleep deprived, it's not that they've kept themselves awake until midnight, it's that their drive to sleep hasn't kicked in until midnight. If they need to get up at 6:30 to catch the bus and be on the bus for a long time, and they're supposed to be wide-eyed and bushy-tailed doing algebra, it's just not working. But what does this mean practically? We know from our own experience as adults that we can't just make ourselves go to sleep. If we have to get an early flight, we wake ourselves up a million times. Then we can't just make ourselves go to sleep again. I believe that education systems need to really think deeply about the adolescent brain and about when learning happens to realize that many teens are sleep deprived. Perhaps more schools should give support to the complex decision around having the school day start later for teenagers.For parents, I suggest that they let kids sleep in on the weekend. Mowing the lawn and doing their chores can be done in the afternoon rather than first thing. Let them catch up on their sleep. They will thank you for it and may be even less surly.

I know these are challenging times. There's a downside to all these key messages about adolescence. In 2020, there's a world of fast cars, readily available drugs and plenty of enticing messages about sex. Teens can get drugs easily. If they have access to sex and drugs, kids really need a lot of adults and peer support. We can't just advise them to say no to drugs. It doesn't work. They need support to help them make better decisions. Now that we've legalized marijuana in Canada, particular kids are going to be more susceptible to psychosis—to delusional thinking, hearing voices and seeing things that other people can't see. The heavy early use of marijuana can negatively affect the brain. We're also discovering that it's use affects learning. Many kids are in clinics saying, "Well it's legal, so I can do it." I've seen for a long time that many kids self-medicate with marijuana because of anxiety. Reports about anxiety are on the rise. For many kids, the over-use of marijuana starts a cycle of lower school performance, which interferes with working memory and affects inhibition and skills acquisition. Marijuana is not innocuous. It's not as some people who promote its use would have us believe. No, it's a challenge for teens. Adolescence is a time of great opportunity, yet there is great vulnerability.

CONCLUSION

I hope that I've been able to communicate that an adolescent brain is a thing of beauty. It's amazing. It's capable of creativity, energy, excitement and emotion. Some of the passion expressed by adolescents comes from the development of their dopamine pathways. There are more dopamine receptors being wired up during this age, there's thrill and thrill-seeking that happens during the teenage years. Dopamine is our reward neurotransmitter. The baseline level of dopamine is lower in adults but the buzz they get when they're excited is higher because things are coming into equilibrium. We're learning from other countries that kids who have the strongest sense of life, of belonging and connection to peers and adults will do better during adolescence. We need to be thinking about the high-quality, frequent relational contacts with all our kids, but particularly with kids who are at the greatest risk. We know that love builds brains. Teenage brains need our love and our adult attention.

A central message for this chapter on the adolescent brain is that we need communities and societies that reach out to kids so that more of them feel that human connection—so they can thrive. My friend Steve de Groot has worked with thousands of kids who have challenging lives and he talks about how adults can learn to stop and ask themselves what they know about a problem from the child's perspective? Too often, we're quick to jump in and manage behaviour that may have nothing to do with what the young person thinks is going on. The act of being present, of listening without judging, is unbelievably important. But listening to our own thoughts is equally important. We listen to where our own mind is going, as we listen to a young person. Reflection is important. As we listen, we ask the question, what would make it safe for this kid to question me and to question what's going on? Making it safe is essential.

In my opinion, as a society, we need to value our families more than we do. Bruce Perry is a child psychiatrist from Texas. He talks about the poverty of relationships. I agree with him. We need to be creating a declaration of interdependence for families, rather than a declaration of the Independence of adolescence. Harvard professor, Robert Putnam wrote the book *Bowling Alone* to say that societies who have more connectivity through club activities and religious institutions are more civic and more democratic. They operate far better than communities that are isolated and fractured. This is the kind of environment that adolescents need in order to thrive.

We need to be reaching family doctors to be giving this message. We need to identify the people who touch children's lives so that they can give this continuous message: Your love builds their brains. We can be more aware of what we're doing and engage more often in that back and forth, that serve and return social interaction that builds relationships. We need public awareness campaigns. We need governments to say this really is important. In the meantime, I think we need to be looking at our teacher education programs. We must include social and emotional skills training into our educational programs at University.

In one First Nations' teaching, there's a picture of the palm of a hand. The message of the image is, "I hold the child in the palm of my hand." The message this image provides is to say that children need five adults who care about them, like the five fingers of that hand. This image conveys that each child is held in the palm of this hand. I wonder how we can have more adults step forward and say to our young people, "I see you, I value you. You matter. I'm here for you." That is my vision, that we see all kids as having a promising life.

8

The Contexts for Developing Self-Regulation

INTRODUCTION

The previous chapter focused on adolescence as an important time of brain development and human growth. This chapter takes us back to the early years and also covers childhood and adolescence. The topic is self-regulation and the contexts required for its development. The way I've often described self-regulation when I'm with young people, is that it's becoming the boss of their thoughts, emotions and behaviours. Self-regulation is a bit more complicated than this but kids seem to know what I'm getting at when I say it that way.

The development of self-regulation occurs over time, starting in the early years and carrying on into adolescence and beyond, so I want to keep in mind some key messages from the last chapter. The heart of the messages is that kids are growing and developing, and that growth and development are very much influenced by the environment and their relationships. So, recall that kids will do well if they can, kids are under construction, and they need time with adults whose eyes light up when they enter the room. In addition, it's important to keep in mind that our thoughts ABOUT children and teens, shape what we feel about them and influences how we act towards them.

In this chapter, I want to re-emphasize some other key messages. These messages include that the brain is built by serve and return interactions, like the back and forth of a tennis match. We also have lots of science to show that kids aren't learning from television or iPads in the same way, or as deeply, as they learn through face-to-face encounters. Because there's so much brain development in the first year of life, scientists consider the first year to be like an external womb, due to the intensity of this growth. This is called *secondary altriciality*,[1] which refers to the immaturity of the brain at the time of birth. For other mammals, at the time of birth, the brain is fully formed. With humans, it is only about 1/3 of the size of an adult brain.

The implications of this growth are profound. Babies cry because they have a need, not because they want to manipulate their parents. So, you can't spoil a baby. If adults respond to a baby's distress their response begins a process that allows a child to develop self-regulation. It's a process that begins by experiencing co-regulation with the adults in their lives. It's really important for parents to learn to read their baby's cues because babies are born helpless. Given this dependency on adults, it's necessary that the environment be nurturing and low in stressors. The effects of toxic stress are most profound during the early years, as discussed in previous chapters.

If children learn to self-regulate, to be boss of their thoughts, emotions and behaviours, by first being co-regulated, then adults need to understand where children's behaviour comes from and realize that a child's behaviour is due to their developing capacities. How well parents and caregivers participate in this development has a lot to do with the adults' mind set and the support they receive themselves from their own communities.

In this chapter I first ask the reader to consider their own view of the child and what environments they consider optimal for child and youth growth. We know from the work of the *Search Institute*,[2] which I discuss later in the chapter, that kids thrive when adults view child and youth development through a positive lens and see a role for themselves in that development. Under these conditions, while working together, adults help kids develop their personal assets. That means that environments matter. After I discuss Search Institute research, I'll focus on how adults see their role as a parent. As I look at two different ways to think about our parental role, as a gardener or as a carpenter, I'll explain how these two ways of parenting affect the experience of young people. Again the parental mind set affects how adults see their role in helping kids develop self-regulation.

I also will ask whether the current educational system is meeting the needs of children and preparing them for the world of today and tomorrow. I suggest we need a paradigm shift in thinking that has at its heart the development of agency and self-regulation through relationship. Finally, I dive more deeply into the role of attachment as the basis of self-regulation and I'll look at the work of my dear friend and colleague Canadian scholar and professor emeritus at York University in Toronto, Dr Stuart Shanker..

ENVIRONMENTS FOR GROWTH

I want to say more about the fact that how we view children shapes how we feel about them and motivates how we act towards them, because there's another dimension to this message. How we think, feel and act towards individual children also directs how we establish the environment in which we expect children to learn self-regulation—or anything else for that matter. As part of developing my understanding of self-regulation, I studied the work of an organization called *The Search Institute.* That group has interviewed millions of young people. In doing their research, they identified positive attributes that young people felt allowed them to live a healthy life. The researchers at the Institute organized these responses into 40 developmental assets.[3]As I was learning about this assets-based approach, and I wanted to pass the idea on to others, I used an exercise that I discovered in their materials. In the exercise, I invite a group of people to stand in a circle. I'm also in the circle and I hold a large ball of yarn. People in the circle are asked to say aloud what they think young people need in order to do well in life. As we stand in the circle, when someone indicates they have a suggestion, someone else throws them the ball of yarn, while still holding on to the piece they have in their hand. Once someone makes a suggestion, they throw the ball to another person in the circle. So, for example, suppose someone says, I think kids need positive relationships. Someone else says, I think they need a safe place to stay. A third person might say, I think they need to work hard at school. A fourth person might say that liking people is an important asset. The yarn is repeatedly tossed across the circle until the group creates a web in the middle of the circle with the strands of yarn.

When the web is partly formed, as facilitator, I introduce a balloon by bouncing it onto the web. People in the circle try to keep the balloon in the air, but of course, there are gaps. Then I say that, if someone has few assets, the balloon will fall through the holes in the web. As those of us in the circle increase the strands of yarn (internal assets e.g., working hard at school) and external assets (e.g., having a safe place to stay), the web becomes more filled in, more secure and it's less likely for the balloon to fall through to the floor. Then we talk about the connection of this exercise to kids' lives and also to their experience of community.

An assets-based approach takes account of internal assets, what the young person contributes to their own well-being, as well as external assets, what the community brings for support. Internal and external assets work together. As some examples, Internal assets may include: I want to work hard, I like school, I like helping other people; external assets may include: I have adults in my life who care about me, I have a spiritual community that sustains me, my school teachers help me learn—all these assets work together to make positive outcomes more likely.

Even as we consider the notion of self-regulation, and its positive development, we need to be creating supportive communities that are represented by people who are connected around the circle and hold on to the yarn. Connection is key. Helping people understand that a child needs many adults who care about them is an essential part of what I do in my role as knowledge translator and child advocate.

MINDSETS MATTER

But we always need to be humble and reflective. No one is an "expert" in parenting because no two children are alike. Just when you get it right with one, along comes another child who is so temperamentally different from the first one that you begin to wonder about your parenting. What's essential to healthy parenting is that you have an appreciation and deep reflective understanding of how you view your role in rearing or in teaching children. As I've been saying, environment is key, but the environment includes how you view the child and how you view yourself.

To explore the point I'm making, I read a book called *The Gardener and the Carpenter*, by Dr Alison Gopnik.[4] She's a philosopher and child development psychologist. In the book, she asks us to think about our role as parents, and I invite you as teachers to think about this as well. Do we see ourselves as carpenters, who take wood and decide in advance what to make? If you're a carpenter, you produce a particular outcome. You use your tools to make it happen. You use strategies to secure that end result. Your aim is to get the specific outcome you've envisioned ahead of time. You decide to make a piece of wood into a chair or a table. As adult carpenters in relationship with children, for example, you may expect to have a well-behaved child who holds the right beliefs. Gopnik asks if this is how you see your adult role.

Or perhaps you see yourself more as a gardener who examines the soil and asks how to create an environment where children can flourish. Gardeners pay attention to soil, sunlight, shade, and moisture levels and try to discover how plants flourish in the garden. Gardener adults want to create an environment in which children and youth can be themselves by providing a setting that's nurturing for them. Gardeners are not passively watching what's going on. They prune, fertilize, plant, water and weed. So, let me ask you, my readers, what do you think about your role? As I've worked with many parents and educators and raised this analogy with them, many say they want to be gardeners. It sounds like the right answer to many adults. But I think the reality is, for many people, while they want to garden, they find that, at the practical day-to-day level, they do a lot of carpentry.

Now, I put gardening and carpentry on a continuum. That continuum stretches from thinking we're going to have a fixed product at one end of the continuum to aiming to create an environment in which the child is creative in his or her own right at the other end. I ask parents and educators to try to understand where they are on the continuum so they can become more aware of how they view children and themselves. Because these views affect how we interact with the young, this reflection begins to reframe how parents create an environment for children. Of course, it's not just parents who are well advised to ask the question. If, as an educator, you think your role is to fill the kids up with knowledge based on the curriculum, it's less likely you'll put a big emphasis on the teacher/learner relationship that you build with students. To use another analogy, do you see your role with students as filling the bucket, or, do you see your role as igniting the flame of learning? Do you fill buckets or ignite flames? I use the expression stuffing the duck as a way of talking about the filling the bucket metaphor.

Much of the work we do with children is adult-oriented. In my observation, we want kids to turn out the way we want them to, so we stuff the duck. What would happen if we spent time thinking more about how to create the conditions where kids can manifest their own potential and thereby thrive?

My interest in this question is linked to my interest in my own magnificent grandchildren. As I watch them, given my knowledge of the brain, I can see their brains developing. I see them one week and think to myself, well, they couldn't do that last week. When one of them first used his pincer grasp, I gasped out loud that, hey, his neurons are connecting. I was just too darn busy when I was raising my own children to make these observations, I think. When I did start learning about the brain and doing all the reading and observing, I started to feel guilty. The brain is built by experience: did I create those experiences for my little ones before they were 6 years old? Sound familiar? Well, I see they turned out pretty well so think we must have created a good enough environment for their growth. Like most people, we did the best we could with what we knew at the time.

If I'm totally honest, isn't this a paradox? I'm asking parents to focus on and know about brain development so they can create the best environment for children, but on the other hand, we all do the best we can. So, I don't want to create guilt in parents. The mantra is progress not perfection. There will be days when you're a carpenter and task oriented. Don't beat yourself up.

The key to providing the best environment for children remains what I've been saying in earlier chapters. Parents are the first and most important teacher for their children. I'm certain we need to be helping more and more young parents and families to be supportive in knowing how important they are to their children. It's not about going out and buying this fancy thing or that fancy thing. It's about building relationships. The way you build relationship in the earliest years is through face-to-face interaction. When I'm presenting a talk, I use a little video of one of my grandchildren at 2 weeks of age. In the video, my son sticks out his tongue and the baby's gaze is transfixed on his father's face and magically he sticks out his tongue in imitation.

There are other cultures and earlier times that paid attention to environment. In many ways, we have to relearn what Indigenous elders knew,[5] or learn from those who've known for centuries how to be with children. I've talked about Tom Porter, a Mohawk elder I mentioned in an earlier chapter. His grandmother reared him. It's fascinating to hear him talk about how much he loved her. He talks about grieving her loss even before she died. He considered what the world would be like when she wasn't there. Imagine that kind of connection. Porter said that, in his Mohawk culture, the word for children is 'the one who has the light within'. When we think about children as the sacred ones, as those who have the light within, it compels us to reconsider how to be with each child.

THE SHIFTING ROLE OF EDUCATION...OR NOT

Another influence on the environment we create for children is shaped by the evolution of an education for all. I've been considering the history of education along with its intent and purpose. An education for all children came into being as a reaction to several issues. Adults wanted to get children off the streets and train them for work, for example, for working in factories. Rote memorization, sitting still and upright in a desk with hands folded, were some of the behaviours teachers believed would provide the right sort of training. Are these still the most important reasons for educating children?

The intent of education then was not what education is now. Yet early forms of an education for all are still influential. In October 2019, I was at an educational conference in Fort Lauderdale. While there, I heard about a 5 year old girl who got into a school program for gifted children. It's very hard to get into that school. Now that she's in the program, the little girl approached the school mental health counsellor and also her parents telling them that she had too much homework. Her grandmother told me the story so I asked her what she meant. She said that when her granddaughter gets home from school, she doesn't get to play. She gets home from the gifted program and has to continue her schoolwork.

Her grandmother is one of the leading lights in infant mental health and has been for many decades. She's in a dilemma. She knows how children grow and thrive best and that play figures prominently in healthy thriving. It's doesn't happen by doing homework. This program for gifted children employs the stuff the duck mentality. Does this program still have the wrong view of children? What's more, does this view of children increase their anxiety by putting pressure on them to perform? What does a high-stakes testing approach do to a child's anxiety levels? Piling on homework, using high stakes testing, and many approaches that are similar to these ways of treating children fail to see a child as beautiful, creative and competent. Again, children learn best through relationship, connection and play.

In contrast to the way mass schooling shapes education, some teachers create communities of learning. As I've mentioned in previous chapters, I have the privilege of working with an Ontario-based world-renowned thinker and writer on educational practise and philosophy, Michael Fullan. He talks about young peoples' agency. He wants education to focus on being with children and capturing their desire to help others to change the world by engaging with the world.[6] This approach creates conditions for learning by focusing on the development of 6 competencies, which are: creativity, communication, collaboration, critical thinking, character and citizenship. He places the importance of these competencies in the context of pedagogical practice. He aims to optimize learning environments and relationships and uses the digital world to leverage learning. In this approach, children experience authentic, meaningful and deep learning—and often learn to give back to their community. As they develop these competencies, in an educational environment that focuses on classroom environments and pedagogies that support inquiry, children develop skill in working with others, communicating their ideas clearly, recognizing the emotions of others and labelling and dealing with frustration. All of this learning takes place in environments that create a sense of belonging through relationships. These are truly self-regulating, generative environments and learning experiences.

SELF-REGULATION AND ATTACHMENT

Let's link what I've been saying about environments, educational philosophy and a child's context so we can understand self-regulation more fully. Human beings are wired to connect. If our brain is socially attuned to what's going on around us, I wonder if we're providing the kind of support to families that's needed for them to provide that connection. What kids need to learn is how to get along with others. They need to learn how to know what their brain is telling them to think and feel. They also need to learn how to reflect on what their brain is saying to them. The old view of the brain was that it was a fixed structure and had a set number of brain cells that declined over the aging process and were seriously damaged by physical trauma.[7] The new view makes us aware of brain plasticity—a brain that's capable of change and is enhanced by experience.[8] For those of us who work with children and youth, this is a phenomenal reality. It means that kids have experiences early, but if these experiences haven't been the greatest, there's hope that new experiences can rewire the brain. This is the primary message of this book: there is hope. But that hope depends on building relationships with children and youth. These relationships are effective if they focus on building connection, belonging and empowerment. If we pay attention to thinking about children and youth in these ways, the environments we create for them will allow them to grow and repair themselves. As we think about how we think about children and youth, our capacity for hope is central.

So if this is the way the brain is built, how should we think about helping children develop self-regulation? We have a view in western society that sees kids as empty vessels. But there is a different perspective. I have learned about and I'm very involved with the work and thinking of Loris Malaguzzi. He was the educator psychologist who shaped the approach used in Reggio Emilia in Italy. What he encourages in people across the world is to see that kids are not empty vessels. They have a hundred different languages of expression. For him, babies and children are powerful, resourceful and full of potential. This view of the child is an important philosophy in the Ontario school system because kindergartens now have children for a full day. That means that 4 and 5 year olds are in public education for all those hours during the week.

But the Ontario education system is based on a Reggio Emilia approach that says the kids are competent, capable and resourceful. They don't have a curriculum that's sitting there for them to learn. In contrast, they use a play-based, inquiry-driven curriculum. That means kids are spending a whole lot of time in play and exploration that's facilitated with their teachers. In that context, teachers know children have ideas and so they listen to those ideas. The Learning Experience is created around the children. This approach is referred to as an Emergent approach. I was involved in the development of some of these educational documents because it was important for me to participate in creating an educational system that was paying attention to more than just cognitive development. I know it's crucial to develop literacy and numeracy. It's essential for survival. But we need to spend more time thinking about social and emotional development and pay attention to the well-being of children and youth.

The focus for this type of educational environment is to think about how our kids learn to get along. I wrote a paper along with others a number of years ago called "Supporting Ontario's Youngest Minds".[9] That research looked at infant and early childhood mental health. The research included looking at literature from other countries. We landed on the following definition from the organization Zero to Three, as cited below:

Infant-Early Childhood Mental Health (I-ECMH), sometimes referred to as social and emotional development, is the developing capacity of the child from birth to 5 years of age to:

• Form close and secure adult and peer relationships;
• Experience, manage, and express a full range of emotions; and,
• Explore the environment and learn — all in the context of family, community, and culture (Cohen, Oser, & Quigle, 2012).[10]

When you look at the definition, it makes all kinds of sense. We shifted the dialogue from mental health to well-being. What kids have to accomplish in the first 6 years of life is to learn how to form close and secure relationships with adults and peers.

As part of this learning, a baby's emotions need to be read by others and regulated by nurturing, positive, warm interactions. We call this the development of attachment. What we know from attachment research is that when babies are separated from their most important caregivers they become distressed. They get sad. They withdraw. I address attachment more fully in chapter two but the connection between self-regulation and attachment is very important. Babies need to learn how to read the signals of a significant person in their lives and to send signals, which are then reciprocated by that person.

There's so much that can interfere with the sending and receiving of these signals early in life. Most of the research we have identifies problems in attachment from the mother's side of things. For example, maternal depression interferes with these exchanges, as does addiction.[11] Mothers with mental health issues or who lacked adequate early years nurture themselves can create difficulties for the relational back and forth social interactions that infants need. But we also know there are factors within the baby that can affect the sending and receiving of these signals. Autism is one example. Children with autism may not give out understandable cues that help a parent to reciprocate.

It's very hard for some families who live with children who have autism if they don't get the signal that their baby likes what they're doing. Parents look for smiles and giggles from a baby to reinforce a sense that these interactions are pleasant and welcome to the baby. These signals are important for their ongoing relationship building, but may be absent with a child who has autism. A family needs to be supported in keeping these interactions going, even if a child has autism. It will make all the difference in the world. Although a parent may not see the responses, this social send and receive messaging is still forming those little brains—whether the child sends it back or not.

As I said, essential for the development of self-regulation is the formation of secure adult and peer relationships. It's really funny watching our grandchildren who are twins. As I observed them at 22 months of age, I watched the development of their relationship as they became much more aware of each other during that 18 to 22 month period. They also exploded into language. What's interesting is that their development didn't focus on learning one thing here and another thing there. Learning tended to jostle along together. In addition, learning didn't just happen in one location or another. It's not just something that happens periodically at playgroup, as one example—it was happening all the time.

As twins, they've got this sense of togetherness. They were at our house in the living room. It used to be an adults' space but it quickly became a children's space with books, trucks and toys. Among all the kid things available, they decided to play with my knitting measuring tape. It's one of those devices you can pull out and push the button and it zooms right back in. So Nana made the big mistake. I showed them how to pick it up and make it go in. I made a little noise so I turned the measuring tape into a toy.

Of course, there was only one of them and there were two boys. What next? Whose turn would it be? One twin had a bit of language but it wasn't well developed yet. So he came over and took the tape from the other. The one who lost the tape yelled no! I suggested they try taking turns. My daughter thought of using a timer to help them. They were too young for this strategy, but... oh well! My daughter found a little funny sounding timer on her phone. She decided to call it 'the big noise'. So there were the boys, at 22 months, taking turns and exchanging the tape measure when they heard the big noise. The timer sounded every 45 seconds. To my surprise, there was no meltdown. In fact, as the big noise sounded, one rushed over to the other. When it sounded the next time, he ran away at first but then handed it over to his brother.

When we observe children carefully, we can see the possibilities and potential in them. As a sequel to the story, a few days later they were at the childcare centre and they had to tell an adult about the big noise. They kept asking for the big noise. They did it beauteously. They learned what we would have said 22 month old children couldn't learn. They learned a new strategy though the repetitive frequency of being exposed to it. It was amazing to see.

This is an example of how kids learn but it's also an example of their social and emotional development. If kids are plunked in front of the television and don't get exposure to their peers, if they don't get exposed to play, they're not going to develop and learn those things in the same kind of a way. This is due to another big task of early childhood. It's what allows them to learn self-regulation.

That task is learning to experience, manage and express a full range of emotions. I've defined self-regulation as becoming the boss of one's own thoughts, emotions and behaviours. Once babies and toddlers experience security with adult caregivers, they can go out and explore the world and discover aspects of themselves. Three-year-old children are absolutely able to label many of their own emotions.

What we know is that when you label your emotions, you move the emotional experience from the limbic system (the emotional primitive brain) to the prefrontal cortex, which is the area we refer to as the thinking brain.[12] In the story about my 22-month-old grandchildren, we see how the twins were learning behavioural boundaries for their emotional expression. They were learning perspective-taking. They learned this by sharing and coming to see that 'my brother wants the same thing I do'. They also learned problem-solving and conflict resolution with peers. How did this learning take place? Adults in the room held a priority for connection—having the boys connect with each other was important to mom and dad—and to nana.

CONNECT BEFORE YOU CORRECT OR DIRECT

I'm always inviting parents to think about how much time they spend connecting with kids and what percentage of the time they correct or direct them. What I remember in my life as a parent is that I spent a lot of time being the party pooper in their lives. I now know I wouldn't do that again if I had it to do over. I wonder if that's what grandparents are for. When our children were little, my husband and I consciously decided we were going to say no as few times as possible. We were going to tell them 'don't do that' as few times as possible. But that took a lot of work because it meant we had to be creating the conditions where yes was meaningful and no wasn't necessary. We were creating the conditions for a lot of play. We didn't have a television for many years so there weren't the conflicts young parents now have over screen time.

Screen time creates a dilemma for young parents. I'm frequently asked how much screen time is okay for children under 5 years of age. Paediatric societies provide guidelines[13] but parents find them very difficult to follow. I know one mom who's looked up the research. She knows she has a dilemma. She knows all about connecting with her little ones but she doesn't want them to fall behind. She doesn't want other kids to have the skills of navigating a phone when her little one doesn't. I'm interested in her dilemma. She asked me when she should let her child have access to screens so that he can keep up with other children. But what some of the research is showing is that little ones who don't have exposure to devices, and so don't have the skills, will pick them up in a snap. What seems to be true is that when children experience good engagement and develop an interest in things, they pick up these other skills quickly. If screen time replaces face-to-face interactions, the problem for developing self-regulation is made worse.

THE ROLE OF FATHERS IN ATTACHMENT AND SELF-REGULATION

In this section, I talk about the role of fathers specifically. I'm well aware that the definition of family has expanded to include same-sex families and other constellations. However, at this point, research I'll share with you is on the role of fathers and I look forward to learning more about other family systems.In this chapter, I've addressed the way self-regulation emerges through co-regulation. Babies need adults in their lives to regulate them by co-regulating them first. As the child becomes comfortable with co-regulation through relationship, they develop the ability to self-regulate. But, as I mentioned at the outset of the chapter, self-regulation is an issue during infancy, childhood and adolescence. Even at 5, 6, 7 to 17 years of age, the young need adult involvement in their lives so they can learn how to be boss of their own thoughts, emotions and behaviours, and learn how to deal with energy they expend when something distressful happens. In addition, adults want the young to do all this, and at the same time, learn to care about other people and care about their own needs as well.

A new area of the research addresses the role that dads play in all this learning and development. Most of the research on parent/child relationships has been done with mothers as the primary caregiver. Only recently has the role of fathers come into view. One reason for the change is linked to the social changes in the family that have taken place over the last decades. Family experience is very different from the time my mom stayed home with us. My daughter and her partner juggle work and childcare as well as managing who's sick and who has to stay home from work.

My parents brought 6 children to a new country. They left Scotland, a known environment, and came to a foreign country, Canada. My dad was a fabulous dad. He was fully present to us when he came home from work as a teacher and then superintendant of schools. He didn't bring work home with him. My parents worked in partnership together in a very different way than did the parents of my friends. I recall some of my friends telling me they really didn't know their dads. They told me he was always behind the newspaper. That's how they remembered him—always behind the newspaper. For them, dad was the disciplinarian—"just wait until your dad gets home"—was the message they heard. Dad was the punisher. Have you watched the television series Mad Men? That series demonstrates many of the attitudes that characterized the 1960s and 1970s in North America.

As they co-regulate children, it's important for parents to ask themselves about factors that affect how they came to be parents. What are the roles and expectations that shape their idea of what it means to be dad or mom? A parent's history, issues around mental health, beliefs about gender, medical knowledge or knowledge in general, all of these aspects of what it means to take care of children will influence how parenting works. It's essential to notice how parents work together as they establish a home environment. As mentioned at the beginning of the chapter, environment is central in teaching children to self-regulate. The family is an environment, so we need to ask how it works.

Like the culture of Mad Men, the absence of the father in North American families has received a good deal of study. We know a lot about absentee fathers. But there hasn't been as much research on their positive role, until recently. It's become clear that dads have a massive influence on child development. Fathering has, as we've always known, huge positive impacts. The quality of father involvement is an absolute key in the social and emotional development of children. One of the ways to look at a dad's influence is to consider how the mother/father dyad works. How does the relationship between mom and dad function to create a home environment? In examining the dyad, there are patterns and influences that overlap. But there are unique differences between how dads and moms interact with kids.

As researchers look at these patterns, the theme is *Vive La Difference*[14]—long live the difference between mom and dad interactional patterns. Some differences are sociological, for example, they're based on gender socialization. But there are also biological differences that are only now being identified. Some of the research focuses on the role of dads with children under 3 years old,[15] but observation isn't limited to that age group. A father's pathway of influence can be seen in direct parent-child interactions, such as how they play with, soothe and talk to their children. We can observe the presence or absence of tension in that relationship and note how the positivity of that relationship affects the child. While some research observations indicate very gender-specific patterns, both father and mother contribute to the family system. There are child factors that need to be thought about as well. Unfortunately, when parents bring home babies who have fragile medical histories, the family environment is under enormous pressure and many marriages experience that stress.

Secure attachment depends on expressions of warmth, trust, security and responsiveness. We now know that moms can have an insecure attachment to their babies but dad's can have a secure attachment. Secure attachment depends on the expression of warmth, trust, security and responsibility. We want to be supporting young dads. There are some programs I know about for teen moms that include the dads. For many years, a young dad was not considered (nor even identified) so they weren't included. But some groups are thinking about bringing in the young dads as well.

I've spoken with many young dads who say they didn't know they had a role whatsoever in raising their children. We have to reverse that pattern. Relational synchrony[16] is all about parents getting in sync with their babies' actions and feelings. In relational synchrony, dads are just as capable as are mums. Another myth about the role of dads is that they only want to get engaged with babies when they learn to talk so that they can interact with them at that level. But what we now see is that introducing dad to a baby's cues is just as exciting for these men as it is for mom. They too can speak *parentese*. We can help young couples, dads and partners to become sensitive to a baby's cues so that these cues can be turned into the serve and return interactions that babies need to experience in order to learn self-regulation.

We can identify aspects of the parenting role that always matter. These aspects include the following: effective support, secure attachment, relational synchrony, sensitivity to a child's cues, adult behavioural style, and seeing things from the child's perspective. But there are also different things dads do on average than what moms tend to do. In a whimsical way let's say, I've seen lots of dads toss their kids in the air and then catch them. Very few mums I've observed toss their children in the air. It seems that tossing children in the air may be a behavioural difference between men and women. In general, mother-child interactions tend to involve quieter, affectionate and socially-oriented interactive patterns than father-child interactions. These father-child interactions are often characterized by higher levels of activity, risk-taking, exploration and object-oriented dyadic patterns.[17]Up to know this section has been specifically about dads but we know in our changing society that same sex couples have children and have their own ways of sharing the parenting roles. Another aspect of the family environment that matters is cooperation between parents. It's essential to look at how each parent releases the parenting role to the other. How does each partner respond to the involvement of the other parent? When our children were small, my husband tossed our son in the air and I said, No! Don't do that! It's bad for him. Wow. Is it the Y chromosome? But I was the mother. I knew best. Don't do that, I'd say. Are you kidding? Look at his face. He loves it. My husband and I had to work it out and learn how to accept each other's way of being as parent. When our son played football, I'd go to watch and yell at him to look out! My husband Jim would yell, go get him! If our son was climbing up a ladder, I would say be careful. Jim would say go to the top. Are these behaviours biological or gender-specific? Are they based on our socialization? My point here is the need for reflecting together. I can say that now as an experienced parent. But in the day, I tended to take things more personally than was necessary. I thought I was right. Boy, it took lots of work as a couple to be accepting and respectful.

A key message here is that dialogue between parents is important. Cooperation and warm interaction between parents that includes connection, validation and affirmation all contribute to a positive family environment where we hope to teach children to self-regulate. It took me a long time to be comfortable letting Jim do a lot of childcare tasks. That was 35 years ago. Division of labour is a huge area of study and impacts the family environment dramatically. The heart of a domestic division of labour is healthy co-parenting. When there is healthy parenting, the level of partner involvement increases so that both parents carry out engagement and family work. Some new research indicates that new fathers are influenced by hormonal changes as well. They experience sensitivity to connecting with their newborn child. The baby's birth is a peak emotional experience for dads. When you think about the past, men were never allowed in the delivery room as a child was being born. They weren't involved in the early rearing. They were behind the newspaper. No wonder there was conflict.

Mothers have been the studied models for secure attachment. But the expanded model is wonderful. Fathers have unique pathways to attachment that don't fit mother-child templates. In the mother-child template, the paradigm is called the Strange Situation, which I explored in chapter two. In the Strange Situation, the mother plays with the child, then a stranger enters, and the mother leaves. Once she returns, the child's interaction with her is key to understanding whether the child enjoys secure attachment or not. In terms of father attachment, it may not look the same. The baby may be secure and happy with dad, even if the mother-child attachment isn't secure. Dad may come in the room, smile at his child, play with him or her for a minute and then we see the child go off and explore. So the world is starting to look at how dad's interaction is different. Father-interaction and rough-and-tumble play patterns also provide opportunities to learn self-regulation. I love the Roots of Empathy program in Canadian schools.[18] That program has taught us that, when infants and parents come into a classroom once a month for a year, some of the boys in the room can see for the first time how a dad interacts with his infant. Some of the children, male children in particular, may be seeing the loving approaches of a parent to a child for the first time. They're also experiencing the responsiveness of a baby to them, and through the facilitation of the program, they get to examine what that feeling is like. These overtures lay a foundational identity that conveys to the boys the idea that they too can be a loving father in the future.

SELF-REGULATION: THE SHANKER FRAMEWORK

Let's go back to the experience of the twins and what they were learning about sharing. When one of the twins gets frustrated, he expresses that emotion bodily. I don't think he uses the word frustrated, but he'll be able to say it soon. In this experience, he's learning to be the boss of his thoughts (my brother wants this too), emotions (frustrated) and actions (letting go of the toy). His learning brings us a little deeper into self-regulation. I've already stated my definition (becoming the boss) and it works for me because I'm a clinician. As a child psychiatrist and knowledge translator, I like to keep things as simple and accessible as possible.

I've learned much from my colleague and friend Stuart Shanker. He wrote a book called *Self-Reg*.[19] Stuart looks at self-regulation by examining how the body reacts to stress. He defines self-regulation in the following way: self-regulation refers to the energy expended when we respond to stress and then recover. Our approaches are very complimentary. I help children understand their thoughts, emotions and actions and observe that children have tremendous individual variation in their responses to stress. Stuart, on his part, describes how the reaction to stress uses up different amounts of energy depending on the individual variations in children.

To give a concrete example of individual differences, one of my sons, when a toddler, wasn't very distressed in new situations. Behaviourally, you wouldn't see any challenge. If we ask how much energy he had to exert in new situations, it wasn't very much. He didn't have to accommodate a lot to new situations because these situations didn't cause him stress. As a contrast, one of my daughters found new situations highly stressful. Behaviourally, she appeared very anxious or upset. Her stress system turned on quickly and went right to high. We eventually taught her how to deal with a stressor and recover from it. When she learned to do that, she could relax.

Shanker thinks of self-regulation in terms of the energy exerted and the effort required to once again relax.[20] Given my definition, we can see that individual children will behave differently and will use different amounts of energy to accomplish recovery. This means that individual kids will have different needs for learning self-regulation strategies. Thinking about the twins again, if one doesn't get what he wants right away, he's just cool with that. He seems to think, okay, I'll find something else to play with. The other, however, is intense. He expresses frustration and it takes a while for him to calm down. He uses much more energy in dealing with the stress and getting to recovery. So a big part of self-regulation is learning to see when a child's behaviour is not misbehaviour—it's stress behaviour. I can't emphasize this point too much: stress behaviour is not misbehaviour.

If you see a child having a meltdown or see a child who's yelling, what's your first thought about what's going on? What would change in your response if you thought to yourself, what's causing that child to be stressed? What would be different if you asked yourself, What can I do to understand that stress? We can regularly ask Why? and Why now? What we want to get to, as we work with kids, is for parents and teachers to be calm, focused and remain alert. Why is that? When you're calm, focused and alert, you're optimizing your own self-regulation. In that state, you're able to modulate your emotions, pay attention to what's going on with the child and ignore distractions. That's what it's like to be self-regulated. You inhibit impulses, but you do much more than just inhibit or control those impulses.

Self-control is not the same as self-regulation. Self-control is about inhibiting your impulses,[21] it's an ability to control yourself, in particular your emotions and desires and the expression of them behaviorally, especially in difficult situations. In self-regulation, you inhibit yourself but you also have full access to the consequences of an action. You have full access to your thinking brain. In this state, you can figure out what's going on and be aware of what you're thinking. You can ask yourself what the effects of your thinking, feeling and acting might have on other people. You can feel empathy. With self-regulation, you can improve your self-control.

Self-regulation is about managing the energy you exert and being satisfied with the way you're dealing with that energy. When I present on self-regulation, I show a video about the difference between self-regulation and self-control. The video, based on work by Walter Mischel in the 1960s shows an experiment with children called the Marshmallow Experiment.[22] In the video, four-year-old children sit on a chair in a room with a table in front of them. The researcher puts a marshmallow on the table and tells the child he or she can have a second marshmallow when the researcher comes back in the room if they don't eat the one that's right in front of them. Then the researcher leaves the room for 15 minutes. The video captures the expressions and body language of children as they try to resist eating the marshmallow. When the researcher returns, she gives a second marshmallow to children who've been successful in resisting the first one.

This video is about self-control. It's about the delay of gratification. Self-regulation is about more than just delay of gratification. What's wonderful about the video is that you get a real sense of how hard it is, how much energy kids use up, to resist eating the marshmallow. You see four year olds doing all sorts of things to keep themselves from eating a marshmallow. They swing their legs. The sniff but don't touch it. They gnaw away at a little bit of it. All these behaviours are aimed at trying to inhibit the impulse to eat the marshmallow. That's self-control. The video viewer sees the use of different levels of energy that kids use to keep from eating the marshmallow.

At the end of the experiment, one little boy hears a noise outside the room and turns around quickly. He's on high alert. You can imagine how high his engine is running to keep from eating the treat. And then he released his energy quickly. Suddenly, he's stuffed the two marshmallows into his mouth. Other children sat calmly. Delay of gratification is an executive brain function in the thinking part of the brain, the prefrontal cortex in the top of the brain. Researchers in this experiment followed up on the children who participated. They found that kids who were able to delay gratification at 4 years old, were doing far better at school and in their relationships when they were 15 years old. That was one finding. The whole study has been under scrutiny for some time however as many factors can complicate a child's behaviour. I use it solely to illustrate self-control. Some other experiments looked at pre-conditions affecting children before the experiment took place.[23] In the original Marshmallow Experiment, things were pretty calm for the kids before the experience began. But what if the children were stressed before it began? What if they were poor and hungry? These researchers asked what would happen if kids had to sit in a room where there were fresh baked cookies and were told they couldn't eat them. Their level of stress would be on high at the start, before the Marshmallow Test even began. What did these researchers find out? They discovered this pre-condition stressed the children and most were unable to delay their gratification. In the second experiment, the stress of not eating the cookies was already depleting their energy. As they were faced with a new challenge, they weren't able to be successful.

One of the things I like to use the video for is to explain executive function. Executive function is like the C.E.O. of our brain. It involves impulse inhibition, working memory and cognitive flexibility. It's a higher order function because it involves more of the prefrontal cortex. It's development starts in the toddler, pre-school years and continues into adolescence. The executive function is hugely important for someone to be able to do well in school. For example, a child needs to know why he or she needs to sit still (impulse inhibition). The executive function is employed when we're listening to the teacher and helps us figure out (remember or keep in mind) why we're doing all the things we're asked to do in school (working memory).

So let's go back to the Marshmallow Test. 10 minutes into the experiment, the child asks herself why she's not eating the marshmallow? The thinking brain reminds her that, Oh yes, it's because I'm going to get two if I wait now (working memory). With the use of the executive function, a child has cognitive flexibility. As

175

an example, the child might think: Okay, if I have to sit here for 15 minutes what can I come up with to be able to deal with that stressor. I'll tap my fingers, wiggle my toes, look out the window, think about my mommy and that I'll tell her I didn't eat the marshmallow and then I got two of them. When you think about the challenges of school, being self-regulated allows the child to recognize a situation, analyze a situation and come up with solutions.

Dr Shanker's method is about much more than self-control or delay of gratification. With the Shanker method or framework, he outlines five steps in his strategy to help with the development of self-regulation. These steps include the following:

- Read and reframe the behaviour
- Recognize the stressors
- Reduce the stressors
- Reflect and develop self-awareness
- Respond with self-regulating strategies to promote growth and restoration.

Here is an example of how to apply Shanker's method to a specific situation:

Situation:
Suppose you're in the grocery store. Your young child desperately wants to have a chocolate bar. When he can't have it, he has a meltdown. Some approaches say that the parent should simply ignore the behaviour or just walk away from the child who's rolling on the floor and crying loudly. Let's look at a different approach that's represented in the following interaction between parent and child and that's aimed at building self-regulation.

Conversation:
Child: I want a chocolate bar. He throws himself on the ground and starts yelling.

Step one: Parent looks at the child and thinks to herself that this is stress behaviour and asks herself what might be the stressor. She asks herself what the child needs.

Step two: Parent reflects and says, it looks like you really want a chocolate bar. I wonder if you're hungry?
Child: Yes. The child is still rolling around and crying.

Step three: Parent says, I know you're upset. I know you really want a chocolate bar. But we're not having that just now. I have a snack and a book in the car for you. Let's think about something that will be fun to do when we get home. Parent also thinks to herself: Don't go shopping just before supper with a hungry toddler.

Step Four: Parent arrives at home and says, You were really upset when we were in the grocery store. What was upsetting you?

Child: I really wanted to get a chocolate bar.
Parent: Well, we weren't able to do that today, were we? And look, now you're fine. You were able to handle that.

Step Five: Is not specifically used in this example, but it might include teaching the child deep breathing techniques, or helping the child recognize what helps him to be calm. As a parent, when you respond to the child's use of a self-regulating strategy, you promote growth and the restoration of the child's energy expenditure.

Another strategy in the Shanker method focuses on 5 domains that may be influenced by stress and helps adults ask questions that will ease the situation. These domains include the following: the biological domain (is the child tired or hungry or sick?); the emotional domain (is the child wondering whether my mom likes my brother better, I don't like trying something new, I'm disappointed); the cognitive domain (is the child thinking, I'm stupid and I can't do this math, there isn't enough time to do all this); the social domain (is the child thinking that no one is playing with me at school, I don't want to ignore Janie; and the pro-social domain (is the child wondering, why don't I get other people's jokes, I hate waiting my turn, I'm worried about my friend who's sick and sad).

Here's another example. I had a conversation with a colleague recently and we were talking about Shanker's framework. It seemed to apply beautifully. She has a ten-year-old son. He visits his dad on the weekends. When he comes home on Sunday night, he's supposed to have a shower. When that's presented to him, he typically has a meltdown. On one occasion, his mom's partner used the word stupid. He had a meltdown. Her partner had not been referring to her son, but when she used the word, the boy was extremely upset and demanded to know why she could use the word stupid but he couldn't. The boy said that she had to put a quarter in the swear jar. His mother was flummoxed. What do I do about this? So we walked through the whole scene.

To begin with, we noted that in terms of stressors:

- Physical Stressor: he's exhausted because it's late. He also hasn't eaten yet and is exhausted from having to play nicely at his dad's all the time so he can build on that relationship.
- Emotional Stressor: mom could ask herself whether he's emotionally strung out? Does he have a hard time with mom's new partner who just recently moved in? Is he still grieving the loss of his parents being together?
- Cognitive Stressor: he had to do his homework first. Mom could ask whether he's challenged about the homework. Has he already had to make too many decisions and has decision fatigue? Does he have a learning difficulty?
- Social Stressor: mom could ask herself if there's something going on with peers at school and whether he's worried about Monday morning?
- Pro-social Stressor: Does he worry about some of the kids in the class whose parents have been off work because of Covid 19 so that he can't see his best friend or cousins?

By using Shanker's approach in terms of the boy's behaviour, you analyze the five domains and ask if something is happening biologically, emotionally, cognitively socially or pro-socially to stress him. After this examination, you can start realizing where the behaviour might come from. This is very different from other approaches. In fact, it's an exquisite approach because you dive deeply into where the behaviour is coming from. The parent asks, How might I behave to help relieve stress and offer self-regulation strategies? She asks herself if the behaviour is stress based. She asks where is the stress coming from. She also begins to ask how to reduce the stressors. As well, she asks herself how she might help her son become aware of the stress. What strategies can he use to manage it?

CONCLUSION

In this chapter, I hope I've conveyed that it takes a village to help kids develop self-regulation. The basic building block of attachment is essential for establishing co-regulation. A child learns self-regulation through the face-to-face, serve and return, co-regulating social interactions with adults and peers in their lives. I also discussed the significance of environments we create for children as we aim to support them in learning how to become the boss of their own emotions, thoughts and actions. The family is one of those environments. And it's important to start thinking about the positive role dad's and partners play in a child's life.

Children acquire the ability to self-regulate by first being co-regulated. That developing capacity to pay attention to their caregivers increases a child's internalization and the regulation of intention during the techniques I've presented in this chapter. The child is best raised in a environment of co-operation. As one example, some Indigenous traditions talk about having five adults in a child's life, metaphorically cradling a child in the palm of their hand. In addition, I have to say again, how important it is for parents to dialogue about how each one contributes to family life. In summary, an adult's positive mindset toward children and youth is key to learning self-regulation.

We've also looked at the question of whether the current school system is working in a way to maximize child development and learning. Are we creating the learning environments that kids need to be successful and thrive? In this chapter, I also had the pleasure of sharing with you the work of Dr Stuart Shanker. The MEHRIT centre[24], which he founded in 2012, works toward a vision of calm, alert and flourishing children, youth and adults. My hope is that my readers will look into the MEHRIT Centre's contribution. Their mission is to ground learning and living in mindful self-regulation. I continue to use and champion Shanker's approach because I see so clearly it's positive effects spreading across Canada. It's having great success helping adults understand and practice what children need in order to learn self-regulation.

9

Well Being and Anxiety

INTRODUCTION

There are connections between self-regulation and anxiety I want to draw out in this chapter. In the previous chapter, I defined self-regulation in simplistic terms as becoming the boss of one's own thoughts, emotions and actions. I also described a second way of understanding self-regulation that focuses on the energy exerted when a stress event takes place and someone is trying to recover. I emphasized that environments we create for children and teens, at home and school, have potential to help or hinder their developing self-regulation. My purpose in this chapter is to say that anxiety creates a challenge for self-regulation and I want to offer insight and relief to those who want to help the children and adolescents that they parent and teach.

A common definition of anxiety is the apprehension or excessive fear a person experiences about real or imagined circumstances. Anxiety can be triggered. These triggers might come from inside the body or from outside the body. In this chapter, I introduce the concept of anxiety in children and youth, but I won't delve into different types of anxiety disorder, which would be beyond the scope of this book. Rather, I'll talk about the physiology of anxiety in general.

As we begin to talk about anxiety, we first need to consider how we understand mental health. The World Health Organization talks about mental health as a state of complete physical, mental and social well-being.[1] Mental health isn't merely the absence of disease. That's a really important concept. In order to be well, we need balance among the physical, mental, social and spiritual aspects of our lives. In this chapter, I begin by stating principles that apply to how we understand anxiety in children and teens. I want to say again how important connection is to helping people cope with anxiety. In addition, I'll describe normal anxiety and clearly distinguish it from anxiety disorders. I'll provide some guidance as to what's going on in the brain when anxiety takes over and offer some hopeful ways to respond to the children and youth who suffer. My goal is to provide practical ways to foster healthy mental health in our adult relationships with children and youth.

PRINCIPLES TO CONSIDER FIRST

Before we start to talk about anxiety in general, I'll describe a number of other principles for understanding the current state of children's mental health by elaborating on the following changes in the way parents, teachers and professionals approach children. In summary, we need to

- Turn away from over diagnosing
- Understand the whole child in his or her whole environment
- Practice and teach children the opening and closing of communication circles
- Demonstrate and teach the human art of repairing relationships
- Understand and apply the practice of a positive psychology approach
- Work with a wellness framework

To start with, psychologists and psychiatrists have spent decades figuring out psychopathology. I was trained in psychopathology. I'm experienced in knowing how to diagnose conditions such as Attention Deficit Hyper Activity Disorder (ADHD), Autism Spectrum Disorder (ASD), Obsessive Compulsive Disorder (OCD), and Foetal Alcohol Spectrum Disorder (FASD). But the biggest issue for psychopathology is OLD—the Over Labelling Disorder. We've become experts at diagnosing, but not at understanding the dilemmas or life circumstances children and youth experience. What we haven't become expert at is identifying the strengths in a person's life and finding what's positive in that life. I know I can diagnose a kid pretty quickly with criteria I have at my disposal. In contrast to the psychopathology approach, others have thought that we should focus on developing positive attributes of children's lives. Our pre-occupation with pathology has not helped diminish the number of children with problems. As we come to the topic of anxiety, it's essential to think about the consequences of a focus on diagnosis as part of the dilemma. We've been using psychopathology's approaches for many decades, but, in that time, we haven't improved the over all well-being of Canadian children. We know so much about diagnosis. We know so much about drugs. We know so much about evidence-based treatments. But we're not moving the needle forward on the well-being of Canadian children. In fact, I can show the statistics on anxiety. They tell us that anxiety disorders have gone up from 9% to 13% in the past three decades, but the perception of having anxiety struggles has tripled.[2] So we need to shift our model. We need to be thinking about creating positive mental health, right from the start. We need to be thinking about giving kids the skills they need to deal with the bumps that every child will experience along the road. We're not doing that—we're not teaching children those skills. Hopefully, we're starting to, but we're just at the beginning of that movement. In order to improve the mental health of children, we need to do different things, not just do things differently.

What I've learned in my 30 or more years of clinical practice is that it doesn't matter how good I am at organizing behaviour into diagnostic categories. If I don't understand the dilemma of the family and the child, I can't really help them fully. I need to understand the context that a child and family are living in. If I don't understand all this, I might as well just be a computer—just fill in the Jean screen and click a button to get an answer! So it's really important to understand the whole picture that includes the child, the family and even the neighbourhood.

Another principle I want to explain has to do with a particular way of thinking about communication that was introduced by an American psychiatrist, Stanley Greenspan. He was a lovely man who died too soon and who really helped change our view on how social and emotional development unfolds. As part of the work he did, he describes opening and closing circles of communication[3] For example, a child smiles and gurgles at a parent. That's opening the circle. The parent smiles and coos back. That's closing the circle. In order for people to be happy in their social and emotional development, it's important that they experience and know how to open and close a communication circle. We can understand this development very easily in the early years but it's absolutely essential throughout childhood and adolescence. Many of us in my field worry that social media are having a significant influence on this core human need of opening and closing communication circles and may in fact be leading to more anxiety.

Another principle has to do with a human capacity for repairing relationships. As parents or clinicians who have an ongoing relationship with family members or clients, we always have an opportunity to repair disruptions in personal connections. Human beings would be lost without our capacity to repair and therefore restore our relationships. Repair is made possible by building emotional connectedness so that kids feel felt by you. If you can establish a secure connection with kids, you can admit you screwed up during a particular interaction. If you have that connection, you can say, hey, I didn't get that quite right. I'd like to stop and rewind what I said (or did). You can also ask for more information from the other person, if something between you goes wrong.

But if you think of the example of the mom and child in the last chapter on self-regulation, it's harder to repair an interaction if you've already given the kid the chocolate bar that they threw the tantrum to get you to buy. The ability to repair an interaction is different from automatically saying no all the time and it's different from saying yes all the time. An opportunity to repair requires some of the same adult self-regulation outlined in the previous chapter. In order to help children stay calm, we need to lend them our calm.

The ability to lend our calm to children requires that we're able to take a positive approach and have self-awareness. Martin Seligman, a US based psychologist, was one of the founding fathers of the positive psychology movement. He has a model of well-being and happiness that's made up of the following 5 core elements. It's called the PERMA model.[4]

- P stands for positive emotions, feeling good
- E stands for engagement, finding flow
- R is relationship, authentic connections
- M is for meaning, purposeful existence
- A is achievement, a sense of accomplishment

He says that for us to have psychological well-being and happiness we need to have all 5 of these elements in our lives.

As I think about anxiety and wellness, I'm also drawn to the First Nations' Mental Wellness Continuum Framework.[5] In that model, mental wellness is a balance among the mental, physical, spiritual and emotional aspects of being. This balance is enriched as individuals have the following:

- Purpose in daily life, whether through education or employment
- Care giving activities, or cultural ways of being and doing
- Hope for their future and those of their families, grounded in a sense of identity
- Unique Indigenous values and having a belief in spirit
- A sense of belonging and connectedness within families, community and culture
- A sense of meaning and understanding about how their lives and those of their families and communities are part of creation that's built on a rich history.

The parallels between these two ways of thinking about mental health are easy to see.

So in the same way that it's important for adults to express self-regulation as they teach children self-regulation, it's important for adults to ask questions about their own mental health. I think about this a lot when I examine my own life. Am I creating the conditions for me to be well? Am I thinking about whether I have a sense of purpose? Do I have a sense of hope and belonging? Do I have meaning in my daily life? These questions are a mental health check up and are especially important at certain stages of life.

As one example, my husband is approaching retirement. We'll be asking ourselves these questions a lot more than we usually do. In terms of retirement, we'll likely ask ourselves whether there's something in his world, as he changes from being a doctor who loves to teach to someone who no longer does that, that will continue to provide meaning and purpose. How can we create conditions for his well-being? When we think about kids with mental health challenges, we also need to think beyond symptoms they express to reflect on their whole lives in terms of the issues named within these two frameworks for wellness. We need to be thinking about life situations from a holistic perspective, and as Seligman proposes, we need to think from a positive psychology approach.

THE NEED TO CONNECT

As we think about wellness generally in discussing anxiety, there's scientific research to show that people who spend time being grateful actually rewire their brains and are happier. One way I've heard people express this practice is in terms of taking in the good and being grateful. When we take on practices like this, we express gratitude and give thanks as part of our daily routines. I've heard many people treat this kind of advice as airy-fairy, frivolous or not serious. But we're aware now that finding activities that engage us in gratitude is important to mental health.

In terms of well-being, we can ask whether we've got meaningful activities, tasks, relationships and events going on in our lives? What does it look like to have meaningful activities going on? Let me use myself as one example. I used to use a sewing machine a lot. Recently, I came back to sewing, so I'm taking a quilting course. Previously, I looked at quilting and thought it was too detailed a craft and I wouldn't like it. But now I sit and put together little pieces of cloth and I'm being so accurate. I enjoy the whole process. As I quilt, I realize I'm in what Hungarian-American psychologist Csikszentmihalyi called Flow[6] - time passes for me without me knowing it. I'm completely absorbed. I love the quilting work I do. I get something very different from creating quilts than I do when I'm making a presentation to groups of people. Both of these aspects of my life are important and offer support to each other. I feel connected to myself when I'm quilting. I feel connected to myself and others when I'm presenting.

We also need relationships that create authentic connections. I feel blessed by my many friendships with people who understand how to connect with me. When I spend time with them, we feel felt by each other. That feeling of togetherness is at the core of what allows us to relax. As I travel across the country, I've noticed that, as anxiety increases, so does social isolation. People seem to have fewer and fewer meaningful connections. Where are those places where you sense and enjoy unconditional love and where what you do matters to people that you see regularly? As we talk about how to address anxiety, activities that provide meaning and relational connection are very important.

In terms of wellness, we need to seek meaning and purpose in life and enjoy a sense of accomplishment. When we think about mental health, we can think of it as a disease or we can think of it as a continuum that moves from well being on one side to having emotional problems or concerns to experiencing mental illness at the other end. All of us are on that continuum. It's not an either-or experience. It's not that one person has mental health issues and another person doesn't. Many of us, myself included, have struggled with depression. Yet I function very well. So where am I on the Continuum? In the old disease model, I'd be diagnosed with mental illness and other people would have mental health. What I understand now is that we can have well-lived lives even if we struggle with various illnesses, including anxiety.

A CLOSER LOOK AT ANXIETY

Sometimes parents or kids wonder whether they're experiencing an anxiety disorder. As one example, a senior high school student might tell me: "I get so nervous before a test. I need to get exempted from this exam." As I sit with this student, I can help him realize that what he's experiencing is pretty normal. Everybody gets anxious when they're going out on a first date or sitting for an exam. When I'm with a student like this one, I would first explore with him what his fear is about in terms of the exam. I would ask him about other aspects of his life to hear how anxiety is interfering with those aspects. What we're seeing so much of today is that young people are experiencing uncomfortable feelings and worrying that there's something wrong with them. They wonder if they have a disorder.

I'm very much enjoying the work of Mark Bracket and his book Permission to Feel from the Yale Centre for Emotional Intelligence[7]. He has developed a model called RULER for understanding our emotions

R: Recognizing emotions in self and others
U: Understanding the causes and consequences of emotions
L: Labelling emotions accurately
E: Expressing emotions effectively
R: Regulating emotions effectively

I think that Marc has it right. Many people, including children and youth, have never been taught or developed the social and emotional skills they need to manage and cope with the challenges of everyday struggles. Teaching these skills is a direction we need to see schools moving toward.

So what is anxiety? First of all, it's something all of us experience at some point in time. It's also different for different people. For example, when I think of my 5 children, some of them are more prone to worry or anxious thoughts than others. It seems to be in their nature. I remember when one son was three years old and was going over to the little wading pool near our house. He was worried about going into the water. I asked him what he was worried about.

He responded by saying that maybe the lifeguard forgot to tell us one of the rules. As I listened to him worry about not knowing all the rules, I wondered what I did wrong as his parent. I thought to myself, so how did I screw up my child? Isn't that the joy of guilt in parenthood? But I know I'm not alone. As I learned more lessons about temperament and from the rest of my kids, I came to realize how ordinary were my three year old son's worries.

An example of the differences among my children is captured by this story. When one son was starting High School I couldn't drive him for some reason. I don't remember why. So his older brother drove him to the new school. The older brother was much more anxious about his younger brother starting High School than the younger boy was. My younger son assured his older brother he was fine, everything would be fine—he could deal with it. As I was writing a paper on the feeling of belonging at school, I asked my kids about this experience. As we talked about the event, I asked the younger son what it was like to start High School. He remembered his brother taking him and said he was a bit nervous but knew he'd make new friends. These two sons are different from one another, biologically and psychologically.

Part of these differences is built by experience. The older boy had more anxiety starting High School and worried about who he would sit with at lunchtime. The younger boy is an extrovert. He was sure he'd find somebody to hang out with. All of us experience anxiety at some time. It's a normal developmental pattern that exhibits itself differently as children grow older. We may see more anxiety in younger children on average as they're trying to figure out the world.

In addition, anxiety can arise from either imagined or real circumstances. When I was working in Ontario as a consultant, I worked in urban and rural settings. I recall one city patient who was afraid of tornadoes. He'd never experienced a tornado or even seen one. He only watched the news. Then I worked in a rural area and met a kid who was afraid of tornadoes. But his fear was based on the loss of 6 of their cows that were taken up in the vortex of a tornado. What's real and what's imagined is very much contextually based. Both of these children experienced the physical reactions of anxiety.

As mentioned at the beginning of the chapter, a common definition of anxiety is the apprehension or excessive fear a person experiences about real or imagined circumstances. Anxiety can be triggered and these triggers might come from inside the body or from outside the body. It's essential to help children understand that anxiety is normal. When you've got a normal trigger, a first date, preparing for an exam, a first concert, going outside and being afraid of bugs at 4 years old or giving a speech—all these things create the biological response I'm going to describe in this section.

A biological response gets turned on if a person's stress system is triggered. This creates a feeling of apprehension, edginess and may even create sensations of nausea. With normal anxiety, these feelings and sensations are transient. They go away. They don't significantly interfere with daily life. The typical experience of normal anxiety doesn't prevent a person from achieving their goals and so it doesn't hinder their developing solid sense of well-being.

As I encounter the number of young people who are concerned with anxiety, I have a hypothesis: I suggest that many are labelling themselves as having anxiety disorder, when what they have is a typical anxious response. At this point, there's no stigma attached to having an anxiety disorder, as there was in the past. We've also been very clear about its symptoms. I suggest that young people experience normal anxiety and they worry that it's 'a thing' they have rather than a transient experience that everyone goes through. These young people are unaware that anxiety disorder is very different from transient anxiety.

Anxiety disorder interferes with a person's ability to live a well-rounded life. By its diagnostic criteria, it has to be interfering with daily life. If people have anxiety disorder, it will preoccupy them. It will stop them from going to school or out with friends. Earlier I mentioned the young man who felt he had a disorder. In particular, he felt he couldn't do exams at university. So to get the full context, I asked him if he was going out with his friends. Yes, he's doing that. I asked if he was playing hockey? Yes, he's doing that. He has anxiety. I'm not sure it's a disorder. Does he enjoy multiple aspects of life? If his answer is yes, the anxiety is transient, not a disorder. I focus on this for two reasons. Firstly we know that educating young people about their bodily reaction to anxiety can help them develop strategies to combat anxious thoughts, and secondly, the treatment of the disorder often includes the use of medication.

Unlike this young fellow, I've spoken with others who are paralyzed with fear about being in any crowded space. They can't go to school, the mall, or interact with friends apart from online. This we would classify as anxiety disorder. To be clear, both of these young people experience significant distress. But how they think about their symptoms affects how they feel and affects how they act. It's different working with the university student than with the other young people. The university student may benefit greatly from some strategies to reflect on how he thinks about exams and develop strategies to combat the negative thinking. We call this cognitive behaviour therapy (CBT). The others are more severely affected and may need a combination of CBT, exposure therapy, or even medication.

Anxiety can run in families. I remember a good friend of my husband's who worked with him. This man told my husband he wanted to talk to me about his daughter. She felt a lot of anxiety. She wasn't going to school, could hardly sleep and worried all the time so that her life was very much affected by worry. He told me that her situation was agony for him because he recalled feeling this way when he was her age. In their case, those genes are pretty strong. The great thing is that, as I was talking with him, I asked what helped him at her age. As we discussed his experience, I asked if he could bring that help to his daughter. He thought he could.

Is there a reliable estimate for the number of young people with anxiety disorder in Canada? We have to ask two other questions before we can answer this one: What is normal? What is a clinical anxiety disorder? We know that in available studies on anxiety disorder in Ontario, the number of children with anxiety disorder shows up around 13% of children and adolescents.[8] Anxiety disorder among young people is high at 13% That's one young person in seven with anxiety disorder. Based on this research, how many children in a typical school classroom are going to have significant mental health problems? What's so difficult is that 75% of the children and youth who are affected, in some of the current research studies, don't get help.[9] When we look at all of this, many kids have symptoms of anxiety but don't meet the criteria for a disorder. In the same way that I think we don't give kids the tools to deal with self-regulation, we're not giving kids the skills they need to help them recover from transient anxiety. If kids have those skills, thought processing might learn will sound something like the following personally reflective inner dialogue: "Okay, I'm feeling anxious. I'm identifying that my thoughts are taking me down a route that's just going to get my gut going. If my gut starts, it's just going to make me not want to go to school."

Anxiety has to do with thoughts, feelings and actions, as conveyed in the following example. In anxiety disorder, thoughts, feelings and action all work together to interfere a person's ability to carry on with ordinary life.

Thought:
• I'm going to fail this exam
• I'm going to be a disaster
• I'm never going to graduate from high school

Feelings
• Apprehension
• Tightness in the stomach
• Pain in some part of the body—starts to really hurt

Thought:
• Something bad is going to happen
• I'm sick
• I can't go to school

Action
• The young person doesn't go to school or go out with friends or play soccer.

Making the Right Distinctions

When we're trying to figure out whether a child or adolescent is experiencing anxiety disorder, rather than transient anxiety, we can ask questions about the object of their anxiety—what they're anxious about. For example, we ask whether this particular object of anxiety is one that a child at this age is normally worrying about. It's very common for 4 and 5 year olds to be afraid of death. It's pretty normal for them to be afraid of bugs or going down basement stairs. It's common for 8 year olds to be afraid of changing their clothes in front of other people. Suddenly, they have an awareness of personal differences and a fear of changing in front of others. As we consider anxiety, we look at the timing and intensity of what a child is feeling and expressing. We can ask if the degree of distress is realistic or unrealistic, given the child's developmental stage and the object of concern.

So it's unrealistic for the child who lives in the city to be worried about tornadoes to the same degree as the kid does who can't find his 6 cows. Does the city kid's intensity regarding his fear of tornadoes make a whole lot of sense? What about the kid who worries that all the kids at school will be talking about her because she has a pimple, so she won't go to school. What can we say about the intensity of her worry? Does the anxiety interfere with the child's daily life? We can also ask whether the child or teen can rebound from it?

Here's the real challenge. We've got a large percentage of children who actually have the disorder. Up to now in this chapter, I've been talking about a large group of young people who don't have the disorder. The good news is that we have strategies to help kids with anxiety disorder. But kids aren't getting into therapy. The wait lists in Canada are very long. Why is that? It has to do with whether our society recognizes and responds to the problem.

When the Mental Health Commission looked at spending in Canada on health and mental health, their conclusion was that mental health has been an orphan in the health care system—it was no one's offspring.[10] If we look further into health care spending and focus on child and youth mental health, we realize this category is treated as an orphan of the orphan, evidenced by how little money is spent on child and youth mental health. How can we reach young people in Canada and help them with anxiety disorder—even though we know we could help them—if we focus so few resources on their concerns?

STRESS, ANXIETY AND THE BRAIN

In order to go deeper into what anxiety means, we need to understand the physiology of stress. We used to think that when we experience a stressor, it came from inside or outside the person. As an example, we have a thought that stresses us: we see a bully walking down the road toward us and we're all alone. When we see the bully, a physiological or bodily sensation of arousal affects much of our body. This is also when the immune system can be activated, which I will describe later on.

When there's a problem with the immune system, people are more likely to get other immune system issues as well. A physiological response begins in our brains. Signals are sent and the pupils in the eye become dilated. The face becomes flushed. The heart races. This is a body response to getting ready for fight or flight. That's what the stress response system is—preparing for action to stay safe. You breathe faster. You sweat more. You've got less blood going to your hands. You've got more blood going to your legs so you can run away. You have less blood flow to your digestion.

All of those reactions are turned on when someone is exposed to a stressor. These are the normal physiological responses that get turned on whether the stressor is that I've lost my keys or a sabre tooth tiger is chasing me. It's the same stress system that gets turned on. But its amount is very different. It stays on longer if a tiger is chasing me than if I've lost my keys. The Harvard Center on the Developing Child is a good site to visit because they talk about levels of stress.[11] Positive stress, which is good for us in order to do well in life, helps us get up in the morning, get to work, stay at work and keep going through the day. We need this positive stress and it's tolerable.

But here's a big difference. Tolerable stress is buffered by supportive relationships. When my brother was dying, he had a very nasty disease, Parkinson's and dementia. It was very hard for my family, but we were able to manage due to the support we gave each other. It was very stressful for me because when he was dying, I couldn't walk. I couldn't move. I had injured my knee and was in constant pain. That was incredibly stressful for me. But my family were around me. They understood. My sister would go to visit him and tell him that I couldn't be there, but that I loved him. She made a very difficult time tolerable for me. I was able to cope and eventually recovered from my physical pain.

What we really worry about is toxic stress. This is stress that's prolonged. The stress system is activated but there are no protective factors. In chapter three, I discussed the nature of stress and described the approach of Sonia Lupien who uses the acronym NUTS[12] to identity that a stress system is activated in a situation that is

- Novel; something is new
- Unpredictable: no way of knowing whether it might occur
- Poses a Threat to the ego: a feeling that your competence is questioned
- Sense of control; a feeling that you have little or no control in a situation

Stress is NUTS under these conditions.

A dominant feeling (fear) that's connected to these situations is that something bad might happen. When you think of situations in which kids are having meltdowns, one important response is to ask what makes the situation NUTS for them. When they're having difficulty and demonstrating challenging behaviour, try to figure out what's NUTS for them. When someone gets stressed, the amygdala deep in our brain sends a signal through the hypothalamus, the pituitary and the adrenal cortex (the HPA axis). There's a release of different neural factors. So we've get a cascade of chemical messengers telling the body: "Be prepared. Get on guard. This is a dangerous time! Under these conditions, adrenaline releases so that someone can run. Cortisol, which helps with healing if it's at the right dosage, is released so that you can keep on running. It's a body chemical that causes the vessels to constrict. In a stress situation, adrenaline and cortisol work together.

For example, if you're out picking blueberries and you run into a bear, you don't stop and say, "Oh my goodness is that blueberries on your tongue or is that blood?" You're going zoom—"I need to get out of here." The physiology of the body is exquisitely tuned so that when we see something scary like a snake, we're not going say how very interesting that slithering object is. We're going to say, "I need to get out of here right now." Our stress response system keeps us safe. But we need to be able to turn the tap off. The body's way of turning off the tap is through the hippocampus, the new learning and memory part of the brain. It has the capacity to turn off the stress by turning off the adrenalin and cortisol taps.

There are receptors on the hippocampus that are sensitive to cortisol. How many of those receptors a person will have on the hippocampus is very much determined by how much stress a person experienced early in life. If you don't have many cortisol receptors, there's no place for it to go, so it hangs around longer. This situation also has an impact on some of the blood products in our bodies that help fight inflammation. Some of these blood products include white blood cells and cytokine, which make up part of our inflammatory response system. So you can imagine if they're being turned on all the time, it will have negative impacts on the body and may lead to conditions such as autoimmune diseases like fibromyalgia.

All these body responses are interconnected. Because the hippocampus is affected early by high stress, and if it doesn't have enough receptors to suck up the cortisol and so that cortisol hangs around longer, the potential for high stress to have negative impacts is high. Two areas that are affected by high, continuing levels of cortisol are the hippocampus itself and the prefrontal cortex, both essential areas for learning. As a consequence, we need to be pretty anxious about hearing that our kids are talking about anxiety.

Why do we need to be anxious? As I discussed, the brain is affected by all the experiences that occur. If young people are bathed in anxiety, that anxiety is going to change their brain. I've mentioned that areas acutely sensitive to these chemicals are the top part of the brain where thinking happens, where problem-solving and impulse inhibition all reside. So you put that together with one 2017 Toronto Star report that almost 50% of Ontario's youth say they miss school because of anxiety, and you have a serious problem.[13]

In Ontario, the Centre for Addiction and Mental Health does a large survey every two years. In the survey they ask students from grades 7 to 12 a series of questions about drug use and mental health.[14] They ask these students whether they've ever experienced moderate to serious psychological distress in the past year. In 2015, the data identified that 34% of students reported moderate to severe psychological distress. This percentage increased in 2017 to 37%. Likewise, when asked about their serious distress, it too increased from 14% in 2015 to 19% 2017. So our kids are the canary in the mineshaft. Recall that this phrase comes from using canaries to detect toxic levels of gas in a mine. If the canary dies, miners know the level of gas is toxic for them as well. The canaries give us a warning. Our kids are giving us a warning that there's something in the environment that's harmful to their development.

Anxiety is experienced on a large scale. Children who live with too much stress can become anxious. Those kids are my main concern. Stress can exist in the family or in the neighbourhood, but one thing teachers across the country are telling me is that they worry parents may be inadvertently contributing to making kids more anxious. For example, teachers tell me that they have confidence that some kids are capable of writing an exam. But rather than giving the child this opportunity, parents come in and insist their child has an anxiety problem that needs to be identified so their child can be exempted from the exam. These parents believe that their child can't do what teachers believe they can do. These parents appear to be very worried but also perhaps overprotective.

RESPONDING TO ANXIETY

As I explain anxiety to a child, I use porcupine and hippo puppets to help me. I want children to understand what's going on when they feel anxious. I say that symptoms of anxiety have thoughts, physical feelings and behaviours. The nice part about breaking it down is that I have three ways to target the help I want to offer children.

So I try to talk about the physiology of how the body turns on. I hope it helps them to be able to think about what it means if they have a tummy ache. I've had so many patients referred to me because they're not going to school. When I start getting their history, I find out they've been complaining about tummy aches for a long time before they stopped going to school. I ask when the tummy aches started. In fact, tummy aches are a sign of anxiety and are very commonly experienced. Other symptoms, generally in youth, include heart palpitations, abdominal pain, nausea, headaches and perspiration—all of which result from having adrenaline and cortisol turned on.

Anxious youths experience more physical difficulties and complaints due to the thoughts they begin to have about what's wrong with them. They're more sensitive to physical sensations, which in turn is due to thoughts they begin to have to explain to themselves what's going on. As an example, a youth might think, "Oh no, this headache I have, I must have a brain tumour. My stomach aches. I must have cancer." As a result, they start to become hyper aware of body sensations. Their tendency is to catastrophize their situation and this reaction is very common.

The good thing is that this tendency to go to the worst case is easier to target with help. That is, it's intellectually easier to target with help. To catastrophize a situation is to blow things out of proportion. For example, an adolescent girl might think, "Mom's late, that means she's been run over by a truck." Or a boy might think, "I didn't do well in this exam. I'm going to be a bum on the street who will never graduate from high school." Overestimating, or expecting the worst will happen, goes along with repeatedly thinking what if, what if, what if. "What if the teacher calls on me? I always get the wrong answer. What if I throw up when I go to school?" In response to these worries, there's a tendency to avoid the situation that might bring them on. So, the youth says to himself, "How can I escape looking stupid? Well, I just won't go to school, so the teacher can't ask me anything." To add to the complexity, in these situations, parents might think that they're a bad parent because their child is refusing to go to school.

So with physical symptoms, very often kids learn relaxation skills while they're in treatment. They learn to use their body sensitivity to focus on realizing, "Hey, my heart is racing. I need to stop what I'm thinking for a minute and just focus on my breathing." The break in that cycle of thinking helps children develop alternate strategies. They learn to move from anxious thoughts to coping thoughts. Thought, feeling and action are all linked together. What we think affects how we feel and affects how we act.

If a child is worried that nobody will talk to them at a birthday party, they may more rapidly get sweaty. When they feel sweaty, they avoid talking to other kids. Their anxiety becomes self-fulfilling. A child who worries they'll do something stupid or embarrassing if they join the group game at recess starts to feel anxious. They don't risk that situation. Adults can intervene by talking to kids about these thoughts, once they ask children what they're thinking. It's fair to ask children about thoughts they're having about a situation. A particular child might say that she's anxious about joining in with a group. An adult asks her what she's thinking about joining in. What might happen? She responds by saying, "They might make fun of me or might not let me join." The adult responds by saying, "Well, what could you do instead?" The child thinks, "I could find someone to play with all the time and bring her into the group with me." In this way, adult and child start to problem solve and they consider the possibility of acting differently.

Children can be very aware of what they're thinking and feeling, while adults only see the behaviour. One little guy told me he was a worrywart. That's what he'd heard people say about him. I asked him if he thought he worried more than other kids his age. "Yes," he said, "There's no question at all. I worry all the time." Another guy I know with autism talked about his worries. This little boy said that it was like his worries and anxieties were like having a mountain of worms in his tummy. He told me he couldn't climb up to get them quieted. It was a beautiful description. When I'm working with kids with anxiety, I try to help them imagine their thoughts, feelings and actions. I also teach them to imagine what they have in their brains to help them with their feelings, thoughts and action. Part of their brain, the amygdala, is on guard against danger. The thing about people that's different from animals is that we can think our way into thinking there's danger. I tell the child, "That's what makes you feel like your heart is pounding and your tummy is sore." I ask him to think of the amygdala as a porcupine and show him my puppet. When the porcupine senses danger, it shoots out its needles and releases adrenaline and cortisol. It tells him to be on guard, to be anxious about something.

Then I tell him that he's got this good buddy the hippocampus that says he doesn't have to worry about it. I might say to a child, "You're worried something bad will happened to your mom. But your mom always comes home. You know you can call her. You can text her. She'll text you back." One young girl told me that when she imagined all this, instead of the porcupine shooting out adrenalin and cortisol, her porcupine had a straw and was sucking back all the cortisol and adrenaline. Isn't that brilliant? The issue with anxiety is that the brain gets tricked into thinking there's danger when there isn't any. Internal thoughts come into play and the brain registers danger, which starts a physiological cascade that leads to the sensation of anxiety.

HOW CAN ADULTS HELP?

I want to say more about what we can do in response to anxiety. The good news is that there are great strategies. There's lots of research that's coming out of the Sick Kids Hospital in Toronto that describes therapy for kids with anxiety.[15] It really works. In an approach called Cognitive Behaviour Therapy (CBT) you're taught to really look at your thoughts and say how they're affecting your feelings and behaviour. This approach is very effective. Doing homework when you're doing CBT is also very effective. The good news is that we can help people who have anxiety disorder. But for parents and professionals, it's first important to acknowledge that there's distress going on in the young person's life.

Too often parents intuitively say something like, "Oh don't worry about it." Or they might insist that there's nothing to worry about. They say this because they want to relieve the child so he or she isn't so distressed. But it's far better to let them know that you notice something is wrong. You can say, "So what's up? I see that there's something going on." In addition, don't overly pressure a child to talk. Make sure they acknowledge back to you that they are worried about something, at least at some point in the future, if not right away. You want to hear them say, "Yes there's something going on. Yes, my tummy hurts."

Once you've got that information, you can start thinking about the self-regulation framework that I described in chapter 8. By using this framework, you help identify the stressors a child is experiencing and acknowledge to the child you recognize anxiety is due to a stressor. You can ask the child to help you identify what the stressor is. Then, you can begin to consider how to go about reducing that stressor. As I suggested above, strategies such as deep breathing, exercise and relaxation are helpful. You also can ask the child to tell you about the worst thing that could happen. Then, ask what might be a less than the worst thing—which is an action the child could carry out that would help her or him to cope.

How should we behave with the child as we respond to stress? Earlier, I mentioned my husband's friend who was very worried about his daughter. He really had to work on his part, which was to becoming calm and reassuring. He identified so strongly with his daughter's anxiety that he thought he was getting anxious himself. His anxiety was feeding her anxiety. So it became a cycle. It's really important that parents recognize they can lend their own calm to a child. It makes a big difference. A friend of mine, Susan Hopkins, does self-regulation work with children. She recommends that adults bring their "soft eyes" into the situation.[16] She promotes being positive about a child's ability to manage the situation with help. She suggests we tell children they can deal with the situation. In a collaborative spirit, adults assure children they'll come up with things that are going to help. It's very important to convey the hope we have for children and youth so they can reframe the situation positively. It's good to break strategies into small steps that you work on together.

Suppose a child is afraid to go to the mall. She's afraid of going out in public because she has panic attacks. One of the ways people deal with stress is to take their response in small steps. So, her parent suggests they go for a drive around the mall to see if that's helpful. Then, they might come closer to the wall but not go into it. Once the child has some positive experiences, she gets desensitized to the mall and her brain doesn't fire as much. Then, the parent suggests, let's just walk to the mall door. At another point, they walk into the mall. This strategy is carried out in these small, gradual steps so the child's brain can relax in that environment.

Remember to celebrate when a child does well and knows they're doing well. Adults are good at picking out what kids don't do. One of my sons taught me many things. I remember coming into the kitchen after I'd ask him to tidy it up. There was still a huge box in the middle of the floor. I said to him, "I asked you to tidy up the kitchen." He replied, "I did Mom." Then I said, "What about that box?" He said, "What box?" He didn't even notice it. It was huge, big enough for someone to get lost in. I said, "That box there." Then he said to me, "Mom, why is it that you notice the things I don't do, but you don't recognize the things that I do?" Oh, that really got me. Then he jokingly said, "You know, it's no fun being the child of a child psychiatrist."

I have a few more key messages for coping with anxiety. Be a model for your child on how to manage your own anxieties. Help children avoid avoidance by establishing a planned, gradual exposure to the things they fear. Teach your child positive self-talk. There are some really great websites to help with finding strategies. One site is called *Anxiety Canada* (it used to be called *Anxiety B.C.*).[17] Go online and click anywhere there's a plus sign. What you see and hear are stories from the field. Kids who experience anxiety tell their stories. They talk about it. As one example, I saw, "This is Millie, most likely to panic." On the video, she talks about what it feels like to have a panic attack and what she's done to help overcome it. The *Anxiety Canada* site is about kids, for kids and done by kids. Families I've worked with have absolutely loved it. I can't say too often that relationships matter. Being there is hugely important for children and youth. Go places with your child. Provide a set of strategies that are good for kids. Someone told me once that we should give children five positives for every negative. Have one-on-one time with each child. I know that's really hard. But it's important to have fun with and laugh with your children—to convey to them that you enjoy each other.

But I've observed a problem I need to say something more about. Perhaps one parent might express the problem this way: "My child is perfect at school but he's a hellion at home. No one at the school has any idea of how difficult he is at home." What might help the parent to understand is that, at school, these kids use up their self-regulation energy. When they get home, it's all spent. At school, they're using energy to fit in, to not cause trouble and to listen carefully. When they get home, they're completely depleted. When someone is depleted of energy, they may revert to old ways of being. They get cranky. What does that mean for parents?

When kids with anxiety come home, it's important to have a Chill Zone. You want a place where they can just unwind and *chillax,* as they say. It may be a time when you want to have a positive zone with them, but it's more likely they need their own downtime. This might happen by sitting in a reading space. If they like to read, create an area in their room or in the living room where they can just sit and be still. Often, families find that playing video games is a soothing activity but they need to be nonviolent ones, not activating ones. With all the negative interaction that a child with anxiety can experience, it's important to be intentional about making time for fun.

The following ideas summarize a positive response to children and youth who suffer from anxiety:

• Provide positive, active responses whenever possible.
• Listen more than you speak.
• Validate the primary emotion.

One of my colleagues from Walpole Island First Nation told me a story her grandmother used to tell her. Her grandmother told her that people have two ears and only one mouth for a reason. We should be listening at least twice as much. I see families who, when they know that a child is going to be discombobulated by a situation, their response is to think or say, "Well, I'm not going to take them out in that situation." Anxiety becomes a self-fulfilling prophecy.

One of the strongest research findings about school refusal is to not let it start.[18] Have kids go back to school, even if it's only for a short time. Find somebody else to take them to school if the anxiety is very high at the beginning. Don't start the habit of school avoidance. While this is a big demand for parents with children who experience anxiety, recall the self-regulation pattern from the previous chapter. Assert yourself calmly. Connect before you correct or direct. We can think of these encounters as an opportunity to be emotional coaches to your kids, rather than to be a parent who corrects them or intimidates them.

Another key message when working with anxiety is the idea of emotional banking. Stephen Covey, in *The 7 Habits of Highly Effective Families*, first described it.[19] If you think of every interaction as being part of a bank account, when you say something positive, when you smile or acknowledge somebody and give them your attention, you're making a deposit in your shared emotional bank account. If you say something negative or ignore a child, that's a withdrawal from the account. With kids, we want to be sure we're spending a lot of time with them, including the kids teachers work with. Just like checking your bank account to see how much money you have in there, reflect on how you present yourselves to your kids. Ask yourself how much you're depositing and how much you're withdrawing from your joint account? When interacting with kids, it's important that we stick to our values, but if we consider their point of view, we make more deposits than withdrawals.

CONCLUSION

In this chapter I've talked about normal anxiety and distinguished it from an anxiety disorder. It's important when we're with children and youth that we understand both types of anxiety and can identify the differences. It also matters that we help the young know about these differences as well.

Strategies and key messages in the chapter can help you establish a much stronger footing as you work with the young, and also as you consider your own life experiences with anxiety.

I hope I've made it clear that approaches to self-regulation and anxiety have a helpful relationship to each other. We need to work together on these two aspects of becoming boss of one's own thoughts, feelings and actions. I've also made a few references to the roles that media culture can play in both a helpful way (e.g., Anxiety Canada) and in an unhelpful way (e.g., using screen time to avoid face-to-face encounters and therefore not learning what can only be learned in serve and return social interaction). In the next chapter, I want to conclude by focusing on digital culture and its multi-faceted impacts on how we connect with children.

10

Growing Up Digital

INTRODUCTION

I want to address the impact of the digital world on young people. What's interesting is that I wrote this chapter during the CoVid 19 pandemic in 2020 and observed that technology is taking on a completely different role. I recognize I'm going to be painting the dark side of digital culture, because that's where my concern arises. No one could do the work I do and not be compelled to raise the alarm about the deep need to find balance in screen use, due to its deep impact on the brain and on development.

At this point my purpose is to provide parents and teachers with information that will help them make informed decisions along with their young people about digital use. Every time I give a talk, parents and educators express their concern about impacts of technology, in particular social media and screen time, and whether there's a negative effect on mental health. They worry about the effects on the kids' social and emotional development. So what does it mean to be growing up digital? This is an area I'm continually learning more about as I read research on the effects of digital culture on young people. The evidence is evolving.

In this chapter, I'll describe studies that conclude that social media is not good for kids. These studies identify sleep disruption and an increase in anxiety symptoms as part of the harm. Yet, since those early findings, it seems the harm has to do with how much social media is used. I'll review what's known and make suggestions about digital culture based on the best evidence that we have today. Sometimes a historical comparison helps us to understand our current context. I came across a story about a four-generation family who live in Sheffield, England. The great-grandfather George was 8 years old in 1919. During his childhood, he was allowed to roam the whole local area on his own and explore anywhere in it. He was allowed to walk 6 miles from his home to the River Valley to go fishing. When grandfather Jack was age 8 years old in 1950, he was able to walk about a mile on his own to spend time in the woods. When his daughter Vicky was age 8 in 1979, she was allowed to walk to the swimming pool alone, about half a mile away. Her son is now 8 years old and is only allowed to walk alone to the end of his street, which is 300 yards. This boy lives in an ever-shrinking circle, but why, and is his mom's action warranted?

Here are four generations who have gone from a 6-mile freedom to roam alone down to 300 metres of free walking. These limitations make sense to people who think the world is a scary place, e.g., they believe that more kids die or more kids get abducted if kids are out of sight. But this is not the case. For the most part, the Western world is far safer for kids now than it was in 1919. But the perception of danger has skyrocketed. Usually, when I speak about changes in habits such as these, people start talking about what it was like when they were kids. Someone might say that, if they look at their own experience when they were a kid, they got up and went out and played all day. One person told me that they came back when the streetlights were turned on. At one of my presentations, one man told me that his mom locked the door when we were gone and we just came in for feeding. That's all we did.

I actually remember that was true for me. As kids, we did things. We explored. I recall going down a gully miles from my house and learning, after I climbed back up the gully with my friends, that they found some explosives or something down there. It was dangerous, but we didn't know it. But we also learned something about taking risks and being careful on our own too. Are children nowadays missing out on this essential life skill—learning how to take safe risks? Is the world actually a scarier place? Or, do we believe or perceive the world to be really scary? I invite adults to ask themselves these questions. What I hope adults will begin to do more often is to reflect on the actual reality and not solely react to the fear that's prevalent in the common perception.

What are the implications of fear we feel about the world as we interact with kids? How does that fear impact what we allow them to do? The sad reality is that kids aren't going outside to play like they used to. Our fear and perception of danger is keeping them closer to us and closer to home. Studies have shown that this is true not only in Canada but also internationally. One thing that's reported as a difference is that there are so many enticements to stay indoors, such as videos and digital devices. Not only are there enticements, children have less time free from adults. Parents ferry them around far more than ever before.[1] The trouble is that when kids aren't outside, many are in the basement playing inappropriate video games such as Grand Theft Auto or, as I'll explore in this chapter, they're spending much more time in front of screens.

The social world has changed. The digital world has come in at an alarming rate. Radio took 30 years to reach 50 million households. Television took 14 years to reach that wide an audience. In contrast, the Internet took four years to reach 50 million households. And IPads, which came out in 2007, took only 80 days to reach 50 million people. When *Pokémon Go* came out, it took 19 days to reach the same number of participants. Parents and teachers that I speak with tell me they just can't keep up with the speed of change. They're finding it really challenging to adjust. So we've got this rapid explosion and expansion of the digital world. And, we've got parents asking what the rules are for its use. I spoke at a conference in York Region, Ontario held by the School Board there. I was really struck by their student participation and particularly one student's presentation when she reported that she learned lots of things at school, but never how to manage her media use. She asked a room of one thousand educators, "How do I learn to be safe on the Internet?"

Parents and teachers want to know how to use devices effectively. What we need to be thinking about is not just a perception of danger, not just how fast things have escalated; we need to focus on the impact of new devices on the developing brain. I'll explain some of the research, but first we need to think about what exactly we're talking about when we discuss the use of these devices.

DIGITAL CULTURE AND KIDS

Dr. Simon Trepel, a child and adolescent psychiatrist from Winnipeg, suggests that we need to focus on the amount of time spent using digital screen technology.[2] The issue of time includes watching television, VT, Videos, YouTube, Netflix, videoing others, texting, chatting, Snapchat, Facebook, smartphone, iPad, computer gambling and also surfing randomly on the Net. For example, let's focus on screen time and look at the increase in its use. Dr. Trepel states that for more than 50% of teens, screen time is with a Smartphone.[3] The Smartphone is a very popular device. It seems that kids start to use a Smartphone at younger and younger ages. With regards to screen exposure, the average age of screen exposure in 2005 was 4 years old. But by 2012, babies at four months old were exposed to screen time In this context, kids are texting a lot. One estimate I've read says that 78% of teens check their phones hourly. Another estimate in the research about texting says that its use is up to an hour per day. That usage amounts to 60 to 100 texts daily and over 3,000 text a month. Personally, I think this may be a gross underestimation. Keep in mind that many of those texts are in response to parents. Then imagine the increase when kids contact their friends. So that means parents have to be able to cover the cost of a good cell phone plan.

These Smartphones are increasingly present in kids' lives. Research shows that kids are getting phones at younger and younger ages. In 2012, kids got a phone at 12 years old on average. In 2016, the age is 10 years old. So lots of kids own them and lots of kids are spending time on cell phones. Ironically, Bill Gates himself didn't let his kids have phones until they were 14 years of age. What did he know that we didn't know?

Some kids may spend more time on devices than they do sleeping, eating, going to school or spending time with family and friends. Then there's texting in class, so school isn't a break from this pattern of time spent on devices. I have an amusing picture image of a guy with his Smartphone at school. His Smartphone is down by his leg. He's using it to text while he has an extra (fake) sleeve on his desk to make it appear as though he's working with two arms on his desk. The digital world is here. And it's here to stay. What we need to figure out is how we're going to prevent the side effects of too much time spent on devices, and maximize the positive aspects.

I'll say more about the very obvious positive effects of digital culture at the end of this chapter, but I'm focusing on negative effects at this point, because they are what adults worry most about. Negative side effects may include an increase in sedentary behaviour, less physical activity, inadequate nutrition, poor hygiene, obesity and deep vein thrombosis (blood clots in the leg). All these negative effects are as a result of over use and inactivity—of not moving from one's position in front of a screen. In addition, I see some of these side effects when I work with young people who have developed an Internet addiction.

One particularly significant and common issue is disrupted sleep. When young people don't get enough sleep, there are ripple effects on learning and on mood. Excessive digital use has been shown to disrupt sleep patterns in several ways. When I say that young people aren't getting enough sleep, I mean that they're getting less than 7 hours per day. If kids are on screen time or using social media for 2 hours in the evening,[4] it takes longer for them to fall asleep. If young people experience decreased evening sleepiness, they also experience a reduced melatonin secretion. Melatonin is the hormone that tells us it's time to go to sleep. If these conditions arise in young people, they experience less REM (rapid eye movement) sleep and also reduced morning alertness.

The condition of poor sleep is a factor that seems related to depressed mood, a decline in self-esteem and difficulty coping during the day.[5] In fact, the mere presence of phones in the bedroom has the effect of disrupting sleep. This disruption is, perhaps, related to the need to constantly check phones and also to the impact of what we call FOMO (Fear of Missing Out). There are other serious issues with the use of devices, including, inattention to hygiene, unsafe behaviours online, one of which is sexting. Physical injuries can also occur due to the repetitive motions made during devise use. These injuries include tendonitis and carpal tunnel syndrome. People also get 'text neck', which is aching in the neck from huddling over the screen. Eyestrain and headaches are common. So, who said too much screen time is a bad thing?

VERY YOUNG CHILDREN ARE NOW USING DEVICES

An alarming statistic to those who work with very young children is the report that younger and younger kids are exposed to screens and are using devices. As one example, the American Common Sense Research Group reported a spike in mobile device use and ownership by children from 0 to 8 years of age between 2011-2017.[6] In their report, children at a very tender age may be exposed to all the side effects named above. The Common Sense Research Group is a very credible source of information. Their mission is to provide parents, educators, health organizations, and policymakers with reliable, independent data on children's use of media and technology. They focus on its impacts on physical, emotional, social and intellectual development.

This research group produced a critical report that was released in 2017 on media use among children aged 0-8 years. This report says that 42% of children age 0 to 8 have their own tablet device, which is up from less than 1% in 2011. These are children under 8 years old—so it's almost 50% of this age group. The average amount of time spent with mobile devices has skyrocketed during this period of time, increasing by nearly 10 times. The data indicate that from 5 minutes a day in 2011 it was up to 48 minutes per day in 2017. The numerical difference between 2000 and 2011 is startling. Children have their own tablet or Smartphone in the home and this has become a norm. Smartphone ownership has moved from 41% to 95%. Remember, this is children under 8 years of age.

So the early years are enormously important for having intentional conversations and intentional practices around the use of screens and cell phones. When we talk about the adolescent brain and digital culture, I've got some good resources for parents. One of the neat developments from the American Academy of Paediatrics is a recommendation they refer to as the Family Media Use Plan. I've already said that brain development is impacted by media use during the early years and what young ones need is face-to-face interactions within the family. But for the adolescent brain as well, its development is best served by relationships and that means face-to-face time, not just FaceTime.

When the Common Sense Census looked at adolescent device use, on any given day, American teens 13 to 18 years old averaged 9 hours per day of entertainment media use. That data excludes time spent at school or homework. The tweens age category, 8 to 12 year olds, on average used about 6 hours of entertainment media daily. You know what? If you are on entertainment media you aren't out playing soccer. Nor are you learning to play the guitar or piano. You're home in your bedroom. When you ask kids about their top activities, they still say that tweens watch TV the most. The percentage of those who watch TV daily is 62%. Listening to music for tweens takes up 54% of their time every day. Teenagers are listening to music for much more time than in the past. They report that they listen to music 73% of the time. So you can see that there's a whole lot is going on.

Will Ferrell, a well-known American comedian and actor, has initiated a public service announcement encouraging families to put down their mobile devices during dinner. Imagine—we live in a world where we have comedians telling us to have device-free family dinners. And we know that family dinner itself is on the decline. Are you not sure this is really an issue? Just go into a restaurant and observe the number of families who sit at their meal, with each person on a separate device. What worries me when I observe this dinnertime pattern is that the brain is under construction during childhood. The ability to learn about others, to read their emotions and learn about their own emotions, is hugely reliant on face-to-face interaction and conversational turn-taking. Are we raising an entire generation or two where these skills are being lost? What's the cost of that loss? A simple suggestion that many experts make is that when you're having family dinner, make it a cell free zone time.

And how do kids experience the flip side of this phenomenon—of parents being on their cell phones or devices too frequently? What's the cost for the young? With extensive adult use of Smartphones and other devices, kids still give lots of cues to say they want their parents' time. It's as if they're trying to say to their parents, Hey, I need your attention. But parents are stuck on their devices. So it's not just an issue of the children using devices, it's also parental use of cell phones.

WHY DO PARENTS ALLOW SO MUCH SCREEN USE?

Why do parents let their kids have so much screen time? The number one response is that kids like it. Because they like it, and want it, parents give it to them. Many parents think about screen time and digital devices as good education. But there's a lot of inferior material that's accessible on-line. Many reading apps are nothing more than repetition. They don't help kids experience deep learning. In addition, there are studies that show kids don't generalize their knowledge from what they learn on screen to what they learn face-to-face. Throughout this book, I've emphasized the importance of face-to-face interaction. When little ones under 8 years are learning, face-to-face experience is hugely important; it can't be replaced by screen time.

There are many other reasons why parents say they allow the use of screen time. Parents use electronic media to provide time for themselves. They also use screen time to help children relax. Some adults use it to bond with a child, so they sit with their children and play games. Grandparents bake virtual cakes with their grandchildren over FaceTime. Sometimes, parents reward children with screen time. But here's the warning: Paediatricians in the US and Canada now say that their first recommendation is that children 2 years of age and younger should not use screens at all. Why? Based on brain development, they're aware that babies need face-to-face time. It's the serve and return of social interaction that builds brains in a healthy way.

Adults who are otherwise occupied and hand over a device to babies aren't forming the right connections with children. In earlier chapters, I explained that brain development is based on a use it or lose it model. That means that what doesn't get used during the early years is snipped away. As one example, I mentioned that in experiment settings, an infant has the ability to discriminate between all the sounds in multiple languages in the first 6 months of life. But the language they develop is the one they hear the most. The ability to discern other language sounds is snipped away. The brain is built by experience. If children spend all their time on media and don't have enough time on face-to-face encounters, is it possible that those areas of the brain that are formed through face-to-face interaction will get pruned away? Are we wiring up for the wrong things?

RECOMMENDATIONS FROM PAEDIATRICIANS

What kids need is human interaction. They need to be outside and engaging the world. They need to have free play. However, the research on best approaches is changing. Research carried out in 2013 showed that no learning occurs with TV watching in children who are under 30 months.[7] I'm not sure they can make that claim anymore because other studies show that kids are learning but they're not *transferring* that learning into other situations. The American Academy of Paediatrics, in their newer version of their statement, says that from birth to 18 months parents adult caregivers should avoid all screen media, which means all phones, television and computers. Except, of course, for Facetime with Nana. It's okay to video chat with grandparents or friends who live far away.

Yet the American Academy of Paediatrics reports that nearly 30% of babies who are under 1 year of age are watching TV and videos for 90 minutes a day. Recall that the Academy recommends 0% screen time for that age group. What are parents actually doing? Clearly not following the recommendations of this organization.

The Academy's recommendation is that 18 months to 2 years of age children can be introduced to high quality children's media, such as Public Broadcasting Services (PBS) and Sesame Street. It's best, however, if adults watch these shows with children and help them understand what they're seeing. That recommendation makes a lot of sense. The problem is, based on some studies, that 64% of 1 to 2 year olds are watching TV and videos for 2 hours a day, unaccompanied by an adult. Pre-schoolers are watching TV and videos for 2 to 4.5 hours per day.

Here's a dilemma. We've got the science. But we're coming up against the reality of how families actually look after little kids in the 2020s given the pressures experienced by young families. What one study by the American Academy of Paediatrics showed is that 97% of 0 to 4 year olds are using mobile devices. Most of them are using it daily while parents are doing chores. The parents of 65% of children use screen time to calm down their children. And 29% of parents use screen time to put children to sleep.

The recommendation is that adults limit 2 to 5 years of age children to 1 hour per day of high-quality programming designed especially for children. And again, they recommend watching for that hour with the child. As adults watch along with their children, they can explain what the child is seeing and how it relates to the world around them. These recommendations came from scientific research that was carried out in 2018.

The Canadian Paediatric Society recommends the following: young children learn best from face-to-face interactions with caring adults. It's best to keep their screen time to a minimum: For children under 2 years of age, screen time is not recommended. For children 2 to 5 years old, limit routine or regular screen time to less than 1 hour per day. The recommendation is to minimize screen time and mitigate (reduce) it's impact, by

- Being present and engaged when screens are used and whenever possible, co-view with children.
- Being aware of content and prioritize educational, age-appropriate and interactive programming.

216

- Using parenting strategies that teach self-regulation, calming and limit-setting.
- Being mindful about your own use of screen time and model appropriate use.

However, we know that these recommendations aren't being followed.

It's clear to me that we must figure out a different message to give parents; one that fits in with their complex lives and perhaps in many cases, it amounts to just pointing out the science of development without blaming or shaming. As one example, even toilet training in the digital world is having an impact. We still have little children who need to learn how to use the toilet. With the introduction of the iPotty, this developmental step is being significantly modified. The iPotty is a little toddler toilet seat with an attachment for a digital tablet. In this day and age, parents are leaning toward the idea that children need entertainment during toilet training. Heaven forbid that we'd be trying to toilet train a child and have nothing to entertain them with, other with than just letting them sit and do their business! What ever happened to encouraging a child to talk to mommy or daddy, who can ask them if they're done yet? I say this to convey the important point that learning to feel one's own body sensations is what toilet training is about. Instead of paying attention to one's own body, and talking with mom or dad, a child can sit for hours and play on an iPad.

With so much screen time use, research studies are discovering consequences to development. One study, between 2011 and 2015 with over 1000 children between 6 and 24 months of age, showed a significant association between handheld screen time and expressive speech delay. There's a group of Paediatricians in France who have done a YouTube talk about the explosion of autism referrals to their paediatric practice.[8] They were receiving referrals for children who were exhibiting autism-like symptoms. When these doctors began to observe the trend, they started to question whether the numbers were possible biologically. They didn't accept that they were seeing an epidemic of autism. So what was going on?

In response to the increasing numbers of children with symptoms, they started taking a media screen use history with parents. They found out that the kids were on screens for hour after hour after hour. The great news is that when they spoke to parents about weaning them off of media time, their kids developed language. In fact, they achieved all kinds of normal and typical development. Not only did the French example show this pattern, but also an important study from the University of Calgary with Dr Sherry Madigan showed similar results. Madigan worked with 2,000 mothers and children. They reported development at 24, 30, and 60 months of age. The research used a developmental questionnaire. What they saw was that the higher the amount of screen time, the poorer the children were on developmental factors. So, the more screen time a child is exposed to, the more challenges there were to their development.

Young children need real world experience. The young need to be going outside or playing pretend and playing, for example, with pots and pans. They need interaction with caregivers not with screens. These results are based on the science we have for how children grow. They need hands-on creative play and time with nature. There's good evidence on so many of these issues. But there's also tension in the family over them as well. One of my colleagues is a researcher in infant mental health (0 to 3 years of age). She was talking to her daughter-in-law, who's a very well-educated person. My colleague runs a home visiting program and told her daughter-in-law she was going to start asking about screen use during home visits. Her daughter-in-law's response was, "Oh, here it comes again, parent bashing."

Parents feel besieged. How can we get the information about negative consequences of too much screen time to parents without having them feel blamed? It's important to let them know—otherwise we let down our children—but it's also necessary to give families support. It's not just about telling parents to avoid too much screen time, and not to give it so easily. It's also about letting parents know of other experiences children need instead. Is it possible to create a play revolution? Can we make interaction and play fun for parents to engage with their children. This is our challenge.

TECHNO-FERENCE: PARENTS AND MEDIA

But there is something else we must be concerned about—distracted parenting. A distracted parent may be a danger to a child. Parents have to ask themselves how their screen time creates distraction and how it impacts their interaction with their children and the child's development. There's a new term that's used to capture distracted parenting—it's called techno-ference.

McDaniel and Radesky, two American paediatricians, wrote a paper on the term to argue that heavy parental digital technology use interferes with parenting.[9] Their article made sense. But now we're gathering evidence that it's true. Think for a moment about the nursery rhyme *Rock-a-bye Baby on the Treetop*. In the present day, the danger isn't that the baby will fall from a tree but that parents may be on a cell phone and miss the fact that the cradle is in danger. As I present on techno-ference, I use a series of pictures to show a real world example.

In the first frame, there's a picture of a young woman on her phone while she's pushing a baby in a stroller. The stroller hits a rut in the pavement and tips over. Items in the stroller fall to the ground. The stroller wheel runs over these items and the baby also slips out because the child wasn't strapped in. What's most alarming is that the woman doesn't move to the baby. She stays talking on her phone. She doesn't appear to be driven to the baby's safety needs as a top priority. What's happened to our parent instinct? I have to be honest and say that my parental instinct would be to toss the phone and get the baby. What's going on? What's going on is that screen time and phone time may take away our parental antennae. While on a device, we may not be as receptive to picking up parental cues from babies. I can't say too strongly that parents need healthy screen habits.

Parents, please take stock of your actual phone needs. Do you need to be checking your phone so many times a day? Do we *need* to be on it? Is it so important to answer every call as soon as it comes in? Some families are having one 24-hour period a week screen free. Another approach to device issues in the family is to involve kids in a discussion of appropriate cell phone use. Write and post the rules on the fridge if you need to do that to get people to pay attention to them. Make sure you're giving kids positive attention. Admit, understand and overcome the fear of missing out on what other people want to convey to you through your phone. Also ask yourself what triggers you to go to your phone. I know the pull of this technology. For me, the very first thing I do when I wake up in the morning is to check my phone. I'm checking my phone to see if my kids have sent me other pictures of my grandbabies. At least that's my excuse.

SCREEN TIME AND MENTAL HEALTH

American psychology professor Jean Twenge is a social researcher who has access to huge datasets through National surveys for 8, 10, and 12th graders. Her interests focus on the correlation between happiness and the use of screen activities versus engaging in non-screen activities. What she found was that for all non-screen activities the correlation between use and happiness was positive.[10] That means that when kids were not using screens they were engaged in more activities that make them happy.

According to her research, if young people were involved in non-screen activities e.g., sports, music and drama, they tended to report being happy. For all screen activities, the correlation with happiness was negative. She conveys from her research that screen use takes time away from activities that make youth happy. The unhappiest group were the teens that use screens for more than 20 hours per week. But 20 hours per week isn't that long if we consider the previous average per day of 9 hours. Adolescent psychological well-being decreases the more hours spent on screens. When these studies came out, Twenge was interested in what makes this age group happy. Positive effects result from sports, exercise, in-person social interaction, religious services, print media and even homework for some young people. Negative effects were described as a correlation with screen time. She's not saying that screen time causes unhappiness. But there's an association.

As I examine these reports on screen time use, I'm noticing that kids who have moderate amounts of time on screens are also

happy, if we're looking at the relationship between screen time and happiness. Of screen time use, those who limited it to 1 to 5 hours per week were the happiest. Those who didn't use screens at all were less happy than those who used it for a couple of hours a week. These statistics make sense if you think of our human need to connect with other people. Those who spent 20 or more hours per week on screens were the least happy. In addition, if we compare kids and teens that use screens for 2 hours or less per day versus kids who use them for 3 hours or more per day, the data show a 34% greater chance of suicide or other related risk factors.[11]
When her study came out, Twenge was asked if her research made a big correlation between screen use and suicidal behaviour. In response, she looked more closely at the data. She asked herself when the overall spike or rise in anxiety, depression and suicidality had occurred. She drew the timing of an increase in these mental health issues with the introduction of the iPhone (2007) and iPad (2010). If someone used screen time more than 5 hours daily, they showed a 48% greater chance of a suicide-related risk factor. What are those risk factors? They include a feeling of hopelessness or the serious consideration of suicide.

For me, as a child psychiatrist, I know many children and youth who express a longing for connection. They may have lots of social media contacts but aren't well connected to other people or themselves. American psychologist Sherry Turkle describes this group as 'Connected but Alone'.[12] They have lots of contacts but not much meaningful connection. They're linked through a device, but don't' experience much *feeling felt*.

What needs to be made clear is that this research isn't talking about all young people. Young people who are more at risk generally for mental health issues seem to be particularly vulnerable when it comes to screen use. This is confirmed by other research that looked at adolescents' mental health and the use of Smartphones. The data in those studies were more positive. What researchers from this research said is that most young people age 11 to 19 are doing well in the digital age. They don't have major psychiatric disorders.So the question to ask is how much screen time is okay? The answer seems to be that it depends on the child and the family. Some research shows that the happiest teens have an above average amount of time spent in face-to-face social interactions and they're below average in screen time. So there may be a sweet spot that has a maximum of 1 to 2 hours daily, which is balanced by time spent in face-to-face interaction.

It's really important to consider what's not happening due to screen time use. Let's recall what's been said about sleep, homework, exercise, play, family time, sports and all the other activities that aren't happening if someone is watching a screen. As mentioned, what's not happening in general is face-to-face interaction. Researchers are adding up all these outcomes of cell phone use and saying that adults need to do something about this trend. People are starting to do something about it. *Growing up Digital*, a Canadian study, is one response that involves research done by the Alberta Teachers Association, the University of Alberta, the Boston Children's Center and the Harvard Medical School.

This study is looking first at what teachers think about media, and then at what parents and grandparents think about the use of screen time. In their research, teachers report that they're worried. One response suggests that technology is good in that it can enhance inquiry-based learning, but in general, kids are more distracted while at school. It seems to be that teachers are also more distracted. Teachers report that kids are disconnected and have more and more emotional challenges. Teachers worry about the impacts of digital culture on their learners. But teachers are also reporting the positive aspects of digital media in education.

THE POSITIVE SIDE OF DIGITAL USE

There's a good side to living in a digital age. It's all about the right kind of use. From a learning standpoint, there are huge opportunities for exciting learning and development. Absolutely! Technology has opened up massive new worlds of opportunity. The digital world allows kids to learn many facts about people in different parts of the world and to actually connect with them. In addition, children may speak out on electronic platforms such as a knowledge forum when they may not be comfortable speaking in person in class.[13] The list is endless in terms of educational value. A recent article from ID Tech,[14] describes many forms of the positive development of digital culture, such as

Creativity and freedom of expression
Independence and empowerment
Problem solving and perseverance

There's an excellent resource called The Center on Media and Child Health, from Boston University and the Harvard Medical School. This resource describes three key benefits of the digital world. These benefits include the following:

Health and Wellness: Mobile devices allow for delivery of personalized health messages (via text or an app) that can help a youth combat obesity or encourage them to quit smoking.

Relationships: Mobile devices can help keep families and friends connected even when they live far away. Whether through text, video chat, or another app, mobile devices have the potential to help children feel closer to those they care about.

Safety & Convenience: No one can argue the convenience of being able to reach your child immediately, or a child being able to reach his parent, in the case of a sudden change of plans. More importantly, cell phones and other mobile devices can be used in emergency situations, and parents can use one of a variety of mobile apps to track their child via the device's GPS.[15] In the unprecedented times of the CoVid 19 pandemic, the use of technology is being reported to be hugely important as teachers reach out to learners, as isolated seniors stay connected to family and as health care workers reach out to their families during their isolation. This would be a completely different experience without technology.

On another note, there are guidelines to help adults select appropriate media and programming for young children. The following guidelines are from Zero to Three, a policy and educational institute in the United States.

That organization offers a very practical way to choose media content for young children by using what they call the E-AIMS. **The E-AIMS stands for**

E Engaging: Is my child Engaged? Is there a learning goal or story as part of the screen experience?

A Actively Involved: Is my child Actively Involved? Does she look like she's really thinking about, and participating in, the content?

M-Meaningful: Is the content Meaningful? Does the content reflect my child's everyday life?

S-Social: Is the content Social? Does this experience encourage my child to talk or respond within the game? Does this experience encourage my child to interact with me as we play together?

As many parents struggle to find the balance of screen use, this guideline will be very helpful, I'm sure.

CONCLUSION

In this chapter, I've outlined a set of side effects of technology use that can't be ignored. We need to respond with action that's well considered and takes careful account of what children and young people need, what they're asking for and what's good for their mental and physical health, as well as what will offer positive support for their brain development.

In response to a need for action, the Alberta Association of Teachers is offering some ways forward. They're clear that we can't just tell kids to put away their phones or put away their iPads. But we can recommend balance. In terms of living a balanced life, we need sleep, exercise, play and technology. We can pay attention to what we include in a day and be mindful about it. We can stop and think about how, as adults, we're using our own technology? Most importantly, we can be present with our kids when we're together. And here are a couple of excellent suggestions:

The American Academy of Paediatrics asks us what are we doing to make sure that kids are getting the sleep and exercise they need. They suggest media free zones at home and time spent communicating with family. They have developed a media family use plan that you can access at https://www.healthychildren.org/English/media/Pages/default.aspx.

In Ontario there's a Healthy Kids Community Challenge that's encouraging parents to "power off and play". They have some wonderful suggestions on games to play, activities to play that aren't too strenuous and don't exact too much of a toll on parents. they emphasize that children learn best through play and relationship.

My closing message really is that the digital world is here and here to stay. We have to make sure that we're learning how to use it and use it well. We need to find ways to convey to parents the truth about screen time's effects on the young. We have to learn how to live with technology. Sometimes people at my presentations will tell me that digital isn't such a game changer. After all, they tell me that people made all these criticisms about TV as well. But I'm certain that the digital world is not just the same as the TV world.

TV didn't influence every aspect of life the way the digital world does. Of concern to me, as has been said throughout the book, relationships and connection are the essential ingredients that make us human. TV didn't significantly interfere with these connections. We must guard against digital use that interferes with relationships. We need to be wise.

What we can be certain about is that brains are built up through face-to-face time between parents and their children and between teachers and their students. FaceTime can't offer the same benefits. What builds brains and fosters relationships is love that's communicated personally. That love is also conveyed when our eyes light up as a child enters the room. This is the kind of interaction that develops the brain and also a child's understanding of other people, of themselves and of the world. It's those kinds of learning that they take into the outside world and transfer to others. That is what must not be lost.

I'm hoping I can inspire a growing awareness to convey this message about human development. Parents need to ask themselves,

Is this the type of relationship I want to have with my child? Am I modelling the kind of relationship I want them to have with other people? Can we take this learning about the digital world, integrate and balance it with play and experiences of nature, which are some of the magnificent ways that children learn.

On a personal note, I love the ability of technologies to keep me connected with friends and family when I'm travelling or when I can only have a limited contact with them. I look forward to every

WhatsApp

from my family. I have also re-connected with long lost relatives— the benefits of technology are many and strong

Last words: Seek a balance in your own device use and in children's exposure and screen use. Think of the development of all aspects of their being, including their physical, social, emotional and spiritual well-being. Keep in mind that we'll all have better health, including mental health when we have that sense of balance that Indigenous elders have been teaching for generations.

End Notes

CHAPTER 1

LET'S START AT THE VERY BEGINNING

[1] Uri Bronfenbrenner, "Social ecology of human development" in F. Richardson (Ed.), Brain and intelligence: The ecology of child development (Hyattsville, MD: National Education Press, 1973), 113-129.

[2] Paul Kershaw, Bill Warburton, Lynell Anderson, Clyde Hertzman, Lori G. Irwin and Barry Forer, "Taking a Social Determinants Perspective on Children's Health and Development" in Canadian Journal of Public Health / Revue Canadienne de Santé Publique Vol. 101, Supplement 3. November/December 2010, S8-S12. The Economic Costs of Early Vulnerability in Canada

[3] www.heckmanequation.org

[4] David Hudson, "Invest in US: President Obama Convenes the White House Summit on Early Education", www.whitehouse.gov/blog/2014/12/10/invest-us-president-obama-convenes-white-house-summit-early-education.

[5] https://www.gov.mb.ca/healthychild/ncd/ncd2010_clinton.pdf

[6] David R. Offert, "Reducing the impact of poverty on children's mental health" Current Opinion in Psychiatry: July 2001 Volume 14 - Issue 4, 299-301 Editorial Review

[7] Chris Power* and Clyde Hertzmant, "Social and biological pathways linking early life and adult disease" British Medical Bulletin 1997, 53 (No 1), 210-22.

(*Department of Epidemiology and Biostatistics, Institute of Child Health, London, UK; Department of Health Care and Epidemiology, University of British Columbia, Vancouver, British Columbia, Canada)

[8] VJ Felitti, RF Anda, D Nordenberg, DF Williamson, AM Spitz, V Edwards, MP Koss, JS Marks, "Relationship of childhood abuse and household dysfunction to many of the leading causes of death in adults", *American Journal of Preventive Medicine*, 1998 May;14(4):245-58.

227

[9] Tom Porter, *And Grandma Said... Iroquois Teachings* (Xlibris, Jul 31 2008).

[10] Babineau V1, Green CG, Jolicoeur-Martineau A, Bouvette-Turcot AA, Minde K, Sassi R, St-André M, Carrey N, Atkinson L, Kennedy JL, Lydon J, Steiner M, Gaudreau H, Levitan R, Meaney M, Wazana A, "Prenatal depression and 5-HTTLPR interact to predict dysregulation from 3 to 36 months--a differential susceptibility model", *Journal of Child Psychology and Psychiatry*, 2015 Jan; 56(1):21-9. doi: 10.1111/jcpp.12246. Epub 2014 May 15.

[11] *www.pbs.org/wgbh/nova/genes/*

[12] R Yehuda and A Lehrner, "Intergenerational transmission of trauma effects: putative role of epigenetic mechanisms", *World Psychiatry,* 2018 Oct;17(3):243-257. doi: 10.1002/wps.20568.

[13] The United Nations Children's Fund (UNICEF) is a United Nations Program headquartered in New York City that provides long-term humanitarian and developmental assistance to children and mothers in developing countries. It is one of the members of the United Nations Development Group and its Executive Committee. UNICEF was created by theUnited Nations General Assembly on December 11, 1946, to provide emergency food and healthcare to children in countries that had been devastated by World War II. In 1953, UNICEF became a permanent part of the United Nations System and its name was shortened from the original United Nations International Children's Emergency Fund but it has continued to be known by the popular acronym based on this previous title.

[14] In keeping with UNICEF's mandate to advocate for children in every country, the Centre's Report Card series focuses on the well-being of children in industrialized countries. Each Report Card includes a league table ranking the countries of the OECD according to their record on the subject under discussion. The Report Cards are designed to appeal to a wide audience while maintaining academic rigour.

[15] https://www.cancer.ca/en/cancer-information/cancer-101/childhood-cancer-statistics/?region=on

[16] Nelson, C.A., Zeanah, C.H., Fox, N.A., Marshall, P. J., Smyke, A.T., & Guthrie, D. "Cognitive recovery in socially deprived young children: The Bucharest Early Intervention Project" *Science*, 2007, 318(5858), 1937-1940. PMID: 18096809

[17] G. Kolata, "What babies know, and noises parents make", Science, 237, (1987), 726.

[18] https://developingchild.harvard.edu/science/key-concepts/

[19] "The Science of Neglect: The Persistent Absence of Responsive Care

Disrupts the Developing Brain" and the Working Paper series from the Center on the Developing Child at Harvard University. www.developingchild.harvard.edu/resources/

[20] A.N.Meltzhoff & M.K.Moore, Science 1977 198 75-78

[21] Emily Sohn, "Babies prove sound learners: Scientists are gaining new insights into why babies are so good at learning languages", (Jan 16, 2008), www.sciencenewsforstudents.org.

[22] https://www.webmd.com/children/video/preventing-premature-births-preemie-miracles

CHAPTER 2

ATTACHMENT IN THE EARLY YEARS

[1] C Holden, "Paul MacLean and the Triune Brain", Science, 1979 Jun 8;204(4397):1066-8.

[2] Robert Sapolsky, Why Zebras Don't Get Ulcers (New York: Holt Paperbacks, 1994).

[3] Sara B Johnson, Robert W Blum, Jay N Giedd, "Adolescent Maturity and the Brain: The Promise and Pitfalls of Neuroscience Research in Adolescent Health Policy", Journal of Adolescent Health, 2009 Sep; 45(3): 216-221. Journal of Adolescent Health. 2009 Sep; 45(3): 216–221.

[4] Daniel J. Siegel, Brainstorm: The Power and Purpose of the Teenage Brain (New York: Tarcher Perigee, 2015).

[5] Sharon Fox, Pat Levitt, Charles Nelson, "How the Timing and Quality of Early Experiences Influences the Development of Brain Architecture", Child Development, Volume 81, Issue 1, January/February 2010, 28-40.

[6] Adrienne L Tierney and Charles A Nelson, "Brain Development and the Role of Experience in the Early Years", Zero Three. 2009 Nov 1; 30(2): 9-13.

[7] Deanna Kuhn, "Do Cognitive Changes Accompany Developments in the Adolescent Brain?", Perspectives on Psychological Science, Vol 1, Issue 1, 2006, 59-67.

[8] Tierney and Nelson.

[9] Margot Sunderland. The Science of Parenting (2nd Edition) (London: DK, 2016).

[10] Mary Ainsworth, "The Bowlby-Ainsworth Attachment Theory", The Behavioral and Brain Sciences, Vol 1, Issue 3, September 1978, 436-438.

[11] John Bowlby, Attachment and loss, Vol. 2: Separation (New York: Basic Books, 1973) 208ff.

[12] Inge Bretherton, The Origins of Attachment Theory: John Bowlby and Mary Ainsworth", Developmental Psychology, (1992), 28, 759-775.

[13] James & Joyce Robertson, Film - A Two Year Old Goes to Hospital, 1952.

[14] http://www.robertsonfilms.info/young_children_in_brief_separation. htm

[15] John Bowlby, "Maternal care and mental health", World Health Organization Monograph (serial No. 2), (1951), 13.

[16] Marinus van IJzendoorn and Pieter Kroonenberg, "Cross-Cultural Patters of Attachment: A Meta-Analysis of The Strange Situation", Child Development, Vol 59, no 1, (Feb 1988), 147-156.

[17] Mary Ainsworth, Mary Blehar, Everett Waters and Sally Wall, Patterns of Attachment: A Psychological Study of The Strange Situation (New York: Routledge, 1978).

[18] van IJzendoorn and Kroonenberg.

[19] Mary Main and Judith Solomon, "Procedures for Identifying Infants as Disorganized/Disoriented During the Ainsworth Strange Situation", in Mark Greenberg et. al, (Eds), Attachment in the Preschool Years, (Chicago: University of Chicago Press, 1990), 121-160.

[20] L. Alan Sroufe, The Development of the Person (New York: The Guilford Press, 2009).

[21] Sroufe, The Development of the Person.

[22] Hans Agrawal et al, "Attachment Studies with Borderline Patients: A Review", Harvard Review of Psychiatry. 2004 ; 12(2): 94–104.

[23] Harvard University, Center on the Developing Child, "Toxic Stress", www.developingchild.harvard.edu.

[24] Bowlby, Attachment and Loss.

[25] Peter Fonagy, "Peter Fonagy and the undermining of old ideas on personality disorder", www.escap.eu.

[26] Agrawal.

[27] Charles Nelson, Charles Zeanah, Nathan Fox, Peter Marshall, Anna Smyke, Donald Guthrie, "Cognitive Recovery in Socially Deprived Young Children: The Bucharest Early Intervention Program", Science, 21 Dec 2007: Vol 318, Issue 5858, 1937-1940.

[28] Sroufe, The Development of the Person.

[29] https://www.rootsofempathy.org/wp-content/uploads/2020/05/Media-kit-Brief-Research-Summary-2020-2.pdf.

[30] Claire Lerner and Amy Laura Dombro. *Bringing up Baby. Three steps to making good decisions in your child's first years* (Washington: Zero to Three, 2004).

[31] Margot Sunderland. *The Science of Parenting (2nd Edition)*, (London: DK, 2016). Foreword by Jaak Pansksepp.

CHAPTER 3

THE SOCIAL BRAIN: SERVE AND RETURN

[1] Paulo Freire, Pedagogy of the Oppressed (NewYork: Bloomsbury, 2000), 32.

[2] Stanley Turecki. The Difficult Child (Random House, 2000).

[3] William Sears and Martha Sears, The Fussy Baby Book: Parenting Your High-Need Child From Birth to Age Five (Winnipeg, MB: Word Alive,1996).

[4] Mary Sheedy Kurcinka, Raising Your Spirited Child Rev Ed: A Guide for Parents Whose Child Is More Intense, Sensitive, Perceptive, Persistent, and Energetic (William Morrow Paperbacks, 2015).

[5] **OCDE** is an international economic organization made up of 34 countries founded in 1961 to stimulate economic progress and world trade. It is a forum of countries committed to democracy and the market economy, providing a platform to compare policy experiences, seek answers to common problems, identify good practices and coordinate domestic and international policies of its members.

[6] **OCDE** is an international economic organization made up of 34 coun-

tries founded in 1961 to stimulate economic progress and world trade. It is a forum of countries committed to democracy and the market economy, providing a platform to compare policy experiences, seek answers to common problems, identify good practices and coordinate domestic and international policies of its members.

[7] Susanne A. Denham, Hideko H. Bassett, Katherine M. Zinsser, Isabel S. Bradburn, Craig S. Bailey, Elizabeth A. Shewark, David E. Ferrier, Kristi H. Liverette, Jessica Steed, Samantha P. Karalus and Saeid Kianpour, "Computerized social-emotional assessment measures for early childhood settings", *Early Childhood Research Quarterly*, 10.1016/j.ecresq.2019.07.002, 51, (55-66).

[8] https://edi.offordcentre.com/category/latest-reports/

[9] Fulvio D'Acquisto, MSc, MRes, PhD

[10] https://ontariochildhealthstudy.ca/ochs/

[11] https://www.camh.ca/-/media/files/pdf---osduhs/mental-health-and-well-being-of-ontario-students-1991-2017---summary-osduhs-report-pdf.pdf

[12] Michael Unger, *Strengths-Based Counselling With At-Risk Youth* (Thousand Oaks, CA: Corwin Press, 2006).

[13] Betty Hart and Todd Risley, *Meaningful Differences in the Everyday life of American Children* (Baltimore, MD: Brookes Publishing, 1995).

[14] Betty Hart and Todd Risley, *Meaningful Differences*.

[15] Anne Fernald and Adriana Weisleder, "Twenty Years After "Meaningful Differences," It's Time to Reframe the "Deficit" Debate about the Importance of Children's Early Language Experience", Human Development 58 (2015), 1-4.

[16] https://youtu.be/Z-eU5xZW7cU

[17] https://youtu.be/apzXGEbZht0

[18] Robert Sapolsky, Why Zebras Don't Get Ulcers (New York: Holt Paperbacks, 1994).

[19] Ferris Jabr, "Cache Cab: Taxi Drivers' Brains Grow to Navigate London's Streets" *Scientific American* (Dec. 8, 2011). Memorizing 25,000 city streets balloons the hippocampus, but cabbies may pay a hidden fare in cognitive skills.

END NOTES

CHAPTER 4

RESILIENCE AND RECOVERY

[1] Michelle Tugade and Barbara Fredrickson, "Resilient Individuals Use Positive Emotions to Bounce Back From Negative Emotional Experiences", *Journal of Personality and Social Psychology*, 86(2), (2004), 320-333.

[2] Ann Masten and J Obradovic, "Competence and resilience in development", Academy of Science, 1094, (2006), 14.

[3] Uri Bronfenbrenner, *The Ecology of Human Development: Experiments by Nature and Design*, (Cambridge, MA: Harvard University Press, 1979).

[4] M Rutter, "Implications of resilience concepts for scientific understanding", *Annals of the New York Academy of Science* 1094 (2006), 1-12.

[5] Washington Post, March 1976

[6] Ann Masten, "Ordinary Magic: Resilience processes in development", *American Psychologist* 56 (2001), 227-238.

[7] http://www.child-encyclopedia.com/resilience/according-experts/resilience-early-age-and-its-impact-child-psychosocial-development.

[8] http://www.child-encyclopedia.com/resilience/according-experts/resilience-early-age-and-its-impact-child-psychosocial-development.

[9] Masten.

[10] Stuart Hauser, J Allen and E Golden, *Out of the Woods: tales of resilient teens* (Cambridge: Harvard University Press, 2006), 39.

[11] Kendra Cherry, "Bowlby & Ainsworth: What Is Attachment Theory? The Importance of Early Emotional Bonds", www.verywellmind.com.

[12] D Olson, C Russell and D Sprenkle, Circumplex model: Systematic assessment and treatment of families (New York, Haworth Press, 1989).

[13] David Reiss, The Family's Construction of Reality (Cambridge, MA: Harvard University Press, 1981)

[14] M Schuster et al, "A national survey of stress reactions after September 11 2001 terrorist attacks", New England Journal of Medicine 345, (2001), 1507-1512.

[15] R Sampson, S Raudenbush and F Earls, "Neighborhoods and Violent Crime: A Multilevel Study of Collective Efficacy", Science 277 (1997), 918-924.

[16] New York Times, January 6, 2004.

[17] F Walsh, "Traumatic loss and major disasters: Strengthening family and community resilience", Family Process 46(2), (June 2007), 207-227.

[18] http://www.psychologytoday.com/blog/nurturing-resilience.

[19] http://resilienceresearch.org/whatworks/.

[20] http://www.hpechildrenandyouth.ca/2016/05/nine-things-all-children-need-to-be-risilient/.

[21] An epigenome is a record of chemical changes to DNA that can be passed down from parents to children. It's influential in how genes are expressed in an individual. Even though it's passed down genetically, the epigenome can be dramatically altered by environment.

[22] A Caspi et al, , "Influence of life stress on depression: moderation by a polymorphism in the 5-HTT gene", Science 301 (2003), 386-389.

[23] Amy Byrd and Stephen Manuck, "MAOA, childhood maltreatment and antisocial behavior: Meta-analysis of a gene-environment interaction", Biological Psychiatry Vol 75 Issue 1, (January 2014), 9-17.

[24] Michael Rutter, "Implications of Resilience Concepts for Scientific Understanding", *Annals of the New York Academy of Science* 1094 (2006), 1-12.

[25] A Deveson, "The importance of 'resilience' in helping people cope with adversity", Australia's e-journal of social and political debate, 2004

CHAPTER 5

CONNECTION IS THE KEY

[1] https://www.brainstory.org.

[2] Roberta Golinkoff, *Becoming Brilliant: What Science Tells Us About Raising Successful Children* (American Psychological Association, 2016).

[3] Jerome Kagan, *Galen's Prophecy: Temperament in Human Nature* (New York: Basic Books, 1994), and Mary Gordon and Michael Fullan, *Roots of Empathy: Changing the World, Child by Child* (Markham, ON: Thomas Allen Publishers, 2012)

[4] Damon E Jones, Mark Greenberg and Max Crowley, "Early Social-Emo-

tional Functioning and Public Health: The Relationship Between Kindergarten Social Competence and Future Wellness", *American Journal of Public Health*, (November, 2015)

[5] MadameNoire, "How Does Texas Determine Prison Facilities? 4th Grade Reading Scores", *Madamenoire* (December 27, 2010), www.madamenoire.com.

[6] http://www.2000days.ca.

[7] First Nations Mental Wellness Continuum Framework - Summary Report - December 2014 - Health Canada and Assembly of First Nations.

[8] https://www.reggiochildren.it.

[9] Youssef Nagy, Laura Lockwood, Shaoyong Su, Guang Hao, Part Rutten, "The Effects of Trauma, with or without PTSD, on the Transgenerational DNA Methylation Alterations in Human Offsprings", *Brain Science* 8(5):83, (2018).

[10] A Weisleder and A Fernald, "Talking to children matters: Early language experience strengthens processing and builds vocabulary". *Psychological Science, 24*(11), (2013),2143-2152.

[11] https://earlyyearsstudy.ca.

[12] The **amygdala** is an almond-shape set of neurons located deep in the brain's medial temporal lobe. Shown to play a key role in the processing of emotions, the **amygdala** forms part of the limbic system of the brain.

[13] https://mindup.org.

CHAPTER 6

INFANT AND PRESCHOOL MENTAL HEALTH: THE POWER OF RELATIONSHIPS

[1] https://developingchild.harvard.edu/resources/three-early-childhood-development-principles-improve-child-family-outcomes/#responsive-relationships.

[2] R.C. Kessler, M. Angermeyer, J.C. Anthony, et al. "Lifetime prevalence and age-of-onset distributions of mental disorders in the World Health Organization's World Mental Health Survey Initiative", *World Psychiatry* (2007), 6: 168–76.

[3] J. Clinton, A. Kays-Burden, C. Carter, J. Cairney, N. Carrey, M. Janus,

C. Kulkarni, & R. Williams, for the Ontario Centre of Excellence for Child and Youth Mental Health. (2014). "Supporting Ontario's youngest minds: Investing in the mental health of children under 6".

[4] C. Kulkarni, N. Khambati, P. Sundar, L. Kelly, N. Summers, & K. Short, (2019). "Beyond building blocks: Investing in the lifelong mental health of Ontario's three- to six-year-olds". Ottawa, ON: Ontario Centre of Excellence for Child and Youth Mental Health.

[5] https://files.ontario.ca/books/edu_the_kindergarten_program_english_aoda_web_oct7.pdf.

[6] Scott Davies, Magdalena Janus, Eric Daku, Ashley Gaskin, "Using the Early Development Instrument to examine cognitive and non-cognitive school readiness and elementary student achievement", *Early Childhood Research Quarterly*, (Volume 35, 2nd Quarter, 2016), 63-75.

[7] Damon E. Jones, Mark Greenberg and Max Crowley, "Early Social-Emotional Functioning and Public Health: The Relationship Between Kindergarten Social Competence and Future Wellness", American Journal of Public Health, (November 2015), 105(11): 2283–2290.

[8] Charlotte Waddell, Cody Shepherd, Christine Schwartz, Jen Barican, "Child and Youth Mental Disorders: Prevalence and Evidence-Based Interventions", A research report for the British Columbia Ministry of Children and Family Development, (June, 2014).

[9] http://www.fcd-us.org/PDFs/NationalPreKExpulsion Paper03.02_new.pdf.

[10] V.J. Felitti, R.F. Anda, D. Nordenberg, D.F. Williamson, A.M. Spitz, V. Edwards, M.P. Koss, J.S. Marks, "Relationship of childhood abuse and household dysfunction to many of the leading causes of death in adults. The Adverse Childhood Experiences (ACE) Study", *American Journal of Preventative Medicine*, (May 1998), 14(4):245-58.

[11] Damon E. Jones, Mark Greenberg and Max Crowley, "Early Social-Emotional Functioning and Public Health: The Relationship Between Kindergarten Social Competence and Future Wellness", *American Journal of Public Health*, (November, 2015) 105(11): 2283–2290.

[12] https://ontariochildhealthstudy.ca.

[13] https://www.zerotothree.org/espanol/infant-and-early-childhood-mental-health.

[14] Andrew N. Meltzoff and M. Keith Moore, "Imitation in Newborn Infants: Exploring the Range of Gestures Imitated and the Underlying Mecha-

nisms", *Developmental Psychology*, (November, 1989), (6): 954-962.

¹⁵ Elizabeth A. Shuey and Miloš Kankaras, "The Power and Promise of Early Learning", OECD Education Working Paper No. 186.

¹⁶ Personal communication.

¹⁷ Robin C. Williams, Anne Biscaro, Jean Clinton, "Relationships Matter: How clinicians can support positive parenting in the early years", Canadian Paediatric Society, Early Years Task Force. *Paediatrics and Child Health* (August, 2019) 24(5):340-347.

¹⁸ https://gritasap.ca/about/.

¹⁹ Jenna Bilmes, *Beyond Behavior Management: The Six Life Skills Children Need* (St. Paul, MN: Red Leaf Press, 2012).

²⁰ https://nrfr2r.com/about-nrf/.

²¹ Nancy Cohen, Mirek Lojkasek, & Elisabeth Muir, "WATCH, WAIT, AND WONDER: An Infant-led Approach to Infant-parent Psychotherapy", *The Signal* (2006), 14.

CHAPTER 7

THE ADOLESCENT BRAIN UNDER CONSTRUCTION

¹ Personal communication.

² Daniel J. Siegel, *Brainstorm: The Power and Purpose of the Teenage Brain* (New York: Penguin, 2015).

³ https://www.livesinthebalance.org/kids-do-well-if-they-can.

⁴ Personal communication.

⁵ https://ihuman.org.

⁶ This knowledge of iHuman's core values for staff members is based on my visit to the site on Friday, October 19, 2019. The information was provided by Katherine Broomfield, the Executive Director at iHuman.

⁷ Siegel, *Brainstorm*.

⁸ https://www.goodreads.com/quotes/63219-the-children-now-love-luxury-they-have-bad-manners-contempt.

⁹ Shakespeare, *The Winter's Tale*: Act 3, Scene 3. 2.

[10] Norman Doidge, *The Brain that Changes Itself: Stories of Personal Triumph from the Frontiers of the Brain* (New York: Penguin, 2007).

[11] https://www.naturalstacks.com/blogs/news/76618565-why-bdnf-is-miracle-gro-for-your-brain.

[12] Sara B. Johnson, Robert W. Blum, Jay N. Giedd, "Adolescent Maturity and the Brain: The Promise and Pitfalls of Neuroscience Research in Adolescent Health Policy", *Journal of Adolescent Health* (September, 2009) 45(3): 216-221.

[13] J.J. Arnett, "Emerging adulthood: A theory of development from the late teens through the twenties", *American Psychologist*, (May, 2000), 55(5), 469-480

[14] M. Fullan, J. Quinn and J. McEachen. *Deep Learning: Engage the World. Change the World.* (Thousand Oaks, California. Corwin, 2018).

[15] Laurence Steinberg, *Age of Opportunity: Lessons from the New Science of Adolescence* (New York: Houghton, Mifflin, Harcourt, 2014).

[16] https://www.search-institute.org/wp-content/uploads/2017/12/2017-Relationships-First-final.pdf.

[17] https://www.paulekman.com.

[18] Todd Yurgelun-Todd, & W.D.S. Killgore, "Fear-related activity in the

CHAPTER 8

THE CONTEXTS FOR DEVELOPING SELF-REGULATION

[1] http://www.self-regulation.ca/uploads/5/6/2/6/56264915/child_links_self-regulation_and_mental_health.pdf.

[2] https://www.search-institute.org.

[3] https://www.search-institute.org/our-research/development-assets/developmental-assets-framework/.

[4] Alison Gopnik, *The Gardener and the Carpenter: What the New Science of Child Development Tells Us About the Relationship Between Parents and Children* (NY: Macmillan Publishing, 2016).

[5] Tom Porter, *And Grandma Said... Iroquois Teachings* (Xlibris, July 31, 2008).

[6] Michael Fullan, Joanne Quinn, Joanne Mceachan, Deep Learning: Engage the World Change the World (Thousand Oaks, CA, 2018).

[7] Norman Doidge, *The Brain that Changes Itself: Stories of Personal Triumph from the Frontiers of the Brain* (New York: Penguin, 2007).

[8] Ibid.

[9] Supporting Ontario's youngest minds: Investing in the mental health of children under 6. (Policy paper from the Ontario Centre of Excellence for Child & Youth Mental Health). https://www.cymh.ca/Modules/ResourceHub/?id=AF13E20F-F63B-40B8-A2E4-84C98FF479DF.

[10] https://www.ourkidsnetwork.ca/Public/Page/Files/97_WTG_PolicePractice_Social-Emotional-Dev%2012.05.14.pdf.

[11] Micol Parolin and Alessandra Simonelli, "Attachment Theory and Maternal Drug Addiction: The Contribution to Parenting Interventions", *Front Psychiatry*. (2016; 7: 152).

[12] Jared B. Torre and Matthew D. Lieberman, "Putting Feelings Into Words: Affect Labeling as Implicit Emotion Regulation" (March, 2018), https://doi.org/10.1177/1754073917742706.

[13] Canadian Pediatric Society position statement, American Academy of Pediatrics position statement.

[14] Tine Steenhoff, Anne Tharner, Mette Skovgaard Vaever, "Mothers' and fathers' observed interaction with preschoolers: Similarities and differences in parenting behavior in a well-resourced sample" (August, 2019), https://doi.org/10.1371/journal.pone.0221661.

[15] Ibid.

[16] Ilanit Gordon and Ruth Feldman, "Synchrony in the Triad: A Microlevel Process Model of Coparenting and Parent-Child Interactions", (December, 2008), *Fam Process*, 47(4):465-79.

[17] Steenhof.

[18] Roots of Empathy. https://rootsofempathy.org.

[19] Stuart Shanker, Self-Reg: How to Help Your Child (and You) Break the Stress Cycle and Successfully Engage with Life (Penguin Canada, 2016).

[20] Ibid.

[21] https://www.psychologytoday.com/us/blog/self-reg/201607/self-regulation-vs-self-control

[22] https://www.youtube.com/watch?v=QX_oy9614HQ

[23] https://www.theatlantic.com/family/archive/2018/06/marshmallow-test/561779/.

[24] https://self-reg.ca.

CHAPTER 9

WELL BEING AND ANXIETY

[1]World Health Organization, "Mental Health: Strengthening Our Response", (March 30, 2018).

[2] J. Comeau, K. Georgiades, L. Duncan, L. Wang, M.H. Boyle, & the 2014 Ontario Child Health Study Team, "Changes in the Prevalence of Child and Youth Mental Disorders and Perceived Need for Professional Help Between 1983 and 2014: Evidence from the Ontario Child Health Study", *The Canadian Journal of Psychiatry*, https://doi.org/10.1177/0706743719830035, (2019).

[3] https://affectautism.com/2018/07/02/circles-of-communication/.

[4] https://positivepsychology.com/perma-model/.

[5] https://thunderbirdpf.org/wp-content/uploads/2015/01/24-14-1273-FN-Mental-Wellness-Summary-EN03_low.pdf.

[6] Mihaly Csikszentmihalyi, *Flow: The Psychology of Optimal Experience* (NY: Harper & Row, 2008).

[7] Marc Brackett, *Permission to Feel* (NY: Macmillan Publishers, 2019).

[8] Ontario Child Health Study.

[9] Ontario Child Health Study.

[10] https://www.mentalhealthcommission.ca/sites/default/files/C%252526Y_Evergreen_Framework_ENG_1.pdf.

[11] https://developingchild.harvard.edu/science/key-concepts/toxic-stress/.

[12] https://humanstress.ca/stress/understand-your-stress/sources-of-stress/.

[13] https://www.thestar.com/news/gta/2017/11/14/almost-half-of-ontario-youth-miss-school-because-of-anxiety-study-suggests.html.

[14] https://www.camh.ca/en/science-and-research/institutes-and-centres/institute-for-mental-health-policy-research/ontario-student-drug-use-and-health-survey---osduhs.

[15] M.D. Katharina Manassis, *Keys to Parenting Your Anxious Child* (NY: BES Publishing, 1996).

[16] https://self-reg.ca/author/administrator/.

[17] https://www.anxietycanada.com.

[18] https://www.health.harvard.edu/blog/school-refusal-when-a-child-wont-go-to-school-2018091814756.

[19] Stephen R. Covey and Sandra M. Covey, 8 *The 7 Habits of Highly Effec-*

tive Families (NY: Golden Books, 1997).

prefrontal cortex increases with age during adolescence: A preliminary fMRI study", *Neuroscience Letters*, (2006), 406, 194-199.

[19] https://www.kpbs.org/news/2013/sep/09/brains-trial-alan-alda/.

CHAPTER 10

GROWING UP DIGITAL

[1] Jean M. Twenge, iGen: Why Today's Super-Connected Kids Are Growing Up Less Rebellious, More Tolerant, Less Happy and Completely Unprepared for Adulthood (And what that means for the rest of us) (NY: Atria Paperback, 2017).

[2] https://www.cbc.ca/news/canada/manitoba/digital-age-screen-time-addiction-youth-1.4645490.

[3] Ibid.

[4] Michelle D. Guerrero, Joel D. Barnes, Jean-Philippe Chaput & Mark S. Tremblay, "Screen time and problem behaviors in children: exploring the mediating role of sleep duration", *International Journal of Behavioral Nutrition and Physical Activity* (2019) Vol. 16, Article number 105.

[5] Elia Abi-Jaoude, Karline Treurnicht Naylor & Antonio Pignatiello, "Smartphones, social media use and youth mental health", *Canadian Medical Association Journal* (February 10, 2020) 192 (6) E136-E141.

[6] https://www.commonsensemedia.org/research/the-common-sense-census-media-use-by-kids-age-zero-to-eight-2017.

[7] Canadian Paediatric Society, Digital Health Task Force, Ottawa, Ontario, "Screen time and young children: Promoting health and development in a digital world", *Pediatric Child Health Journal* (2017).

[8] "Virtual Autism: A New Threat to Toddlers", https://www.youtube.com/watch?v=9-eIdSE57Jw.

[9] Brandon T. McDaniel & Jenny S. Radesky, "Technoference: Parent Distraction with Technology and Associations with Child Behavior Problems", *Child Development* (January 2018) 89(1):100-109.

[10] Jean M. Twenge, "What Makes Teens Happier? Hint: It doesn't involve their phones", *Psychology Today* (December, 2018) 12:271-283.

[11] Jean M. Twenge and W. Keith Campbell, "Associations between screen time and lower psychological well-being among children and adolescents: Evidence from a population-based study", *Preventative Medicine Reports* (December, 2018) 12: 271–283.

[12] Sherry Turkle, "Connected but Alone?" TED Talk, www.ted.com.

[13] Personal communication with student.

[14] Ryan, "Benefits of Technology and the Right Kind of Screen Time for Kids" (May 10, 2018), https://www.idtech.com/blog/benefits-of-technology-for-children.

[15] Ibid.

Index

D

E

G

H

I

J

P

R

233, 234
Risley 59, 60, 232
River Valley 208
Robert Putnam 150
Robert Sapolsky 64, 229, 232
Romanian orphanage studies 14
Roots of Empathy xv, 21, 22, 39, 171, 234, 239
Ross Greene 133

S

Sapolsky 64, 229, 232
schoolification 96, 106
screen time xiv, 166, 167, 205, 207, 210, 211, 212, 214, 215, 216, 217, 218, 219, 220, 221, 222, 225, 242
Search Institute 154, 155
secure attachment 24, 31, 35, 38, 43, 169, 170, 171
securely attached 29, 33, 36, 38, 43, 119
Securely attached 35
self-control 52, 174, 175, 176, 239
self-efficacy 86, 99
self-esteem movement 99
Self-Reg 172, 239
self-regulation xiii, xiv, 18, 28, 38, 43, 51, 52, 53, 68, 93, 106, 107, 112, 120, 121, 136, 153, 154, 155, 156, 161, 162, 163, 164, 165, 167, 170, 171, 172, 173, 174, 176, 179, 180, 181, 184, 185, 186, 192, 201, 203, 204, 205, 217, 238, 239
Seligman 185, 186
separation anxiety 28, 34
serotonin 85
serve and return 19, 20, 21, 22, 38, 46, 47, 61, 63, 121, 122, 150, 154, 170, 179, 205, 214
Shakespeare 136, 237
Shanker xiv, xv, 155, 172, 173, 176, 177, 178, 179, 180, 239
Shanker method 176, 177
Sheffield, England 208
Sherry Madigan 218
Sherry Turkle 221, 242
Siegel 39, 120, 130, 135, 143, 146, 229, 237
silos 114, 115, 124

T

Y

York Region 209
York University 155
Yurgelun Todd 144

Z

Zero to Three 40, 118, 163, 223, 231